DIGITAL LIBRARIES
Challenges and Prospects

DIGITAL LIBRARIES
Challenges and Prospects

Editor

R.C. Ganguly

ISHA

ISHA BOOKS

Delhi-110009

Digital Libraries: Challenges and Prospects

ISBN: 81-8205-427-3

Published in 2007 in India by
ISHA Books
B-63, 1st Floor, New Gupta Colony,
Near DDA Market,
Delhi-110009
Phone: 9212142040
ishabooks@hotmail.com

Laser Type Setting by: Rudra Computer Graphics, Delhi
Printed at: Salasar Imaging System, Delhi

Preface

The information media constantly manifests itself in various forms, and amongst the numerous manifestations which are being prophesied and which are on their way to becoming reality, are those of digital libraries. Digital libraries have already made their presence felt in the West, and it would not be an exaggeration to state that they would soon be a part and parcel of the way information is accessed in India too. A library is an organisation which is constructed keeping in mind certain aims, such as providing information to a large number of people without delay, and enhance access to information technologies. They act as bridges linking the past to the present, and as guides for the future. These aims have been constant since the beginning of libraries themselves, and show little scope of changing in the future. Digital libraries in this regard are a step forward in adhering to these aims.

Libraries have always represented considerable expenditure in both the cost of books and their maintenance. Access until the latter half of the twentieth century was therefore limited to until recent times; even now the term reference library implies that its material is available for consultation only. However, as the information explosion takes place constantly, rapid advances in information processing, storage and communication technologies have revolutionised the role of worldwide libraries in disseminating services to users. In an age where "fast" is the byword for any kind of service, libraries have to continuously brace themselves to face the onslaught of the needs and demands of information seekers who have little patience with traditionally printed, cumbersome books, and have to be appeased with information in digital form, more suited to their desktop PCs and modern sensibilities. As a result, libraries are facing new challenges, competitors, demands, expectations and users who want everything tailored to meet their wants and needs. This book seeks to present before the readers a full fledged discussion of these challenges and what they entail, and the opportunities that which can be grabbed and utilised by libraries through transforming their services, information products, incorporation of technology, trained personnel. etc.

It is hoped that the book will be useful as a reference document for information professionals aspiring to go for digital libraries.

Editor

Contents

1

Introduction

The libraries of the period before 1850 can be characterised as private libraries of physical artifacts. The artifacts were expensive and only the rich or well organised could afford to provide access to a prescribed set of users. Homogeneous access methods sufficed since the set of users was well known. These libraries might be characterised by "the best reading for our prescribed set of users at the least cost." Architecturally, the private library was a centralised, real world facility. In order to have access to the information bearing entities, patrons of the private library had to collocate in the real world with the physical artifacts of the library.

The libraries of the period after 1870 until the present can be characterised as public libraries of physical artifacts. The artifacts were still expensive but accessibility of the information was deemed "in the public interest" and taxes were levied to maintain public ownership, control and funding. Heterogeneous access methods were necessary since the set of users was no longer well known. These libraries might be characterised by "the best information resources for the largest number of users at the least cost." Architecturally, the public library was (is) a centralised, real world facility. In order to have access to the information bearing entities, patrons of the public library had (have) to collocate in the real world with the physical artifacts of the library. The libraries of the near future can be characterised as being personal and group libraries of digital (either electronic or digital representations of physical) artifacts. With terabyte stores available in the next few years, individuals and groups will be able to have million volume repositories if they desire.

The artifacts will be inexpensive and access methods will become personalised. This library might be characterised by "the best information resources for the individual or group at the least cost." Architecturally, the future library will be (is) a distributed, virtual world facility that may be either public or private. In order to have access to the information bearing entities, patrons of the digital library do not have to collocate in the real world with the physical artifacts of the library; instead the digital artifacts collocate with the user on demand through global networking.

The process of conducting scholarly work is radically changing due to the addition of computer-based tools that support critical thought. These tools include those that produce electronic documents and allow electronic publication, as well as the repositories of digital artifacts discussed above and their computer-based finding aids. We are seeing a shifting of responsibilities for reading, writing and publishing across the dimensions of time, space and process. For example, writing is shifting from a mostly personal process done in the same place and time to a collaborative effort among authors distributed in both geographical space and time, and publishing is changing from a communal or social effort to a more personal process.

Electronic documents have many characteristics that are not shared by paper documents. We may include new types of publishable artifacts in our electronic documents including simulations of physical processes, original data, active citations, and entities that have previously been embedded in different media (video, audio, etc.). The structure of electronic documents is available for querying and full-text indexing can be a natural by-product of storage in an electronic repository. These documents are more fluid, in the sense of being changed easily, and multiple versions may be stored and referenced. New computer-based tools and global networking are bringing the capability to publish to the individual and small group.

Time to publication of an accepted work is approximately halved in electronic publication due to the elimination of production time from the existing publishing cycle. Serious problems exist concerning the ease in which plagiarised and derivative works can be made, and workable economic models for electronic publishing have yet to be discovered. Copyright Intellectual property rights are possibly the most difficult problem we face in the information age. Copyright goals of promoting the progress of science, publishing and public access to knowledge must remain our utmost concern, but our copyright laws must be rewritten for the new realities of electronic publishing and digital libraries. Phrases such as "fixed in a tangible medium" and "work distinct from embodiment" in copyright laws need clarification when being applied to virtual artifacts. In addition, the doctrine of "fair use" must undergo refinement.

World-wide information resources are now available to local schools and, indeed, to many homes. Local and regional perspectives are now mixed with global perspectives and local libraries are struggling to find the right mix of access to physical and electronic artifacts. Librarians and educators are finding that ownership is not as important as it used to be, but that access to the most up-to-date information has become critical. Educators (and students!) are beginning to build personal digital libraries of electronic artifacts and references to Internet information resources. Collaborative inquiry-based learning (learning as one tries to find the answer to an outstanding question of real importance) strategies among teachers and students in the shared information space of the digital library is becoming commonplace. In these changing times, professional societies are scrambling to remain solvent as much of their income has traditionally been derived from publication products. The Association for Computing Machinery (ACM), a professional society dedicated to the computing profession, has developed a publication strategy that it will follow in the near future. ACM's strategy provides a good example of the changes occurring in professional society publishing.

ACM's publication strategy includes provisions for: digitising all back issues of all journals, a single publication repository, a single subscription fee, networked-based access, user profiles, multiple versions of articles, and the capability for automatic notification to potentially interested users when an article is placed in the repository. More interestingly, they are encouraging self publication before or at the time of submission to the ACM. If accepted, an archival copy is sent to ACM and a standard statement indicating ACM as the copyright holder is attached to the personal, self-published version. For many reasons, archaic work practices of varying "inappropriateness" to modern scholarship linger on despite their known flaws.

In information-intensive fields, the derivation of possible new work practices can be suggested by differentiating those aspects of current practice that are archetypal to the problem addressed from those artifactual to the technologies currently employed. In particular, orality-literacy studies are here proposed for this purpose in fields where the mutable cognitive artifacts that scholars employ are known to be poorly reflected in the static artifacts produced by pre-electronic work practices for pre-electronic distribution methods.

Many believe that we are entering an era where electronic tools for storing and manipulating information will be considered indispensable for everyday thinking and remembering. Douglas Engelbart expressed this belief when he described a "certain progression of our intellectual capabilities," from concept manipulation (manipulation of concepts in the mind alone) to symbol manipulation (expression of concepts through language) to manual external symbol manipulation (manipulating linguistic symbols using writing) and finally to automated external symbol manipulation (manipulation of symbols using computers).

Engelbart's second stage corresponds with the concept of "primary orality," and his third stage with "pervasive literacy." We extend the concept of orality and literacy by positing a new property of culture, pervasive hyperliteracy or simply hyperliteracy, corresponding to Engelbart's fourth stage. Why posit hyperliteracy? If we are indeed entering an era where automated external symbol manipulation tools have become prerequisites of serious thought, then the designers of such tools should be interested in which aspects of thought are intrinsic to language-using human beings and which aspects are products of the use of non-electronic writing, since some of the latter may decrease in strength or disappear altogether in the residents of this new era. These artifactual properties are not trivial, and they are precisely the concern of orality-literacy studies. A curious aspect of some scholarly work practices is that often, these practices are known to depend on false assumptions or over-simplifications of a problem. In some cases, such as in certain economic models, these false assumptions are taken as reasonable because they produce good results and make the models tractable.

In other cases, however, these false assumptions are simply products of tradition, based in part on artifacts of old technology and literate mindsets. We take as one very specific example our experiences with botanical taxonomists. For several years, we have worked together with botanists to build a digital library of herbarium collection data. We have been able to observe several common current work practices that have changed as our botanist colleagues both gain access to new technology and re-evaluate those parts of their old technology that dictated how they did their jobs. As a particularly good example of a current work practice dictated by current technology, consider that there are botanical journals that use taxonomies that everyone acknowledges are outdated.

The editors of the journal, however, are reluctant to correct the errors in this standard taxonomy, partly because some of the fixes are not universally agreed upon, but also because changing the taxonomy now would "invalidate" articles just published. The current common practice, then, is for researchers to carry out their work using a more realistic taxonomy, and then literally "uncorrect" their terms to match the journal standard. For reference, the object of taxonomic classification is the taxonomy, which consists of taxa, which themselves consist of other taxa or specimens. Taxa are composed in a hierarchic fashion. Taxa at different levels in the tree have different names, such as family, genus, species, etc. We briefly describe three interesting problems we observed the taxonomists encounter in their current work practices.

Different groups of taxonomists produce different taxonomies, even if the specimen set examined is identical. Groups in which particular specialists work on a given taxon may show more detail in the expansion of that taxon, or different groups may use different measures of similarity when composing taxa, weighting various kinds of evidence differently. It seems contradictory to have multiple solutions to a classification problem. Separate taxonomic groups produce separate taxonomies, which are then identified with the groups that produced them. This identification is despite the fact that the taxonomy may always be used in conjunction with other taxonomies, or that it is based on the prevailing attitudes in the community. It seems contradictory that a communally defined, communally used product is identified with a small set of taxonomists.

The products of the work are often taxonomies, not simply revisions to existing taxonomies. Whether updates or new full revisions, the products are viewed as closed, well-defined entities, representing an opinion of a group at some time. However, new evidence, new analysis methods, and new interpretations are constantly being introduced. It seems contradictory to produce a well-defined, static analysis of an ill-defined, dynamic phenomenon. One artifact of literacy is the notion of single-valued, static truths. The work practice of developing and publishing taxonomies separately from one another is a particular instantiation of this artifact. The product of this work is a taxonomy, a "taxonomic fact" or truth, presented and interpreted as such. However, the notion of truth is changing from the literate view of static and single-valued to the hyperliterate view of dynamic and multi-valued.

Literacy promotes the concept of idea ownership by the individual, even when the idea represents a communally held truth. In this case, taxonomies are identified with their producers or publishers. There is no way to recognise the contextualisation of a taxonomy in itself. However, the notion of authorship is changing from owner of a document and by extension its ideas to recorder of ideas that are the product of several people, past and present. Consider an analogy from the business world - the growing role of the analyst. The analyst provides a filtering or ordering function for data that is oftentimes already available. Many new companies focus no longer in the production of information, but its compilation. This reflects a situation in which the problem of information is what to do with the overabundance of it, and not how to find and retrieve data.

One artifact of literacy is closure of ideas. The product of taxonomic work is a well-defined, discrete entity. Products no longer must be closed. They may exist as changing entities over time, with poorly defined borders. Consider World Wide Web sites with links to many other sites. These sites have no closure per se. Where one chooses to draw boundaries is contextually and individually defined. This is in opposition to the closure engendered by books and other written entities. As above, one new possibility is a communally maintained set of taxa, with various notes, modifications, and addenda separately maintained over these taxa. The boundaries of the communal knowledge could only be determined by a given consumer at a given moment. What implications can we draw from the above for the health sciences? Organisational tasks will be to provide and organise access to global information resources for their users. The necessity for ownership will decline and the organisation will act more as a filtering agent that provides regional perspectives on the global information space. Professionals, researchers, and educators will have to take responsibility for personalising and maintaining access to global information resources. They must also recognise the fluidity of digital artifacts and will be responsible for synthesising the multiple points of view for their constituents.

Digitisation in Libraries

Libraries and archives are society's primary information providers and were early users of the new digital technology with respect to cataloguing and processing management, and later for providing information on their collections to the www-community. Besides preserving and providing access to 'born digital material' a great number of archives and libraries nowadays have also turned to creating digital surrogates from their existing resources. It is for those libraries and archives that these guidelines have been compiled. Many libraries and archives would like to plan digitisation projects but lack experience There is a need for a practical guide as a working tool for planning digitisation projects. The reasons for implementing a digitisation project, or more precisely for digital conversion of non-digital source material, are varied and may well overlap. The decision to digitise may be in order to:

— To increase access: this is the most obvious and primary reason, where there is thought to be a high demand from users and the library or archive has the desire to improve access to a specific collection

— To improve services to an expanding user's group by providing enhanced access to the institution's resources with respect to education, long life learning

— To reduce the handling and use of fragile or heavily used original material and create a "back up" copy for endangered material such as brittle books or documents.

— To give the institution opportunities for the development of its technical infrastructure and staff skill capacity. From a desire to develop collaborative resources, sharing partnerships with other institutions to create virtual collections and increase worldwide access

— To seek partnerships with other institutions to capitalise on the economic advantages of a shared approach

— To take advantage of financial opportunities, for example the likelihood of securing funding to implement a programme, or of a particular project being able to generate significant income.

Since digitisation is both labour intensive and expensive it is important to capture an image in a way that makes it possible to use it to serve several needs. The key components of a digital imaging project are:

— Selection policy
— Conversion
— Quality control programme
— Collection management
— Presentation
— Maintaining long term access.

All these components are equally important - the chain is not stronger then its weakest link. Digital technologies are undergoing rapid and continuing development and many issues are unresolved, giving rise to a delusive reliance on the "wait-and-see" approach. The basis of a commitment to going digital is an acknowledgement that the technology will change and change often. The crucial management decision is therefore less about the "when", or the "whether" to begin. It is rather a question of whether the institution can afford to ignore the opportunity to reach wider audiences in a global community, in a manner afforded by the technology to improve access to and the preservation of cultural and scholarly resources.

Digitisation will be a costly exercise, requiring detailed planning and the establishment of an infrastructure to ensure continued access to the digital file. Institutions in countries of the developing world especially should consider whether the costs and time involved will be commensurate with the benefits. Such institutions should for example be prepared to resist encouragement in the implementation of a digitisation project by outside donor agencies, when analysis shows that for example the use of microfilm would be adequate, even preferable.

Obviously, the user plays an important role in the decision to begin a project, but which role, is very often hard to define. Indeed the specific demands of the user may be difficult to know. In most cases there is a supposed user's group, and it is the aim of the institution to increase its services and expand its approach and influence. The user group may differ, depending on the type of institution and the mission of the organisation. Institutions of higher education fulfil faculty staff and students needs. Public and national institutions must satisfy a large and more diverse population. This influences not only selection but also the forms of presentation and accessibility.

Digitisation is not preservation: digitisation is not cheaper, safer or more reliable than microfilming. Unlike a frame of high quality microfilm, a digital image is not a preservation master. The only way that digital reformatting contributes positively to preservation is when the digital surrogate reduces physical wear and tear on the original, or when the files are written to computer output microfilm that meets preservation standards for quality and longevity. A digitisation project is therefore no replacement for a preservation programme based on reformatting on microfilm. This is in general true. But there may be specific circumstances, for example in developing countries, that can turn this notion on its head.

If an institution with no experience nor facilities for preservation at all, wants to preserve a specific collection, it may decide to invest in digital instead of microfilming equipment, thus avoiding the high expenditure on microfilming cameras and processors and realising that this digital equipment and the developed staff skills will serve other purposes as well. This shifting from the generally recommended method of preservation microfilming into digitisation with its risks in the long term is perhaps not the ideal solution for the problem of nineteenth and twentieth century paper decay but can serve as a practical way of providing protection to certain documents. Digital technologies offer a new preservation paradigm.

They offer the opportunity of preserving the original by providing access to the digital surrogate; of separating the informational content from the degradation of the physical medium. In addition, digital technologies liberate preservation management from the constraints of poor storage environments typical of the tropical and sub-tropical climates in which many developing countries are located.Cost saving Digitisation does not result in cost savings for collection management. A digital surrogate can never replace the original item or artefact. If an institution wants to save space by deaccessioning the brittle newspapers, it would do better to create microfilm copies rather than digital images.

The whole process, selection, scanning, creating records etc. requires heavy expenditure and the long-term maintenance of the digital assets has its own high costs. An institution may wish to investigate the possibilities of cost recovery by marketing digital copies. Preservation of digital information is undoubtedly expensive and requires highly skilled technical staff and equipment. Individual libraries embarking on digital projects should seek co-operation within regional, national and international agreements and should look to conclude agreements with trusted repositories. Whether to use a digital process which reproduces the image, or to use OCR (Optical character recognition) or actual keying in of the source text. It is likely that users will want searchable texts, and that means OCR or re-keying.

On the other hand, depending on the type of users and the kind of text, many users will want to see the page images as well, and experience a touch of the original. This may lead to the conclusion to use both methods but in most cases this would be cost prohibitive. Then the best way is to choose page images. Whether to produce digital files capable of handling every job traditionally carried out by conventional photographic services. Selection is important to see digitisation as a series of choices where competing requirements and demands have to be balanced.

The selection therefore has to be conducted in such a way that it will assure that not only issues like the value of the selected material and interest in its content are considered but also demands concerning technical feasibility, legal matters and institutional conditions. Issues involved in the selection of material for digitisation will be examined from two perspectives: 1) Principal reasons for digitisation (to enhance access and/or preservation) 2) Criteria for selection. As noted in the Introduction there can be several reasons for increasing accessibility:

— Enhancement of access to a defined stock of research material
— Creation of a single point of access to documentation from different institutions concerning a special subject
— Implementation of the "virtual re-unification" of collections and holdings from a single original location or creator now widely scattered
— Support for democratic considerations by making public records more widely accessible
— Extending the availability of material in support of educational and outreach projects

The key point is to evaluate the contribution that increased access could make to a defined user community. If the institution planning a digitisation project is a private one, it is normal for it to focus on specific needs and to target a specific user group. If however a public institution is involved, it will probably have to satisfy a larger population and more diverse demands. The way that it is intended to use a digital image is of vital importance in shaping the technical requirements. When digital conversion deals with source materials which are endangered or damaged, the purpose is, in the first place, to create accurate reproductions of these originals on a long-lasting medium and not to select materials according to demand. These reproductions need to satisfy both users of today and future potential users, and must therefore both be of high quality and possess a physical stability that can be maintained over time.

One method of selecting source materials for preservation is to classify them into three categories:

— Rare, unique or fragile documents, archives and other objects of artifactual value that need to be retained in their original form: Digital conversion can provide high quality surrogates with quick and broad access which in most cases will protect this kind of material from handling. This can be difficult to achieve using some kinds of microform.

— Source material with an important intellectual but relatively low artifactual value, highly used and damaged or fragile: Digital images are normally good replacements for serving immediate demands. If the source materials are deteriorating and, therefore, need to be replaced permanently, archives and libraries sometimes prefer to produce microfilm for preservation purposes and digital copies for access.

— Mostly brittle source material of high intellectual but low artifactual value and with a low level of use. This is not material that will be of interest for digitisation in the first place. If it is brittle material that needs to be replaced by surrogate copies to allow use, then microfilm is still the normal choice in many countries being stable, cheap and easy to store.

In the future, when researchers discover this source material and perhaps use it more frequently, there will always be the possibility to digitise the microfilm Many institutions have not yet accepted digital technology as being stable enough for long-term preservation. The reasons are often that they feel the threat of technical obsolescence of the digital medium and an uncertainty both about the legal status of electronic documents and about the future costs of preservation of such documents. While waiting for the problem of digital longevity to be solved, most institutions are creating archival images of what can be called "preservation quality". That means that they:

— can be used for different purposes

— are created at a quality level that will minimise the need for rescanning.

The fact that a surrogate has been created is certainly not enough to justify disposal of the originals. Even to be accepted as the text for consultation by the reader rather then the orginal the digital images must:

— have a guaranteed authenticity

— be a part of a preservation plan.

Disposal of original source documents after digital conversion is sometimes used in records management programmes but only for documents that have already been appraised and scheduled for disposal, and which have been digitised to facilitate heavy use during their intended life time. It is useful when planning a digitisation project to look at policies established by other institutions for their own projects. Many of these are now available for consultation on the Web.

Another example is the Library of Congress where the selection for preservation digital reformatting is based on value, use, characteristics of the original item, and appropriateness of digital reproduction for use and access. Regardless of the purpose for implementing a digitisation project, the selection of source material will always be more or less content driven. In fact, intellectual value is the basic question in all kind of selection: does the content of this material justify all the efforts, costs and other resources that will be needed? Therefore, every digitisation project or programme ought to have its own definitions of value based on the goals it trying to achieve.

During the last ten years scholars have started to build up virtual collections of scanned documents, books, museum artifacts etc. The selection is normally based on the intellectual content of the material, but it could as well be built on the physical appearance or on other factors like age etc. The purposes of building virtual collections may differ. It could for example be to re-unify scattered collections and holdings or to enhance research by integrating different source material that otherwise would have remained separate items located in different parts of the world. The possibilities of providing widespread access over the Internet plays an important role here.

To make a digitisation project worthwhile requires a certain minimum volume of information. Otherwise the research value will be too low to attract enough either planned or potential users. An important question is, therefore, if a selection is being made based on content, should all of a collection be included or only parts of it? Normally the value of archival material, photographic collections etc. is higher as aggregates rather than as single parts taken out of context, but if individual documents or objects have significant research value, even a few of them can form a critical mass of information. The level of demand is of course of great interest when selecting source material for digitisation. If the purpose is mainly to enhance access, the likelihood of significant use of a digitised.material will probably govern the selection process. Involving scholars and other researchers in the original decision is therefore a traditional selection methodology.

Sometimes an active user group for a specific source material may be spread all over the world and because of that it can be difficult to define or even detect. Materials in special collections often run the risk of being looked upon as little-used, which is not necessarily true since a small specialist group can generate a great deal of important research. To balance the demands of different user groups many institutions have boards of scholars and other researcher to help them select material that is most urgent to digitise. When an institutions digitising activities are being developed from general proposals to specific projects covering whole collections or types of documents or objects, these advisory boards can be strategically important. For cultural institutions starting their first digitising project, a good rule of thumb is that selecting the most heavily used parts of their collections will normally give the greatest added value because it will satisfy the majority of the people they try to serve.

Selection of material for digitisation will be affected both by its physical condition and by the existing quality of the bibliographical descriptions available for it. Material which is fragile, damaged and in poor condition may present too many risks of further damage being caused by handling to allow it to be scanned without special care, or some basic conservation treatment. This will involve additional costs, and the institution will need to consider whether other collections in better condition should have priority, or whether the costs of preparation and conservation should be built in to the costs of the overall digitisation project. Similarly, if the material being considered as a candidate for digitisation lacks detailed cataloguing or descriptive data, it is essential for future access to such material to create such data, and it will therefore need to be considered whether the necessary costs of doing this can be included in the overall budget of the digitisation project.

A digital image is an "electronic photograph" mapped as a set of picture elements (pixels) and arranged according to a predefined ratio of columns and rows. The number of pixels in a given array defines the resolution of the image. Each pixel has a given tonal value depending on the level of light reflecting from the source document to a charge-coupled device (CCD) with light-sensitive diodes. When exposed to light they create a proportional electric charge, which through an analogue/digital conversion generates a series of digital signals represented in binary code. The smallest unit of data stored in a computer is called a bit (binary digit). The number of bits used to represent each pixel in an image determines the number of colours or shades of grey that can be represented in a digital image. This is called bit-depth.

Digital images are also known as bit-mapped images or raster images to separate them from other types of electronic files such as vector files in which graphic information is encoded as mathematics formulas representing lines and curves. Source documents are transformed to bit-mapped images by a scanner or a digital camera. During image capture these documents are "read" or scanned at a predefined resolution and bit-depth. The resulting digital files, containing the binary digits (bits) for each pixel, are then formatted and tagged in a way that makes it easy for a computer to store and retrieve them.

From these files the computer can produce analogue representations for on-screen display or printing. Because files with high-resolution images are very large it may be necessary to reduce the file size (compression) to make them more manageable both for the computer and the user. When a source document has been scanned, all data is converted to a particular file format for storage. There is a number of widely used image formats on the market. Some of them are meant both for storage and compression. Image files also include technical information stored in an area of the file called the image "header". The goal of any digitisation programme should be to capture and present in digital formats the significant informational content contained in a single source document or in a collection of such documents.

To capture the significant parts, the quality assessments of the digital images have to be based on a comparison between those digital images and the original source documents that are to be converted, not on some vaguely defined concept of what is good enough to serve immediate needs. However, the solution is not to capture an image at the highest quality possible, but to match the conversion process to the informational content of the original - no more and no less. At capture, consideration has to be taken both of the technical processes involved in digitisation and of the attributes of the source documents. These attributes could be of varying dimensions and tonal range.

Source documents can also be characterised by the way in which they have been produced: by hand, by a typewriter or printer, or by photographic or electronic methods. The physical condition of the source documents can affect the conversion in different ways. Fading text, bleed-through of ink, burned pages and other kinds of damage sometimes destroy the informational content but more often set physical limitations on the possibilities of catching information during a scan. Therefore, the need for pre-scanning treatment of the source documents has to be identified. Neglecting this can not only be a threat to the documents themselves but can also limit the benefits and results of digitisation and increase the cost. Ordinary steps to prevent this are for example to carry out preliminary elementary conservation treatment, and to use book cradles for bound volumes, and routines to control lighting and other environmental conditions during the actual scanning.

If the source documents have artifactual value they will normally need to be examined by a conservator before scanning. When the risks of damage to the source documents are high and the documents are of special value or in bad condition, it can sometimes be better to scan from film intermediates instead of from the original documents, if such film is available. Image quality at capture can be defined as the cumulative result of the scanning resolution, the bit depth of the scanned image, the enhancement processes and compression applied, the scanning device or technique used, and the skill of the scanning operator.

Resolution is determined by the number of pixels used to present the image, expressed in dots per inch (dpi) or pixels per inch (ppi). Increasing the number of pixels used to capture an image will result in a higher resolution and a greater ability to delineate fine details, but just continuing to increase resolution will not result in better quality, only in a larger file size. The key issue is to determine the point at which sufficient resolution has been used to capture all significant details in the source document. The physical size of a source document is of importance when determining the resolution. When the dimensions of the document increase, the number of pixels needed to capture required details in it will increase too, as well as the file size.

Large files can cause problems for users when viewing the images on a screen or in sending them over networks, because the file size has an important impact on the time it takes to display an image. One way to decrease the file size is to decrease the resolution. This is a critical decision, especially if the source document has both a large physical size and a high level of detail, which can be the case with oversized maps and drawings. Bit depth is a measurement of the number of bits used to define each pixel. The greater the bit depth used, the greater the number of grey and colour tones that can be represented. There are three kinds of scanning (digital sampling):

— bitonal scanning using one bit per pixel to represent black or white

— sgreyscale scanning using multiple bits per pixel to represent shades of grey; the preferred level of grey scale is 8 bits per pixel, and at this level the image displayed can select from 256 different levels of grey.

— colour scanning using multiple bits per pixel to represent colour; 24 bits per pixel is called true colour level, and it makes possible a selection from 16.7 million colours.

The choice of bit depth affects the possibility of capturing both the physical appearance and the informational content of a source document. Decisions about bit depth therefore have to take into account whether the physical appearance, or parts of it, have an added informational value and need to be captured. This can be the case when the purpose of the digitisation project is to produce facsimiles of the source documents.

Image enhancement processes can be used to modify or improve image capture by changing size, colour, contrast, and brightness, or to compare and analyse images for characteristics that the human eye cannot perceive. This has opened up many new fields of applications for image processing, but the use of such processes raises concerns about fidelity and authenticity to the original. Image processing features include for example the use of filters, tonal reproduction curves and colour management tools. Compression is normally used to reduce file size for processing, storage and transmission of digital images. Methods used are for example to abbreviate repeated information or eliminate information that the human eye has difficulty in seeing.

The quality of an image can therefore be affected by the compression techniques that are used and the level of compression applied. Compression techniques can be either "loss less", which means that a decompressed image will be identical to its earlier state because no information is thrown away when the file size is reduced, or "lossy" when the least significant information is averaged or discarded in this process. In general "loss less" compression is used for master files and "lossy" compression techniques for access files. It is important to be aware that images can respond to compression in different ways. Particular kinds of visual characteristics like subtle tonal variations may produce unintended visual effects.

Digital images reproduced from photographic formats have a wide tonal range, commonly resulting in large files. Another technique besides compression that can be used to reduce file size is to limit the spatial dimension of the digital image. This can be done when the image is intended to be an archival reproduction rather than a facsimile replacement of the original. The equipment used and its performance has an important impact on the quality of the image. Equipment from different manufacturers can perform differently, even if it offers the same technical capability. Operator judgement and care always have a considerable impact on image quality. In the end it is decisions taken by humans which decide what quality will be achieved.

Quality Control Programme in Digital Imaging

Quality control is an important component in every stage of a digital imaging project. Without this activity it will not be possible to guarantee the integrity and consistency of the image files. Steps need to be taken to minimise variations between different operators as well as between different the scanning devices in use. Scanners most also be regularly controlled to verify accuracy and quality. A quality control program is needed both for in-house projects and for projects where all arrangements or parts of them are outsourced. An important difference is that in a partly or totally outsourced project the quality requirements often have to be formulated before a contract is signed, due to its legally binding nature. In-house projects can built up their quality control programmes step by step as a part of their project activities.

Although quality control is a crucial factor to ensure the best results, there is no standard way to ensure a certain image quality at capture. Different source documents require different scanning processes, and this has to be considered when developing a quality control programme.

However, in most programmes it is enough to set up a sampling plan covering for example 10% of all images produced by each scanning device during a certain time period (day, week, month). If a specified percentage of the chosen images is found to be incorrect then the whole batch will have to be subjected to control. A quality control programme always covers the master files that are produced and in most cases will also cover other out-puts such as access files, microforms and paper copies. The automated image evaluation tools that are available today are normally not sufficient for materials that are required for cultural and scientific purposes. Therefore, visual quality evaluation has to be done:

— either from on-screen or print-outs

— based on a mix of on-screen evaluation and print-outs (film or hard copies)

Technical limitations that can affect the evaluation must be considered, beginning with the possibilities of getting good quality printed hard copies of grey scale and colour images. Before a scanner is bought, vendors should be required to deliver measurable digital results from relevant digital image quality evaluation tests. When a digital imaging project is running, scanning quality control measures must be set to enable operators to ensure that the scanning device is operating within anticipated tolerances.

Issues of main concern in performance are: spatial resolution, tonal reproduction, colour reproduction, noise, and artifacts detection. In projects which are scanning oversized material, such as maps and plans, geometric accuracy is also an important factor. A common definition of spatial resolution is the ability to capture and reproduce spatial details. It covers both input and output devices and that is probably one reason why the concept of resolution is one of the most misunderstood and misused technical specifications applied to digitising equipment. Resolution is often specified in terms of dpi (dots per inch).

However, dpi should normally be used only for printers, as "d" always refers to printed dots (e.g. ink jet printers and laser printers). For input resolution (i.e. scanners and digital cameras) and on-screen resolution (i.e. monitors) pixels per inch (ppi) normally should be used. A pixel is in general a much smaller physical unit than a dot. When it says that a scanner has a maximum resolution of for example 600 dpi, it means in practice that the scanner optically samples a maximum 600 pixels per inch (ppi). But the optical sampling rate of a scanning device only delineates the maximum possible (optical) resolution in the direction of the extension of the CCD unit.

It will not guarantee that the scanner in reality can spatially resolve details to the same degree that the optical sampling rate would imply. The reason is that the optical sampling rate of an input device is only one component of the concept of resolution. Other components of importance are for example the quality, focal range and mechanical stability of the optical system, the input/output bit-depth, the vibrations of the source document and the CCD, and the level of image processing applied to the image.

There are several methods for evaluating resolution. Commonly used are the following:

— Resolution targets, which were originally made for use in micrographic and photographic industries. They are normally used to measure the reproduction of details, uniform capture of different parts of a source document, image sharpness etc. The results can sometimes be not fully trustworthy, but resolution targets are still practical tools to use especially for bitonal conversion.

— The Modulation Transfer Function (MTF), in which the spread of light in the imaging process (line spread function) is measured. This is a more reliable and objective way to evaluate how well details are preserved and suits best greyscale and colour systems.

— Spatial Frequency Response (SFR), which means measuring the ability of the scanner to transmit high-frequency information by means of a specified transfer function (in practice equivalent to MTF)

Tonal Reproduction

Tonal reproduction is the most important of all image quality metrics, because it gives the conditions for the evaluation of other image quality parameters. The effectiveness of these indeed assumes a satisfying tonal reproduction. In practice tonal reproduction determines how dark or light an image is as well as its contrast. Due to various (electronic) noises in the scanner there will always be losses in the bit-depth during a scanning process. It is therefore important to capture an image with a higher bit-depth than is needed for the digital output, for example at least 12 and 14 raw bits/channel to get an 8 bit output (greyscale).

Tonal reproduction is evaluated by a tone reproduction curve that relates the optical density of a paper document or a microfilm reproduction to the corresponding digital count (tone value) in the digital reproduction. In digital systems this curve is called the Opto-Electronic Conversion Function (OECF). Tonal values can also be assessed with a histogram which graphically shows the distribution of tones in an image and also the tonal range of it. Clippings in highlights or shadows compared to the tonal values of the source document can indicate that there are limitations in the dynamic range of the scanning device. Dynamic range can be described as the range of tonal difference between the lightest light and darkest dark and its value therefore shows the capacity of a scanner to distinguish extreme variations in density.

Normally, the dynamic range of a scanner should meet or exceed the density extremes of the source documents. It is important that no tonal compression is made in a scanned image at capture. If tonal compression is implemented at this stage of the conversion process, an image can never be restored to fully tonal value again. The scanner gamma value (brightness setting) should therefore always be set to 1.0 in the scanner software. This is sometimes called "linear tone reproduction" The main challenge in digitisation of coloured source documents is to reproduce them with maintained colour representation on screen or on printouts. The main problem is that monitors as well as operation systems and system applications display colour in different ways.

Human colour perception also differs between individuals There are several colour models for defining the properties of the colour spectrum. The most used are RGB and CMYK. RGB stands for red, green and blue and is the model used by monitors and scanners. The idea is to simulate a wide range of colours by combining different amounts and intensities of red, green and blue light. Each of these three colours is defined as a colour channel, and on a 24-bit monitor each channel has 8 bits representing 256 shades. In 1996 a special standard RGB, called sRGB, was created for the Internet, and it is often used for monitors as well as scanners, digital cameras, and printers. However, criticism has been made that sRGB is too limited and cannot reproduce all colours. Therefore, it is important to consider before buying a digital capturing system (camera or scanner) if this limitation is of significant importance in relation to the output required from the digitising project.

The CMYK model is based on cyan, magenta, yellow, and black. It is built on the principle that all objects absorb a certain wavelength from the light spectrum and always reflect an opposing wavelength. Printing and photographic systems are built on the CMYK model which also is called subtractive. At the beginning of the 1990s a consortium of vendors created the ICC (The International Colour Consortium) with the purpose of developing vendor-neutral and standardised colour management systems. Their ICC standard profile can be used in different operating systems and be embedded in colour images. However, not all colour image management systems support embedded ICC profiles.

In digital imaging systems noise often has its origin in the CCD unit and in associated electronics. Noise is usually measured by calculating the standard deviation of pixel count values over a certain area as a signal to-noise ratio. The greater the deviation, the greater the noise which will reduce the quality of an image. Image software that can measure this is available. Examples of artifacts that can have an impact on the quality of an image are dust, scratches, and streaks. They all create a visible non-random fluctuation in light intensity, but how this affects the image quality differs depending on the out-put requirements.

In most cases it is enough to use existing software to detect artifacts, but sometimes visual examination is needed. There are many single elements that can influence the quality of an image when displayed. Firstly, the brightness and the colour purity vary between the centre and the corners of the display. Secondly, the choice of LCD (liquid crystal display) or CRT (cathode ray tube) display can have an effect; the latter is still seen as the best when it comes to image viewing. Thirdly, colour management production needs regular calibration of the monitor according to a standard. Calibration tools are sometimes included in software applications. Calibrating a monitor means setting two values: the light intensity of the monitor (gamma) and the so-called white point (when all three RGB channels are illuminated). Set the gamma value to 1.8 -2.2 and the white point (colour temperature) to cool white (5000 kelvin). It should be remembered that settings of these values which are ideal for the evaluation of image quality may not be optimal for normal viewing by users.

Image evaluation always needs a controlled environment. It is also important to adapt this environment to the requirements for viewing, which differs between the monitor and the source documents. Monitors are best viewed in low light, but not darkened rooms, and source documents in bright light. Surround effects like reflections can affect the evaluation and have consequently to be minimised for example by using a neutral background (grey) and neutral colours (grey, black, white) on the operator's clothes.

The possibility of being able to use a collection of digital images in the way it was intended depends not only on conversion standards and quality controls, but also on how the collection is managed. If the purpose is to meet not only short term needs but also to provide accessibility over time, steps have to be taken to satisfy both current use and the expectations of future users. Plans must be made for example to:

— make scanned images appropriate to the ultimate intended use

— up grade distribution of images and user interface functionality

— transfer images to new technical platforms to meet increasing capacity for processing and handling of digital information

— migrate digital images to new file formats or physical media to ensure long-term accessibility

To make scanned images usable, great concern should be taken relating to their storage. All image files that are produced by a digital image project must be organised, named and described in a way that fits the purposes of the project. Before a name and a description of an image file is considered is has to be decided how it should be stored.

Normally, the source documents being scanned are physically organised according to principles of archival or library arrangement. Holdings of documents are often divided into series, volumes and issues, and collections of manuscripts and photographic items have numbers.

The easiest way to handle this question is to translate the main principles of how the source documents are physically organised into a logical disc hierarchy in the computer. This should be done as far as possible according to existing standard systems. This is important to ensure the compatibility of file naming structures between different technical platforms. It must also be possible for the collection of image files to grow, and the way of organising them has therefore to be scalable.

Computers are not able by themselves to interpret logical relationships in a collection of source documents as for example sequences of folders and pages. Therefore, this has to be mirrored in the way the scanned image files are named. There are two approaches for this:

— to use a numbering scheme that reflects numbers already used in an existing cataloguing system, or

— to use meaningful file names. Both approaches are valid, and what best fits a certain collection or group of source documents should be chosen.

Every digital imaging project has also to adopt conventions for names, for tables of signs and for rules relating for example to punctuation and to the use of capital letters. It is important that these conversions are uniform. A standardised vocabulary is one of the corner stones in managing a collection of digital images. File extensions are also important when giving names to image files. Many extensions have standard meanings and are employed widely, but care has to be taken when dealing with non-standard extensions.

To describe digital images there is a need for metadata, that is structured data about data. Metadata can also be defined as data that facilitates the management and use of other data. This is nothing new for archivists and librarians. The use of metadata is closely related to rules for the description and cataloguing of printed publications, archival records, and artifacts. The difference is that in the digital world additional categories of metadata are required to support computer navigation and the management of data files. Metadata describing digital images can contain information of different kinds. Descriptive metadata for description and identification of information resources Structural metadata for navigation and presentation.

Every digital imaging project, however, must choose a designated metadata solution based on its own goals. There are two main approaches to metadata solutions: data management techniques and document encoding. The level of descriptive metadata always determines the level or possibilities of retrieval. Therefore, it is of crucial importance at the time that a digital imaging project starts to decide the deepest level at which the digital images will be searched. Moreover, existing metadata like finding aids, indexes etc. has to be surveyed, and if adequate, linked to the image files. It also has to be considered if and how metadata generated in the digital conversion process should be accommodated. Today, TIFF (Tagged image file format) is the most common file format for storing master versions of digital images.

In TIFF, but also in other graphic formats such as GIF, the software used by the scanner automatically creates a number of tags with technical and administrative information which is recorded into the file header, in other words directly into the file itself. The information in the TIFF header is stored in ASCII format and in that sense is platform independent. The practice of recording metadata into the TIFF header is widespread, and the advantages are obvious: it ensures a close connection between the source document, the conversion process and the image file that is the result of the conversion. Building up collections of digital images also means that efforts have to be made to make them accessible to people. Libraries all over the world have for decades used MARC (Machine Readable Cataloguing) as a metadata standard, but it has not been adopted by other cultural sectors. To meet new demands in retrieval, initially for the Web, the Dublin Core Metadata Initiative at the beginning of the 1990s presented a set of 15 descriptive elements of metadata. These elements are intended to be simple, international and cross-sectoral. Dublin Core is today one of the most widely accepted metadata standards in the world.

Today many digital projects and programmes use SGML (Standard Generalised General Markup Language) or parts of it like XML (eXtensible Markup Language). The purpose is to bind together images and give access to structural elements in single objects or in whole collections. Document encoding can also be used in systems where data are taken from underlying databases and transformed into standardised representation for exchange. There are some disadvantages with SGML. It is for example not supported by many software applications, and XML has more and more taken over as the most used markup language.

A well-known initiative using SGML is TEI (Text Encoding Initiative), which has developed DTDs (Document Type Definitions) for encoding individual texts in the field of humanities. For encoding entire archival collections or holdings of objects, the Encoded Archival Description Initiative (EAD) has developed a DTD for encoding finding aids. Running a digital imaging project means balancing the needs of known and potential users, the technological infrastructure used by the project, and the demands on available human and financial resources. Therefore, the technological capabilities of image capture devices and workstations (scanners or digital cameras, operating systems, internal memory, storage, display quality, networking capability, and speed) must be clear before a project starts, as well as the means of delivering image data to users.

An analysis of technical needs for a digital imaging project is usually conducted within the framework of a pilot project or study. It gives a project a chance to investigate, on a small scale, the feasibility to (1) carry through their plans and to (2) introduce digital technology into a library or an archive, if it is the first digitising project for the institution in mind. Technical needs focus primarily on hardware and software, both dynamic in development for the foreseeable future. Although any list of minimum requirements is almost immediately obsolete and therefore must be fairly general, the following basic information and communication technology package should be sufficient to conduct a digitisation project on a basic level:

— An ordinary level PC (Intel Pentium Processor or equal) with the following additional characteristics:

— At least twice the random access memory (RAM) recommended for current office requirements. The RAM type should also be at least a Synchronised Dynamic (SDRAM)

— At least 1 Gigabyte free hard drive memory space additional to what is needed for installed software and the operating system (Windows or equal). Image processing is memory hungry, and long delays will negatively affect productivity.

— A CD-writer, which is an essential peripheral to provide the means to copy the digital product to CD-ROMs, especially if storage space is a problem or if CD-ROMs are planned for resale.

— A modem or an Ethernet network card for Internet access

— An A3 flatbed scanner optically capable of true resolution of 600 dpi (ppi) or higher. Interpolated results to achieve a higher resolution can result in an unacceptable loss of details. Smaller A4 flatbed scanners are not able to capture the full dimensions of imperial foolscap documents of which many archival collections are comprised. A transparency adapter is another useful optional extra for the capture of film-based materials and glass negatives in large formats.

— An office level black and white laser printer (600dpi) is required if print-outs will be used for quality control. If images are to be printed for sale this will require a high-resolution colour photo quality printer.

— A power management unit (UPS) is recommended in areas that experience uneven electrical power supply.

The acquisition of equipment should also incorporate a maintenance contract for a minimum of three and possibly even five years. It is generally considered that after three years the equipment will require upgrading, and after five years it will be obsolete and need to be replaced. Software selections should be based on a serious consideration of open source solutions. Support of open source software under the terms of the GNU General Public License builds a digital library user community independent of market forces, limiting software obsolescence where it is not feasible to sustain expensive licensing structures attached to commercial products.

Proposed software developments of an XML base class in the Greenstone software suite are eagerly anticipated as a promising open source solution to collections management of images and related metadata. The requirements of imaging software focus on the provision of standard file formats offered, notably .TIFF and .JPEG. Sophisticated graphic software tools should be used judiciously to preserve archival integrity, with image enhancement limited to automatic settings of the scanner software. Institutions intending to embark upon a digitisation project need to be aware at the outset that they must investigate the copyright situation involved for each item that they intend to scan, and also the legal position affecting access by users to the images that will be created by the project.

This will be particularly true if the institution intends to develop a business plan to market access to and copies of the images as a cost-recovery exercise. They need also to consider the issues involved in ensuring the authenticity of the digital images created if they are to serve as surrogates for the original source materials. Copyright means that an author's right to an original work of literature, music and art is legally protected. The time span for copyright depends on when the work was created and can differ between countries. Copyright gives the owner an exclusive right of disposition over his or her work, in other words to do or to authorise copying and public distribution or performance of any kind.

Transfer of copyright must be made in written form and signed by the owner of the copyright. If the work is (1) made by an employee as a part of his or her employment or (2) by contract defined as a work made for hire, the person or body employing the creator or giving the contract is considered the copyright owner. Copyright has also a moral element that gives the owner the right to be mentioned, for example when the work is published, and should prevent the work being changed or corrupted. Many archives, libraries and museums have in their custody collections which have been donated and where the copyright has passed to the heirs of the creator. If the copyright owners are unknown to the institution, it can be impossible or at least very time and money consuming to obtain copyright permission.

One of the advantages of digitisation is the possibility of opening up collections and holdings for wider access, which can be in opposition to the protection of intellectual property rights. It is, therefore, recommended that the first issue to address in a digitisation project or programme is the legal conditions for making digital copies. To protect institutions from possible litigation where it has proved impossible to identify the copyright holder, it is recommended that access to the digital collection is reliant upon acknowledgement of a copyright disclaimer. Opinions about what authenticity stands for and how it can be achieved differ between scholars. The core issue is, of course, that a document or an image is what it purports to be, free from manipulation or corruption. In the analogue world a document is trustworthy when its identity is reliable, which means that the following facts have to be established:

— The creator

— Time and method of creation

— Circumstances of origin

If this trustworthiness is maintained over time, the document is authentic. When it comes to digital files the situation is more complicated. There is always a risk that something untoward happens whenever such files are transmitted across time or space, in other words when they are stored off line, when hardware and software used to process, communicate or maintain them is replaced or upgraded, or when they are sent between persons, systems and applications. For this reason, a reliable identity is not enough to guarantee the authenticity of digital files. Their integrity must also be intact. It must be established what actions have been undertaken to maintain the files, who has been involved in these actions and what tools have been used. Furthermore, it must be confirmed that no unauthorised changes have been made in the physical representation or in the intellectual content of the files.

Today, there are different kinds of methods in use to prevent or detect unauthorised changes in digital files.

Digital signatures and digital seals, built on cryptographic technology, and so called "watermarks" placed inside the images as identifiers are some examples. If digital images are accepted as replacements for source documents and are intended to serve that purpose, it must be guaranteed before conversion that:

— The source documents have no intrinsic value

— The informational content (and if needed the physical appearance) of the documents has been adequately captured

— The legal requirements are met

— The means for retrieving and preserving the digital images are in place

However, in most digitisation projects and programmes source documents or analogue surrogates of them are kept and can be rescanned if the digital images are lost or corrupted.

Digital Conversion

The cost of the technical infrastructure required for the conversion is determined by the media selected. Bound volumes may need to be scanned face-up on a planetary scanner, loose documents on a flatbed scanner. Transparent media, (slides, negatives) may be captured with a transparency adaptor on a flatbed scanner, but optimal image quality might be secured in the inclusion on the budget of a film scanner. Included in the hardware cost estimate is the maintenance contract to support maximum production. The objective of digital conversion for cultural heritage institutions is authentic representation rather than image enhancement for desktop publishing. Image capture software is normally bundled with the capture device, and subsequent image management can be effected with high end products like Adobe PhotoShop, Corel PhotoPaint) or demonstration packages on the Web (PaintShopPro). Once a digitisation process has been chosen for the source material selected, the cost per image can be analysed on the following basis:

— *Source type*: Turning pages and repositioning of bound materials will take longer to scan than loose sheets; the large pixel dimensions in scanning oversise maps or newspapers slow production rates, and may need to be outsourced where technical infrastructure is not available.

— *Quantity*: total volume of images to be scanned.

— *Process*: direct scans or intermediate, OCR conversion to ASCII text. o Standard: resolution, bit-depth, tonal range will affect resultant file-size, and ultimately, the cost of disk storage.

— *Cost per item*: Where resolution is constant, cost per item is affects by physical dimension of the source material, resulting in variations in file-size, and cost of disk storage.

The processes to make collections accessible, either in a catalogue or on the Web are determined by the selection of a metadata standard, based on the following factors:

— Extent of existing collection-level description.

— Need to modify metadata for various user audiences.

— Compatibility to make collection visible through a Gateway.

The cost of metadata or indexing processes are disproportionately high (60% of total cost), as they are conducted by qualified information specialists, who often need to be re-skilled in the use of new standards. Post capture processing includes quality control against the conversion standard selected and re-scanning where necessary. This can either be conducted on each file, or at specific capture intervals, to ensure consistency of image quality. The creation of smaller derivative files from master tiff files can be automated, to provide low-resolution images for Web presentation. Digital archiving comprises electronic records management functions of providing security, authenticity, and integrity for long-term preservation and access.

While many document management systems will offers these features, it is important that proprietary file formats are avoided at all costs. Files should be stored in a standard file format (.TIFF, .JPEG, ASCII text) that can be migrated to a new platform as required, without loss of data and resultant costs incurred to the library or archive. The identification of a local agent to provide ongoing software support in developing countries is important for cultural heritage institutions. Digital asset management is becoming of increasing importance to the commercial sector, and the strength of the growing market will positively affect pricing, and enhance the availability of local support. The application of digital technologies in providing open access to information demands high levels of capacity in information technology.

Where this capacity is lacking in developing countries, reliance on consultants must be calculated into the budget at market-related prices. The implementation of a storage system to manage document images should enable the management of file relationships, audit trails, version control, and disposition scheduling. The selection of a suitable system requires some investigation of commercial software products for budget purposes. Software evaluation may be effectively conducted by a specialised consultant, working in conjunction with staff to identify the needs of the institution. Apart from the many useful features that many software packages offer, an additional point of budgetary consideration is the license fee, usually an annual commitment to maintenance and updating of the software.

The design of a user interface and management of the delivery system is integral to access. Budgeting for software is open, with solutions ranging from highly sophisticated HTML editors (Dreamweaver, Front Page), to shareware products available on the Web (Arachnophobia, Front Page Express). The budget considerations in managing the storage and delivery system will include the software requirements outlined above, systems administration functions of server acquisition and maintenance, network infrastructure and access control (firewall), backup hardware and media (tapes, CD's etc.). Storage of backup copies and microfilm masters in off-site low temperature and low humidity storage is recommended for disaster recovery purposes. Modest solutions to managing the storage and delivery system can be applied in developing countries. One solution can be found in hiring the services of a commercial Internet Service Provider (ISP), rather than assuming the technical challenge and ongoing costs of server maintenance.

Because of resource constraints, many libraries and archives in developing countries tend to be behind the digital technology curve. Service providers in the education and qualification of library and archive staff have been slow inform students of the new skills they will need to respond to the digital environment. These include not only technical skills, but proposal writing and project management skills applied to the development of technical services. The successful application digital technology is not a matter of hardware or software, but a problem of access to opportunity, which goes far beyond technology. Directors of libraries and archives may fear that because they do not understand the technical details of digitisation, they cannot effectively plan for the implementation of digitisation projects.

It is more important for managers to understand the impact of digitisation on the organisation and its goals. Three main areas of consideration are change management, capacity building, and in developing countries, the social implications of digital technologies. Opportunities for staff development in the implementation and use of digital technologies require managerial support, often less than enthusiastic when faced with the reality of trimming budgets to support new initiatives. Change is basically about people. It may be necessary to analyse the problems of interaction within the organisational culture for obstacles related to territoriality, a lack of informed managerial support and fear of change within the line management, including technophobic barriers to technological innovation. These issues are often underestimated.

The functional units of organisation within the institution may need to be deconstructed to enable change by focusing less on procedures and more on common goals of providing an information service. It is inevitable that existing lines of authority and responsibility will be relaxed. The level of seniority that is age-related in the traditional societies of developing countries has no place in the digital arena, where individuals must be fearless of risk and change, and be self-motivated in learning the limits and opportunities of information technology and communication. In the absence of formal training in developing countries, managers can nevertheless provide leadership in seeking aptitude in these areas to empower the right people in the organisation. For example, a simple manifestation of managerial support for changing institutional cultures might be in making time available to staff, who show an aptitude, to familiarise themselves with computers. Financial assistance in the form of institutional loans for personal computers, modems etc. will serve the institution by extending the learning curve beyond office hours, while taking the threat of change out of the workplace. Even when opportunities abound, people and organisations have a natural aversion to change, especially where it is perceived as daunting, complicated or costly. At the same time there is a natural human tendency to desire what others have. Capacity building is therefore effectively achieved by forming partnerships with early adapters, either institutions or individuals with experience in the use of the technology, and who in their commitment to making it work, ensure the transfer of skills and increase the chances for a successful outcome of the project.

The development of partnerships with similar cultural heritage proposals to collaborate with experienced institutions or individuals on joint initiatives can leverage human development beyond the seniority and gender constraints of the particular institutional culture. Formal training opportunities that might be available include commercial training for the basic office environment, or short courses offered by universities and colleges, some even on-line, aimed to deliver successful technology. Most institutions began operating on the information highway by sending highly motivated delegates to intensive training courses. In the developing world, the training should be appropriate to the particular needs of operating independently with limited IT support. It has become clear that in providing grant-funded specific digitisation training courses that the acceptance of such opportunities also bears with it a level of accountability.

Capacity building then becomes self-motivated, if the individual is empowered to affect change in developing digital technologies. Intensive instruction in digitisation should assume a basic level of IT competency in a Windows environment, and aim instead to provide key skills for digitisation: image capture: to capture a digital image from a physical object OCR (Optical Character Recognition): to convert imaged text into machine-readable format markup languages: standard protocols for adding metadata, e.g. HTML, XML metadata: standard schema of administrative, descriptive, structural and preservation information, e.g. Dublin Core indexing and database technologies to search and retrieve digital resources intellectual property management: the risks and responsibilities of disseminating electronic information user interface design: the interpretation of user interactions with the data web technology: encompasses basic delivery mechanisms of digital data via HTML, XML and use of search engines project management: to achieve goals within set periods of time, and within a specific timeframe. In addition new managerial skills are required in the broader areas of project management, systems implementation and increasingly, in fundraising. The reliance in developing countries on inadequate funding from the national government is broken in providing an information service to the global community.

The goals and objectives of digital projects have to be clearly identified and the implementation carefully planned in order to attract grant funding. Whether digital projects are to be ultimately outsourced or production conducted in-house, the need to develop both technical and managerial skills is essential for effective quality control. An important component of capacity building in developing countries is the opportunity provided to create new job opportunities for the people of the country. Partnerships that support human development are preferable to those that offer quicker, and often cheaper off-site conversion, but which ignore the social upliftment of job creation Human resource development is essentially aimed at breaking the digital divide. The Internet provides global information sharing, changing the way in which users interact with information resources.

2

Digital Information Infrastructure

The 1980s saw the development of the microcomputer, which enabled many libraries and information units to acquire their own computer systems. By the mid-1990s Personal Computers (PCs) have become commonplace in libraries and information units worldwide, and many people also have PCs at home. These PCs may be used for what has become known as 'edutainment', where educational packages which parents hope will improve their children's education are used, as well as encyclopedias on CDROM and games, of which a large number are available.

With the development of the information superhighway many of these domestic PCs can now link to the Internet to access information sources that previously were only available in a library or information centre. Many professionals, including doctors, pharmacists, veterinary surgeons and lawyers, now have PCs on their desks. The battery-powered 'laptop' computer is a portable device that can be used when travelling on trains and planes.

The hardware of a current PC comprises:

— *Central processor:* The speed with which the processor carries out basic instructions (measured in millions of instructions per second (mips) or given as a frequency and measured in megahertz (MHz)) and the amount of main store that can be accessed are factors used to describe a processor. The earliest computers processed up to 10,000 instructions per second and there has been continuous increase in this speed so that current PCs have a processing speed of thousands of mips.

Intel is a major manufacturer of processors and in mid-1996 it announced plans for a 200 MHz Pentium processor which means that it will operate at two to three times the speed of current Pentiums. RISC or Reduced Instruction Set Computer chips have been designed with the aim of speeding up the time taken to process an instruction by limiting the number of instructions to include those most often used.

Another approach to improve speed is to have parallel processors so that the processor is not, as in most situations, processing a set of instructions one after another (or serially), but instead several processors obey instructions in parallel. Although the speed of processing has increased dramatically the cost of processors has decreased equally dramatically.

— *The main memory:* The main memory of any computer is used to store information that is currently being processed. The earliest computers were capable of storing only 1,000 to 8,000 characters of information. The amount of store has increased continuously over the years with a parallel decrease in costs.

  The most common form of memory can be written to as well as read from, and is referred to as RAM (Random Access Memory). The standard PC of today has a RAM of about 8, 16 or 32 MB (the unit normally used to refer to storage of one character is a byte; 1,000 bytes are called a Kilobyte or KB, and 1 million bytes are called a Megabyte or MB).

— *Input:* A variety of input devices may be attached to a computer to enable information in any form (for example, text, voice, image) to be converted into the appropriate binary codes. The keyboard (many of which follow the QWERTY layout developed for typewriters in the late nineteenth century) is often the primary device for entering information.

The original ASCII code was seven bits long and capable of recognising 128 separate symbols. This is not adequate for representing the range of symbols used in languages throughout the world. There are various other standards used. For instance the Arab Organisation for Standardisation and Metrology (ASMO) developed the ASMO 449 for Arabic characters, and the East Asian Character Code is based on work undertaken by the Research Libraries Group (RLG) in the United States for the processing of Chinese, Japanese and Korean ideographic characters.

Unicode is the general name used to refer to the International Standards Organisation (ISO) 10646 standard 16-bit code which encompasses the world's principal scripts and has been developed by a consortium involving computer manufacturers such as IBM and Apple, and software developers such as Microsoft, as well as RLG and ISO.

A major input device of the 1990s has been the mouse, and its use to 'point and click' at sections of the screen is a common feature of current computer systems. Scanners can also be attached to PCs to input images or graphics. Laser scanners are used to input the information from barcodes on books and borrower cards in circulation systems or from journal issues for serials control systems.

Video scanners can be used as input devices so that a videoconference can be set up over linked PCs with the participants able to see each other, or for medical diagnoses. Touch-sensitive screens allow the user to point directly at, for instance, a particular option from a menu of possibilities displayed.

— *Storage devices:* The traditional medium for storing data is based on magnetic materials. Most PCs have a hard disk which is in a sealed cartridge that contains the read/write heads. The capacity of hard disks has increased greatly over the years from about 5 MB in 1980 to as high as 2.5 GB in 1996 (a Gigabyte, or GB, is equal to 1,000 MB).

Data can also be input and output on to floppy disk and most workstations have a floppy disk drive capable of reading and writing 3.5 inch diameter disks. Optical storage media have become increasingly popular in recent years and many PCs now have an integral CDROM reader. The price of CDROM technology has dropped dramatically over recent years owing mainly to the popularity of CDROM as the medium for games and entertainment products

— *Output:* The most common output device is the screen or monitor. Many monitors now do not just display text information but can also display the complex graphics and video that have appeared for games in the home computer market, and are also used in multimedia CDROMs. Speakers can be attached to deliver sound linked to images on the screen so that, for instance, Nelson Mandela's voice or the national anthem of Estonia can easily be heard when using Encarta.

Laptop computers use flat screens based on liquid-crystal display technology as this consumes little power. Hard copy printout is still required and there are now many high-quality laser printers available. Again the technology of printers has developed greatly and prices have decreased over the years.

The July 1996 issue of Personal Computer World published a comparison of what £1,500 would buy at various dates, showing the incredible developments in this area:

— 1979 Research Machines 380Z microcomputer with 16 KB RAM, tape interface and a second-hand teletype printer.

— 1983 BBC Microcomputer with disk filing and 800 KB store on two 5.25-inch floppy disks, a colour monitor and a dot-matrix printer. 1989 PC with 10 MHz processor, 640 KB RAM, graphics capability and a dot-matrix printer. 1992 386SX PC with 1 MB RAM, printer and Microsoft Works.

— 1993 486SX PC, 10 MHz processor, 8 MB RAM, 120 MB hard disk, Works for Windows. 1994 486DX PC, 33 MHz processor, 8 MB RAM, 424 MB hard disk, Works for Windows. 1995 486DX PC, 66 MHz processor, 8 MB RAM, 528 MB hard disk, multimedia capabilities with double-speed CDROM and sound card.

— 1996 Pentium PC, 75 MHz processor, 16 MB RAM, 1 GB hard disk, quad-speed CDROM drive, 17-inch monitor and modem (for Internet connection).

Probably the major recent software development for library, information and archive work has been the use of the Windows interface. In the mid-1980s an operating system known as PC-DOS (PC-Disk Operating System) was produced by the American firm Microsoft for IBM to use with its PC. At about the same time a completely different interface and operating system was developed for the Apple Macintosh computer; this made use of the point and click features of a mouse with different options displayed on the screen in the form of small pictures or icons. This type of interface became very popular with users and by 1990 Microsoft had developed a similar type of interface, known as the Windows 3 interface, for the IBM PC.

Microsoft has also developed a wide range of office support software that is used in many libraries, information units and archives. Simonson describes the use of general word processing and database management software (that is easily and cheaply available) for archive purposes at the

Surrey Record Office in the United Kingdom. He notes that the advent of multimedia computing, networks and the information superhighway places the onus on archivists to find ways of making the information in their custody available electronically.

There is also an urgent need for archivists to understand and get involved in the information revolution that is currently taking place, so that a coherent strategy can be developed for managing the electronic archives of the future. During 1995 Microsoft launched Windows 95, a 32-bit multi-tasking operating system, and this is now beginning to be used in libraries and information units worldwide.

Network Developments

When computers were first used in libraries it was often necessary to link terminals or workstations from remote branch libraries to the main computer system, or to link together various PCs so that they could, for instance, share a CDROM drive or a printer. These activities involved the implementation of some form of data communications network. A network used to link equipment over a limited area is known as a local area network or LAN.

In many universities around the world there are campuswide LANs that enable students and staff from all over the campus to link to, amongst other things, the library's Online Public Access Catalogue (OPAC). Many libraries and information units have also become involved in providing access to a range of CDROMs via a LAN. There are many advantages to this approach:

- Several users may have concurrent access to the same CDROM.
- Library users may connect to a number of CDROMs from their own desktop PCs without having to handle the actual disc.

— Expenditure on CDROM licences may be reduced.

— CDROM discs and drives are protected from vandalism and theft.

— CDROM titles can be centrally updated.

There are various approaches to providing a CDROM network. The CDROMs can be attached to a network file server such as SCSI Express. Another approach is to use an optical server which is dedicated to running a group of CDROM drives. Products which provide this facility include CD-Net, CD-Manager and CD-Connection. A final approach, which is beginning to be popular, is to copy the CDROM data to magnetic disks.

A major recent advancement in this area has been the development of products such as SilverPlatter's Electronic Reference Library (ERL), which provide the user with a seamless way of accessing CDROM databases, local databases and remote databases. CDROM has proved to be very useful in many countries. However, bibliographic databases on CDROM do provide users with information on items that may not be accessible locally and so the number of interlibrary loans rises significantly. National or regional networks that link LANs or other computing facilities are known as wide area networks, the major one being the Internet. Often national libraries act as focal points in helping others in a particular country with this activity. The Conference of European National Libraries (CENL) is involved in the development of Gabriel a World Wide Web server - which provides links to sources of information about the services and collections of members of CENL.

Library Management Systems

Library management (housekeeping) systems typically are integrated packages which include modules for various cataloguing, OPAC, acquisitions, circulation, serials control and interlibrary lending. A detailed description of almost forty such library systems available in Europe is given by Leeves. These systems include those that originate in one of the European countries and are available in others (for example, BIBDIA (Germany), LIBER (France), Pica (Netherlands), SuperMax (Denmark) and VUBIS (Belgium)), as well as those that are non-European in origin, mainly coming from North America.

Great political changes have taken place in Eastern Europe during the 1990s and this has, amongst other things, opened the market for library systems. Borgman reports on developments related to library automation in Croatia, the Czech Republic, Hungary, Poland, Slovakia and Slovenia. The Regional Library Programme of the Open Society Institute in Budapest, Hungary, was established in 1994 to support, promote and advance the information sciences in Central and Eastern Europe and the Commonwealth of Independent States, and has recommended longterm goals for automated access to library information. In order to support these goals a series of library automation workshops has been held in various countries of the region. Some of the library housekeeping systems hold records in the Machine-Readable Records (MARC) format whilst others allow for the import and export of MARC-based records.

There are a variety of MARC formats available and Campos et al. provide an overview of some of the national MARC formats (for example, CATMARC (Catalonia, Spain) and IndoMARC (Indonesia)) as well as the increasing use of the UNIMARC format. Countries that have adopted UNIMARC as a national standard include Croatia, Greece, India, Italy, Portugal and Slovenia. The OPACs of many libraries worldwide can now be searched using the Internet. Some of these OPACs have been designed to be searched over the Web whereas others can be accessed using a Telnet connection.

A special facility known as Hytelnet was developed in Saskatoon, Canada, and is designed to help users in searching OPACs at all Internet-accessible libraries via Telnet. Facilities are available to search by country and by system type, and to look at help files for searching the different OPAC types. The concept of an integrated library house-keeping package with the various modules accessing the same bibliographic record is beginning to be replaced by the concept of deintegration, with libraries buying different packages from different suppliers, and mixing and matching to best suit their particular needs. This has become possible because of various recent developments:

— The move away from the proprietary operating systems used by the integrated systems of the 1980s to open systems based on UNIX; examples include Geac's ADVANCE, Innovative Interfaces' INNOPAC, Fretwell Downing's OLIB, Sirsi's UNICORN and IME's TINLIB.

— The move away from the proprietary database management systems to industry-standard relational database management systems. Examples include Geac PLUS's use of Informix, Dynix HORIZON's use of Sybase and OLIB's use of ORACLE.

— The use of client-server architecture in the design of systems. In the client-server model of computing a division is made between the applications software and the database software. The two communicate with each other over a network using a communications protocol. Processing which involves data manipulation or screen display can be carried out on the client computer and only database queries from the client and responses from the server need be communicated across the network.

— The use of Z39.50. Z39.50 is a 'retrieval protocol which allows client programs to query databases on remote servers, to retrieve results and to carry out some other retrieval-related functions'. Its main impact on libraries is to enable users to search, say, the OPAC of a neighbouring library using the same OPAC interface as in their local library. For this to happen the local system must have a Z39.50 client and the remote system must have a Z39.50 server. Dempsey et al. list some of the library systems which incorporate Z39.50 client-servers; these include Geac ADVANCE, Dynix, INNOPAC, LIBERTAS, OLIB, Talis and UNICORN. Some of these clients are integrated with the standard OPAC (for example, LIBERTAS) while others are available as stand-alone products.

Library house-keeping systems no longer operate in a stand-alone fashion. Libraries which use a system to manage local processing of stock also need to provide their users with access to a range of information services as part of the electronic library; this could include access to networked CDROMs, locally loaded databases, the Internet and so on. Several suppliers now make information about their products and their company available on the World Wide Web. Pachent describes the process of choosing an automated information system for libraries, museums and archives in the county of Suffolk in the United Kingdom. The chosen system provides traditional library management functions as well as access to networked CDROMs, local databases, the Internet and access to OCLC FirstSearch databases.

Information Retrieval Systems

Text retrieval software

For many years a range of software has been available specifically aimed at information storage and retrieval of textbased information. Examples of such software include BRS/Search, CAIRS, CDS/ ISIS, Cardbox Plus, HeadFast, IdeaList and InMagic. CDS/ISIS is very widely used all over the world as it is available free of charge to nonprofit organisations in UNESCO Member States and exists in a number of language versions.

A regular feature on CDS/ISIS is included in Information Development. One recent example given of the use of CDS/ISIS is the DRAiN (Drainage Information System) project which aims to coordinate information from various relevant research organisations in Egypt, France, India, Mexico, Pakistan and Uzbekistan involved in irrigation and drainage research. For many years textretrieval software was used to process bibliographic data, but recent developments in storage technologies have meant that this software can now be used also for fulltext retrieval purposes.

The producers of this software have continued to develop their products and many now run under Windows, can deal with graphical data as well as text data and can be used when creating local CDROMs. The directory by Wood and Moore provides details of about 100 such packages. A special category of textretrieval software is personal bibliographic software which may be used by academic researchers and which offers pre-defined data structures and pre-defined output structures (to comply with bibliographic styles adopted by organisations such as the American National Standards Institute (ANSI)) as well as standard facilities such as Boolean searching and batch importing of records. An introductory essay by David Bearman in a directory of about eighty software packages for use in archives and museums notes that the 'problem with archives software has historically been that the market is too small and diffuse to support a range of products'. However, he points out that the Internet provides an exciting domain for archivists with the possibility of setting up World Wide Web servers of archives holdings which might include images and sound information as well as document delivery services.

Geographic information systems (GIS)

GIS software comprises tools for the collection, analysis,

retrieval and display of spatial information. Technologies that integrate the management and analysis of this type of data are being used in a variety of ways for environmental studies, global change research, transportation planning, urban planning, marine studies, and so on.

As with bibliographic data, there is a need to share resources worldwide and the MARC format is being investigated as one possible solution. One of the projects - Project Alexandria (not to be confused with the plan for the new library of the same name at Alexandria in Egypt) - being funded in the United States as part of the National Science Foundation (NSF) digital libraries programme, is developing a system to access spatial data in distributed databases.

Development of Databases

Traditionally the information that can be stored and retrieved in computer systems used for library and information work has been structured into databases. The growth of databases has been rapid. There is a wide range of organisations involved in publishing databases; these include traditional academic publishers (Oxford University Press, Elsevier), learned societies (Institute of Physics, Institute of Electrical Engineers), commercial companies (Institute for Scientific Information, Derwent), the computer industry (Microsoft) and the entertainment industry (Sega, Disney, Nintendo).

Work on quality issues of publicly available databases has been undertaken by various online user groups, and Armstrong describes the concept of 'database labelling', which would provide the potential user with basic information about the database and the extent to which the information contained could be trusted. As well as the traditional online search services (such as Dialog, DataStar, STN and ESA-IRS) there are now many others ways in which libraries and information centres provide access to publicly available databases for their users.

During the 1980s more specialist services appeared and the existing services broadened their scope. FT Profile, for instance, specialises in the provision of fulltext online information tailored for the business community. OCLC entered the online search service field in late 1991 with FirstSearch, a service designed particularly for end-users.

In the United Kingdom the Joint Information Systems Committee (JISC) of the funding bodies for higher education has organised the establishment of centralised databases for the academic community. By charging a university a fixed annual fee, searching becomes 'free at point of use' for researchers, teaching staff and students.

The rise in the use of the Internet has been accompanied by the development of commercial, consumeroriented online services. Examples include America Online, Prodigy, Compuserve, Genie and Delphi which are popular with end-users as they cover a range of information such as news, general health matters, encyclopedias, business information and magazines.

Growth of Current Alerting Services Instant Article Supply (CAS-IAS)

CAS-IAS provide access to the table of contents of several thousand current journals and also provide means of transmitting requested articles. By making use of CAS-IAS services some libraries are moving from a just-in-case mode of operation with respect to serials holdings to a just-in-time mode. Examples of CAS-IAS include OCLC FirstSearch (with the Article 1st and Contents 1st databases), UnCover (now owned by Knight-Ridder, which also owns Dialog and DataStar) and Inside Information (from the British Library).

Interface Developments

The early online search systems such as Dialog, DataStar and ESA-IRS relied heavily on command languages for carrying out online searches, and this helps to explain why these systems were mainly searched by specially trained intermediaries. With the developments of OPACs and CDROMs in the 1980s, an interface was needed which could be fairly intuitive with searchers and needed no special training.

The technique adopted was to provide the searcher with a menu of options on the screen so that an appropriate option could be selected which would then lead to another set of options or to the data. On the positive side, menus can be self-explanatory, easy for the novice searcher and give a structure to the search. However, they may be slow to work through and irritating for frequent searchers.

With the major move to a Windows environment, many producers of search systems are developing their software to work in Graphical User Interface (GUI) mode. When a screen of potentially clickable items is presented it is not always obvious to the novice searcher where to go next in this two-dimensional environment and so there are many aspects of screen design that need to be borne in mind by the interface developer. Schneiderman outlines eight golden rules for any designer of a search interface. Paraphrased these are: strive for consistency, enable frequent users to take shortcuts, offer informative feedback, give action sequences a logical structure, offer simple error handling, permit easy reversal of actions taken, make the user feel in control and reduce short-term memory load.

Retrieval techniques

Most retrieval software is based on the user combining chosen terms or phrases using the standard Boolean operators AND, OR, NOT in the search statement. Over the years various alternative techniques have been developed by researchers; these are referred to in the literature as best match, nearest neighbour, probabilistic retrieval, fuzzy sets, relevance ranking or ranked output. Some of these ideas are now appearing in commercial services such as Personal Library Software's Personal Librarian, Dialog's TARGET, and FREESTYLE developed for the LEXIS legal service and the NEXIS news service. Evaluating the performance of various information retrieval systems has been a topic of interest for many researchers over the years. A major initiative, known as the Text Retrieval Conference (TREC), involves a number of research groups from around the world testing their information retrieval techniques on the same databases of fulltext items.

Aspects of automation

There are many potential problems related to the use of information technology in archive, library and information work, and these can result in useless, expensive and inappropriate systems. There have been examples of libraries where much time, effort and money is spent on the latest software and hardware but little time has been spent on revising work practices or ensuring that workstations are ergonomically designed for the people who use them. Only about 10% of the literature on library automation covers human aspects, whereas about 80% of the problems that arise in automation projects are thought to be caused by human or organisational matters. It is most important to consider people at all levels when setting up any form of computer system in a library.

The real needs of the users must be taken into account in the design; library staff and computer staff need to know enough about each others' areas of expertise so that they can communicate properly; systems librarians and network managers need to have suitable job descriptions so that they do not become too 'technostressed'; workstations need to be suitably designed for their likely users; users need to have realistic expectations of the new system; and library staff need to be kept informed in an appropriate way. Traditional organisation structures may need to be adapted with the introduction of new systems.

In many countries where legislation is in place to cover the health and safety aspects of, say, working with VDU (Visual Display Unit) screens, managers are being forced to think about the human aspects of automation. There is much to be done in making sure that human factors are considered at all stages in the design of a computer system for use in libraries or information units. The impact on people of electronic libraries (IMPEL) is one of the supporting studies to the e-Lib project.

All librarians and information workers must be able to cope with the vast quantity of electronic information now available as well as to advise their users how to cope with it. Del Castillo reports on the use of information technology in libraries in the Philippines, and notes that problems are due to lack of know-how, lack of direction, lack of funds and a weak telecommunication infrastructure. Some manufacturers make their products available on the world market and have invested efforts in translating the interface dialogue of their systems into various languages.

TINLIB, for instance, is available in about twenty-five different languages and is used in libraries on five continents. ALEPH, from Israel, can handle several different scripts within a single record and has been used in many East European countries, including the Czech Republic, Hungary, Slovakia and Romania.

Multimedia Technologies

During the 20th century, there have been endless and dramatic technological changes in all three major areas of information technology computing, communications and content. We have witnessed the advent of personal computers, world wide packet networks, optical disk and other mass storage media, interactive video technology, image technology, digitising and scanning technology, computer graphic technology, and the growth in both size and number of massive public and private databases bibliographic first, then numeric, and now multimedia. The concept of mixed media or multimedia has been around for some time, the form and its impact having been registered well before the advent of the computer, personal or otherwise.

Hypertext and Hypermedia

At the basic level, a hypertext system is a database management system which permits one to connect screens of information using associative links, and by allowing users to link information together, thereby creating trails through associated materials. At the more sophisticated level, a hypertext system has a software environment which supports collaborative work, communication and knowledge acquisition. When the system's database structure is complex, it is common to supply a special node called a graphical browser which displays the structure of the database and serves to reorient users who are dislocated.

Hypermedia extend the hypertext concept to link textual material to all forms of material - graphics, image, video, animation and sound - that may be digitally encoded for storage and retrieval through computer-based systems. As early as 1988, Casa-Bianca, in his attempt to publish a hypertext-like journal, Hyper-Media, graphically presents a typological framework of hypermedia in what he calls HyperMedia Map.

Multimedia technologies are not one single technology, and there is no single product, or definable market. The term 'multimedia technologies' epitomises technology integration through the use of multimedia tools. In order to summarise the above and facilitate our discussion on multimedia, a simple working definition of multimedia is proposed as follows.

Multimedia extends the hypertext concept of non-linear and non-sequential links of textual material to all forms of material that may be digitally encoded for storage and retrieval through computer-based systems, including images, sound, graphics and animation. Thus, multimedia refers to a synthesis of text, data, graphics, animation, optical storage, image processing and sound. Clearly, multimedia technology is not a single technology, and there is no single product, or definable market.

As librarians and libraries everywhere are still handling largely printed materials, it is important to understand that the information seekers are no longer satisfied with only printed materials. They will want to supplement the printed information with more dynamic sound, music, graphics, animation, photography and video, all of which can now be fed into an ordinary computer where they can be cut, changed, shaped, combined, manipulated, enhanced and reconstructed into all kinds of exciting information products. In order to benefit from the current multimedia environment, one needs to know the multimedia tools available in the marketplace so that they can be used to bring multimedia to the desktop. Currently the marketplace is full of multimedia products, as shown by the thousands of titles included in any directory of multimedia titles, many of which are multimedia CDROM titles.

For libraries' interest, multimedia products of every reference type, as well as subject topics, are available. Because more and more products have incorporated rather large numbers of images, sound and digital videos, much more powerful hardware than the bare minimum requirement for a PC system will be required:

— 80386 CPU.

— EGA/VGA or VGA A Plus Graphics.

— 2 MB RAM.

— Double-speed CDROM Drive.

— Microsoft Windows 3.1.

The general rule is that whenever possible, try to acquire a system with as much speed, hard disk space and RAM as possible. For example, some products will run properly only with a 486 or Pentium processor with at least 16 MB of RAM and a fourspeed CDROM drive. The unfortunate fact is that most multimedia application products are developed for users with the higher-end systems, and few have kept the low-end systems users in mind.

Production tools

Only a couple of years ago, producing multimedia applications was generally difficult, since most multimedia production tools were either not readily available or simply too expensive for general use. But fast technological development has made it possible for many to consider producing their own multimedia applications now.

To facilitate librarians' use of these tools for production purposes, those for both Macintosh and PC systems are included below. Although Macintosh tools are often preferred for the development of multimedia applications, they might not be readily available to libraries in developing and less developed countries. There are simply too many multimedia production tools to cover all adequately. A similar publication including tools for the PC platform is IBM's yearly issue, Multimedia Today: The Sourcebook for Multimedia. The issue for 1995 lists over 600 production tools. For illustrative purposes, the following discussion covers only a very small number of selective tools in some distinctive categories.

Animation

The best known animation tool is Macromedia's Director 4.0 (H) which is available for both Mac and Windows. Macromedia's Director is a powerful animation and authoring tool. Users can create, combine and synchronise graphics, text and animation with audio and video; add full interactivity with buttons and scripts; export and import QuickTime movies, etc. Conversion software is also available to convert Mac Director applications to PC and vice versa. Other notable software includes Adobe's Premier 4.1 (H), Avid's VideoShop 3.0 (M) for Mac, and Gold Disk's Animation Works Interactive 2.0 (L) for PC.

Clip art and photography

In this category, Photo-CD technology has been utilised fully by most producers to store about 100 images of clip art and photographs on almost every subject for both Mac and PC platforms (some store 600 when the top two levels of higher-resolution images are sacrificed). Of international interest, Educorp's International Graphics Library is a CD with 32-bit QuickDraw images (L). These clip art images can be copied and pasted on multimedia applications. More clip art CDs can be found in various software catalogues from Image Club in Milwaukee (United States).

Development tools

The marketplace has over fifty development tools for multimedia authoring and digital publishing. For Macintosh, the most noteworthy is HyperCard (L). It features an intuitive interface designed to guide users through the construction of hypermedia programs and presentations of various media elements such as pictures, paint graphics, QuickTime movies, audio, videodisk sequences and text, where users want them simply and quickly. Other popular ones include Macromedia's

Authorware 3.0 (H) for both Mac and Windows, the Voyager Co.'s Expanded Book Toolkit (L) and SuperCard 3.0 (M). Other PC systems include Aim Tech's IconAuthor (H) and Motion Works' Media Shop (M) and ToolBook (M).

Drawing and painting

Most noteworthy in the drawing and painting category are Adobe Illustrator 5.5 (M), Canvas 3.5 (M), Macromedia's Freehand 5.0 (M), Claris' MacPaint 2.0 (M), and Adobe's SuperPaint 3.5 (M). All are powerful illustration and design tools that simplify the creation, manipulation and refinement of artwork with advanced features for editing, text handling, colour support and more.

Image processing

Adobe's Photoshop (M) for both platforms (Photoshop 3.0.3 for Mac) is the most recognised and most powerful image processing tool. It lets users design artwork with a wealth of powerful painting and selection tools, or retouch and correct true colour or black and white scanned images with image editing tools and filters. It also has a wide range of third-party plug-ins for enhanced image manipulation, most notably Kai's Power Tools 2.1 (L), which provides a set of three dozen powerful extension and filter plug-ins that expand the ability to create computer-generated artwork and manipulate scanned images. Aldus PhotoStyler 2.0 (M) for Windows is also a popular tool for PCs.

Media Catalogues

A number of tools are available for organising and quickly retrieving digital photos in categories.

Modelling and rendering

Numerous powerful tools are available in the marketplace

for creating photo-realistic computer images and animation at an affordable price for the type of sophisticated work that was possible only with mainframe and minicomputers a few years ago. Some powerful tools are Specular International's Infini-D 3.0 (M), Strata Inc's Strata Virtual (L) for real-time renderer, Macro-media's Swivel 3D Professional 2.0.4 (M) and Virtus Corp.'s Virtus VR (L). Tools from Strata and Virtus are for both Mac and PC systems.

Music software

Music is an important element of a multimedia production.Various tools are available as a MIDI (Musical Interface for Digital Instruments) sequencer, editor and performance tool that provides multitrack recording, precise editing of all musical events, etc. These include Unicorn's Performer 5.02 (M) and Opcode Systems' Vision 2.0 (M) for Mac, Midisoft's Studio (M) for Windows and Turtle Beach System's Wave for Windows (M) for PCs. Digi-Design's SoundTool (M) consists of a sound accelerator card and Sound Designer II (software) which allow hours of CD-quality sound to be recorded on to a hard drive and edited with unparalleled precision.

Presentation and videoediting software

Many highpowered software tools are available for on-screen animation presentations with motion, sound and QuickTime, and flexible non-linear editing systems for Mac. For presentation purposes, Gold Disk's Astound and Adobe's Persuasion 3.0 (M) are powerful graphic and digital video software that will produce or deliver data-intensive multimedia presentations. Macromedia's Director 4.0 (H), Adobe's Premier 4.1 (H), and Avid's VideoShop 3.0 (M) are powerful tools providing an economic means of professional video editing. Director and Premier are available for both Mac and PC systems. Other PC desktop presentations include Motion Works CameraMan (L), Eduquest's Linkway 2.01 (L) and Linkway Live! (L), Lenel Systems' MultiMedia Works (L), and IBM's Storyboard Live! 2.0 (L).

Multimedia peripherals

Multimedia requires hardware and software power and speed as well as special capabilities to capture sound, image and video. Thus, peripheral devices which can accelerate any process as well as performing any of the capturing functions are essential. In addition, because all multimedia elements will consume a large quantity of memory and storage space, there will be a need to look into those peripherals that can double memory as well as compress and decompress multimedia files. The following are samples of peripherals which are worthy of serious consideration.

Accelerators

Many accelerators and chargers, such as DayStar Digital's Image 040 (H), can accelerate imaging functions up to 600%. Unfortunately these boards are generally quite expensive (over US$1,000) and are intended for high-end operations.

Audio/video controllers

IBM's M-Motion Video Adapter/A (H) for PS/2 can receive and process analogue signals from multiple external video and audio sources, and then send them to a monitor and external speakers for immediate viewing/listening in multimedia application settings. In this way, a PC can be connected directly to an analogue videodisk device and grab the analogue videos directly to integrate into multimedia applications. The Creative Labs' Sound Blaster 16 boards for PCs provide rich CD-quality stereo sound for multimedia, education, business, home and entertainment applications at affordable prices.

Digital cameras

In the last two years, several reasonably priced high-performance digital cameras have been introduced. Apple, Canon, Kodak and others have produced such digital image capture devices at a cost ranging from $350 to over $1,000. Users should acquire cameras only after studying carefully their need for digital images. These digital cameras can be connected to hardware systems using any platform. Most digital cameras function like regular cameras and therefore are mainly for capturing individual images.

Another type of digital camera which can capture both colour pictures and videos is becoming quite popular. Examples include VideoLab's FlexCam (L) and Connectix's QuickCam (L). These are compatible with all leading video digitising boards. Each is an integrated colour camera and microphone and can produce video output in both NTSC and PAL.

Digitisers and frame grabbers

In addition to software, built-in hardware capabilities or addition digitisers and frame grabbers are required for real-time digitising of sound, images and video. For example, Macromedia's MacRecorder Sound System includes both the digital sound recorder hardware and SoundEdit software for users to record, edit and play back live or pre-recorded sounds on a Macintosh.

Digital frame and video grabbers are abundant in the marketplace. For example, Radius' SpigotPower AV (M) provides full-screen, full-motion capture and playback of interlaced and non-interlaced JPEG video. It is able to capture and save full 24-bit colour data. Creative Labs' Video Blaster boards of different models can bring full-motion video sequences to a PC. Users can capture analogue video sequences at up to thirty frames per second.

Scanners

Scanners are essential for turning hard-copy texts, pictures in both positive and negative forms and films into digital files. Because of these different original formats, there are also different types of scanners. These include:

— *Flatbed scanners,* such as Microtek's ScanMaker II (M) and III (H) models, that convert printed and artwork to digital files. For example, the ScanMaker III (H) is a 36-bit colour high-resolution flatbed scanner up to 1,200 dpi. Generally, a scanner with at least 300 dpi can be quite effective for multimedia application development. Although more expensive and higher resolution drum scanners are also available, they are generally too expensive (some are over $35,000) for general-purpose use.

— *Slide scanners* that will do the same with photographs, such as Microtek's ScanMaker 1850S (M).

— *Film scanners,* such as Microtek's ScanMaker 35t (H), that can scan any 35 mm slide in 24-bit colour mode in up to 16.7 million colours or in 8-bit greyscale mode to capture up to 256 shades of grey.

— *Handheld scanners* (L) that generally provide a lowcost alternative for producing digital images for multimedia applications. However, the resolution of these scanned images is low and the images can easily be distorted.

Information Storage

Library, information and archival work generally deals with very large quantities of information. Regardless of whether information sources are in printed or electronic formats, space is always a key issue. Mass storage is required to meet:

- — The need for a large-volume digital storage system for archival management.
- — The need to provide users with immediate access to the rapidly growing volume of data and information that is stored in digital information systems and is likely to be distributed on optical media in the future.
- — The need to provide users with access to multimedia information quickly and interactively through the integration of technologies.
- — The need to transfer a large volume of data and/or files from one system to another.

Technologies for mass storage

Traditionally libraries have used conventional media like film, microfilm and microfiche to store information materials, but they are bulky and rather expensive. With the advent of computer and optical technologies, mass storage has shifted mostly to electronic media. There are several different technologies available for mass storage on magnetic tapes, high-density floppy disks, portable hard disks with a capacity of over 2 GB, and optical disks. But it is optical media that are the primary ones for mass storage. Because of this, the following section will explore further the different types of optical media.

The various types of optical media offer different storage densities, media formats, transfer rates, capabilities and compatibility among commercial vendors' products. In the last decade alone, a flood of new media and applications - CDROM, laser videodisks, write-once and read-many devices, erasable disks, to name just a few - have been introduced, promoted and utilised. There is a wide range of optical alternatives available to provide the highest application flexibility to end-users.

Optical media can be grouped into three major categories:

— Read-only media.

— Write-once and read-many.

— Erasable.

Under each of these major categories, a multitude of optical storage media can be found. For more detailed information on each of these optical media. All of them are essential for multi-media application developments.

Multimedia operating system

Hardware and peripherals

To enter the interactive multimedia world, a minimum equipment configuration should be more than the bare minimum described earlier. It should consist of the following components:

— A computer system with a minimum of 4 MB of RAM.

— A 350 MB hard disk drive.

— A 14.4 kbps modem (fax modem would be preferable).

— A double-speed CDROM drive.

— A portable videotape recorder.

— A fixed videotape recorder capable of being connected to a computer output either directly or through an appropriate AV card inserted into one of the bus slots in the computer.

— A television monitor for use during taping and playback.

— A scanner.

— Additional hardware in the form of an LCD display panel or LCD projection system is highly recommended.

Multimedia software

The minimum software configuration for using multimedia products is rather low, since most products have plug-and-play capabilities with very few requirements other than the installation processes. However, the following are varying levels of software requirements for producing simple multimedia applications:

— A basic editing software package, such as those available from Adobe, Avid, Radius and others.

— An intermediate-level software system that would include all of the above plus a free-standing audio editing software package, a two-dimensional modelling or rendering software package and a graphic/titling package such as Adobe Photoshop.

— An advanced-level software system that would include all the above plus an advanced-level three-dimensional modelling or rendering software package, and an authorware package for output to hard, floppy disk or to read/write compact disc.

The equipment cost varies greatly from one model to another, and from one configuration to another. Thus it is best to check with the vendors for current price information. However, it is safe to estimate that a PC Pentium multimedia system can be acquired from US$1,500 to $4,000, and a Macintosh Power Mac from US$2,000 to $5,500, depending on the system model, RAM size, hard disk size, and connected peripherals. Whenever possible, efforts should be made to acquire a system with as large a RAM and hard disk storage capacity as possible. The cost of software also varies greatly, ranging from less than $100 to over $1,000. However, powerful software like Adobe Photoshop costs about $600 and Macromedia's Director about $900.

Multimedia applications

The abundant multimedia tools are to be used for creating multimedia applications. Yet how one goes about developing multimedia depends on the nature of the application and how it will be viewed and used. Although there is no multimedia development formula, the process does follow a series of basic steps. These steps include:

— Concept.

— Content and interface.

— Product.

Planning and design

Planning and design is always the most important component of any development, regardless of whether it is technology-related or not. Usually at least half to two-thirds of project effort is devoted to this phase. In other words, the better a project is planned and designed, the more likely it is that it will be successful, effective, efficient and useful. For a multimedia application, after the idea is conceived and a conceptual framework developed, the planning process will have to go into the more minute details of plans and design, so that these will lead to the successful implementation of the application development.

It is important to stress the importance of project design. This includes both the application design and interface design. Remember that an application can deal with 'goldmine' source materials which are rich, relevant and essential, but if the presentation is not well thought out and the interactive feature of multimedia technology is not fully utilised, then the richness of the available knowledge base will not be fully exploited.

On the other hand, even if the presentation of the multimedia application is well designed conceptually, it can still fail if the interface design is either poor or uninviting/ confusing to the user. Few would be willing or able to visit the 'goldmine'. In designing multimedia applications, it is essential to realise that the process of linking multimedia information in a hyperweb environment can be both confusing and disorienting. Beyond the many demanding technical elements that allow multimedia to come together, there is a sense of transcendentalness that occurs during the production process. While combining massive amounts of information, one commonly observes coincidences and encounters baffling developments.

Great care must be taken to separate the intelligent realities from the illusions. Integrating the complex threads of interactive electronic communication requires an emphasis on the relationship between the designer/producers and their reader/listener/user/viewer. New access paths to source material and new procedures for protection and licensing must be developed. Industry standards must emerge to facilitate diversity and universal connectivity.

Multimedia Documents

After the planning, one has to determine what kind of information is to be included and published, and then prepare and process this information. Information sources can include all formats - textual, still images and motion videos, sounds and animation. This step involves information-gathering and preparation, and electronic management. The former determines the format to be chosen for inclusion, and the latter considers how to turn all the desired information to electronic forms and also how to manage them.

Text

The existing text information can be available in both printed and electronic forms. For the printed information, all three popular ways of conversion to an electronic format - keyboarding, imaging (scanning), and optical character recognition - will be used. For the electronic files, once the delivery platform is decided, electronic text files will have to be converted for the chosen platform.

Images

Hardcopy images will have to be scanned and stored in acceptable format for multimedia applications. The most popular format is JPEG (Joint Photographic Experts Group), but PICT (a Macintosh graphics file format, closely related to PCT and commonly supported in Macintosh format) and TIFF (Tag Image File Formats) are also popular with multimedia application software. When multimedia is moving closely with Internet and World Wide Web applications, GIF and JPEG with a very high rate of compression are preferred. Scanned images often need to be processed and enhanced by the use of software like Adobe Photoshop. Video. Using the videocapturing software via a videocapturing board, one can convert video sources from television, video recorder and video camera to digital video and save them in popular formats such as QuickTime movies (in both platforms), or AVI (Audio-Video Interleaved) for PC applications. The standard for digital video is MPEG (Moving Pictures Experts Group). Again, liked the scanned images, captured digital videos will have to be edited by the use of software tools like Macromedia's Director, Adobe's Premier or Avid's VideoShop.

Sound

Through the use of sound recording software and a sound recorder, sound sources from tapes, cassettes and video can be converted to digital sound files, which can also be manipulated and enhanced by means of existing tools.

Data Compression

Non-text files consume a large amount of storage space (for example, one colour image at screen resolution can easily take up about 1 MB of disk space or more); thus the issue of size becomes very significant, and hence compression and decompression. Compression is a widely employed technique to reduce the size of large files without appreciably changing the way a viewer sees the images or digital videos or hears the sounds. Once compressed, the file must be decompressed before it can be used. Compression and decompression can be accomplished by software alone or through the use of a combination of software and hardware. Take image as an example: compression software analyses an image and finds ways to store the same amount of information using less storage space. Compression hardware usually consists of a ROM chip with built-in compression routines for faster operation, or a coprocessor chip that shares the computing load with the computer's main processor.

There are different levels of software compression:

— Lossless compression: no information lost through the compression process. In this way, the file size is generally not reduced much.

— Lossy compression: through the compression, some information is lost. This will reduce the file size more dramatically than the lossless one.

The most common method for compressing image is called JPEG, which is a standard way of reducing image file size that discards information which could not be detected easily by the human eye. In compressing the digital video, the standard is MPEG. MPEG is an industry standard for moving images that uses interframe compression (or frame differencing) as well as compression within frames. There are different MPEG standards, such as MPEG I, which optimises for data rates in the 1 to 1.5 MB/sec range (the common transfer rate of CDROM drives and T-1 communications links), and MPEG II, which optimises for data rates above the 5 MB/sec rate.

Interactivity in multimedia technologies

There are many compelling reasons for using multimedia

for education, training, information delivery, business, entertainment, etc. First of all, the power of pictures is enormous. Only recently, with the advent of multimedia technologies, have we been able to tap the undeniable power of visual images and other non-textual information sources.But equally appealing for multimedia technology is the power of interactivity - a concept extended from hypertext as discussed in the introductory section. Through the ages, information has been presented and absorbed in a linear fashion. Interactive multimedia brings the incredible freedom to explore a subject area with fast links to related topics.

Reusable Model Components of Library

Large-scale digital library (DL) designers and engineers face significant technical challenges in providing adequate response time to users. Substantial advances in hardware technology make the CPU faster and faster every year. However, I/O hardware technology has not kept up. I/O speed continues to be the main hardware performance bottleneck.

Better designs and better tuned configurations may help meet this performance challenge. Building digital libraries with excellent performance requires design evaluation and what-if analysis for which simulation is a very powerful tool.

Although developing a simulation model of a complex DL is an onerous task, recent advances in object-oriented visual simulation enable component-based model development with almost no programming. Component-based development is becoming increasingly important.

The NIST advanced technology program on component-based software lists numerous benefits of component-based development. Such benefits can be realised in visual simulation of digital libraries by way of using the Visual Simulation Environment (VSE).

The VSE technology has been developed over the last decade at Virginia Tech and Orca Computer, Inc. under $1.2 million research funding from the U.S. Navy. VSE enables discrete-event, domain-independent, object-oriented, picture-based, component-based, visual simulation model development and execution for solving complex problems.

NCSTRL (pronounced "ancestral") is a distributed digital library of computer science technical reports from universities and institutions throughout the world. Log data collected at three NCSTRL servers, namely, Cornell, Virginia Tech and UCLA, were used to probabilistically characterise the query inter-generation times (i.e., the time elapsed between the time a server receives a query and the time it receives the next one) for a user population.

Data on query inter-generation times was collected over a period of three days. We used the ExpertFit software product to fit a probability distribution to the collected data. The log data collected at the three servers also was studied in an effort to probabilistically characterise the server response times to queries. However, log entries did not contain sufficiently precise data that could be used for this characterisation.

Therefore, the triangular probability distribution was used to characterise this stochastic phenomena in the absence of sufficient data. The transmission time of requests from one server to another was determined by examining log entries. By collecting performance data at different times of the day, we characterised the network delay at different servers. Broadly, these delays were classified into two categories: normal and heavy.

The library contains nine reusable model components. Each component is described below. Each instantiated component or an object in VSE is given a unique identification called object reference. This reference is used for message passing.

Dienst Server

This component models the behavior of a Dienst server that receives a user query, searches its own repository of technical reports, and simultaneously sends the query to all other Dienst and MIS servers in its region. If some server does not respond within the timeout limit, the Dienst server then sends the query to its region's backup server, if any.

When all contacted servers respond with query results, the Dienst server returns the merged results to the user. This component belongs to the VSE class DienstServer and exhibits the following behavior (methods).

— *replicationStarted*: sends the reference (identity) of the Dienst server to the region it is contained in at simulation start-up. The region collects all the Dienst server references within it and sends the list to each server.

— *receiveServerList*: returns a list of references of all Dienst servers within a particular region.

— *dynObjArrived*: indicates the arrival of a query submitted by the user. If the server status in the model is found to be operational, a "searchFor" message is sent to all other Dienst servers, the MIS server within the region and the system CIS server (if any). The server also sets the number of replies expected to the query. It schedules a "timeOut" event for that query, whereupon it checks if all expected responses for that query are received.

— *timeOut*: checks if all the expected responses to a particular query are received. If not, it accesses the Backup server of the region (if any). It schedules another "timeOut", whereupon a check is made to see if the Backup server has responded within the time limit.

— *backupServerTimeOut*: checks if the Backup server of the region responded to the query. If not, the Dienst server sends all the responses it has been able to collect so far to the user and informs the user of the servers that failed to respond within the time limit.

— *searchFor*: is sent to a Dienst server by another Dienst or Lite server within the region as part of a distributed search for the query received by the other server. If the server receiving the message is up, it schedules the arrival of a response to the query at the sending server after a time which is the sum of the search time and the network delay between the two servers.

— *replyToQueryArrived*: is sent to a Dienst server by all other Dienst servers, the MIS server within the region and the system CIS server (if any) in response to a search request made by the server. It indicates the arrival of a reply to the search from the remote server.

Lite Server

This component models all of the Dienst server's behavior except that it does not perform a search on its own since it does not possess a repository of technical reports. It belongs to the VSE class LiteSite and exhibits the following behavior (methods).

— *replicationStarted*: sends the reference (identity) of the Lite server to the region it is contained in. The region collects all the Lite server references within itself and sends them to each server.

— *serversWithinRegionAre*: returns a list of references of all Dienst, MIS, Backup (if any), and CIS (if any) servers within a particular region.

— *dynObjArrived*: indicates the arrival of a query submitted by the user. The server checks if it is operational by generating a uniform random number between 0 and 1 and comparing it with the probability of its going down, and if so, it then sends a "searchFor" message to all Dienst servers, the MIS server within the region and the system CIS server. It also sets the number of replies expected to the query. It schedules a "timeOut" event for that query, whereupon it checks if all expected responses for that query have been received.

— *timeOut*: checks if all the expected responses to a particular query have been received. If not, it accesses the backup server of the region (if any). It schedules another "timeOut", whereupon a check is made to see if the backup server has responded within the time limit.

— *backupServerTimeOut*: checks if the backup server of the region has responded to the query. If not, the Lite server sends all the responses it has been able to collect so far to the user and informs the user of the servers that failed to respond within the time limit.

— *replyToQueryArrived*: This message is sent to a Lite server by all the Dienst servers, the MIS server within the region and the system CIS server (if any) in response to a search request made by the Lite server. It indicates the arrival of a reply to the search from the remote server.

Merged Index Server (MIS)

This component models a Merged Index server which possesses the indices of the Dienst servers of the NCSTRL regions other than its own. It is accessed by the Dienst and Lite servers in its region. It performs a search on its indices and returns the result to the requesting server. It belongs to the VSE class MISServer and exhibits the following behavior.

— *replicationStarted*: sends the reference (identity) of the MIS server to the region it is contained in. The region then sends the MIS server reference to all other servers within the region.

— *serversWithinRegionAre*: provides a list of references of all Dienst servers within a particular region.

— *allMISServersAre*: provides a list of references of all MIS servers in the system.

— *searchFor*: is sent to the MIS server by a Dienst or Lite server within the region as part of a distributed search to a query received by the Dienst or Lite server. If the MIS server is up, it schedules the arrival of a response to the query at the sending server after a time, which is the sum of the search time and the network delay between the two servers.

Central Index Server (CIS)

This component models a Central Index server which possesses the indices of all the Lite servers. It is accessed by the Dienst and Lite servers. It belongs to the VSE class BackUp and exhibits the following behavior (methods).

— *replicationStarted*: sends the reference (identity) of the CIS to the region it is contained in at simulation start-up.

— *searchFor*: is sent to the CIS server by a Dienst or Lite server within the region as part of a distributed search to a query received by the Dienst or Lite server. If the CIS server is up, it schedules the arrival of a response to the query at the sending server after a time, which is the sum of the search time and the network delay between the two servers.

Backup Server

This component models the behavior of a Backup server which possesses the indices of all the Dienst and MIS servers in its region. It is accessed by a Dienst or Lite server when the server times out on a query. The Backup server conducts the search over its indices and returns the results to the requesting server. It belongs to the VSE class BackUp and exhibits the following behavior (methods).

— *replicationStarted*: sends the reference (identity) of the Backup server to the region it is contained in. The region then sends the Backup server reference to all other servers within the region.

— *serversWithinRegionAre*: provides a list of references of all Dienst servers within a particular region.

— *searchFor*: is sent to the backup server by a Dienst or Lite server within the region if it times out on a response to a search from one or more Dienst or MIS or CIS server in the system. If the backup server is up, it schedules the arrival of a response to the query at the sending server after a time, which is the sum of the search time and the network delay between the two servers.

User Population

This component models the submission of queries from a user group to a particular Dienst or Lite server. It belongs to the VSE class UserGroup and exhibits the following behavior (methods).

— *dynObjectEnteredModel*: schedules the random submission of the next query to the server.

— *dynObjArrived*: indicates the arrival of a response from the Dienst server to the query submitted by the user. It retrieves the query submission time and calculates the total time spent in responding to the query.

— *replicationStarted*: schedules the submission of the first query from the user group upon simulation start-up.

Query component models the characteristics and behavior of a user query in the form of either a dynamic object or an object-oriented message. For the purpose of animating the movements of queries in the system, the dynamic object representation is used. For the purpose of conducting long experiments without animation, the message form is used.

3

Digital Archiving

Audiovisual Archiving

Audiovisuals are not new but have become of increasing importance as art, entertainment and information carriers. In some cases the transmission of sound and visual data has greater value and impact than the printed document - where, for example, there is a literacy or language barrier. Audiovisuals may also be the only suitable records for the oral or sonic transmission of culture and the arts, news and other current items. The spread and development of modern technologies mean an increase in the role of audiovisual data carriers for communication, information and culture. Today's radio and television rely heavily on archive material and it is estimated that more than 60% of radio and television programmes use archival or stock material for programming.

The definitions are still being formulated, but audiovisual materials are to be understood as visual recordings (with or without soundtrack) and sound recordings irrespective of their physical base or recording process. The carrier usually requires a playback device. This definition is meant to cover the maximum number of forms and formats. Audiovisual materials should not be confused with multimedia; the former provide source material for the latter, and multimedia as such are not archival material.

Two features of audiovisual materials add an extra dimension to the principles of collection and preservation: a proliferation both of formats and of systems of production and playback. These cause incompatibility problems between formats and systems. Archives have to maintain original playback devices and employ technical staff who know how to use and maintain the machinery. The Recommendation for the Safeguarding and Preservation of Moving Images, adopted by the General Conference of UNESCO in 1980, provides a basic orientation for integrating and protecting audiovisual recordings as part of the cultural heritage of each nation.

Audiovisual archives are storehouses for a large proportion of the social and cultural heritage of the twentieth century. An audiovisual archive is defined as an organisation or department of an organisation which is focused on collecting, managing, preserving and providing access to a collection of audiovisual media and the audiovisual heritage, applying archival principles. Such archives contain huge treasures of unique material. Archives of audiovisual materials are relatively new, but they have proliferated in the past few decades. The first sound recordings appeared in 1877 and the first sound archive—the Phonogrammarchiv in Vienna—was established as a research archive in 1899, although it was not followed by others until the 1930s. Film appeared in the 1890s and archives began to be established in the 1930s. Photography had appeared earlier in the nineteenth century.

Television was originally recorded on film, but video has been the principal material since the later 1960s. Although audiovisual materials have appeared so recently, time is not on their side and the longer we delay in gathering, conserving and preserving the materials, the less we shall be able to retain. It is vital that steps are taken now to collect and manage audiovisual materials properly before their fragile nature takes a further toll. Already much has been lost owing to ignorance, lack of awareness of the dangers and careless handling.

Audiovisual archives vary in type, purpose and function, and until recently most of them were singlematerial archives: moving image (film or television), sound and still-image archives, the latter frequently housed in more conventional archives of print materials. As the technologies converge so do the archives, to unite effort and conserve resources. Some archives take responsibility for all recorded materials, others take smaller bites and combine one or two of the materials. The larger archives cannot always combine materials in one department; the physical techniques required to deal with each material from the point of view of storage, handling and restoration need different expertise and materials are therefore separated by this parameter alone.

Other functions of collection management can be applied to all the materials: documentation and information retrieval, and selection. Storage vaults may have to accommodate more than one material and the resulting environmental considerations will be different from those more stringently applied to individual materials. Alternatively, an archive may decide that it must apply the optimum storage and environmental values which apply to each material: single-material archives are more fortunate in these cases. Academic archives also house audiovisual materials, many in universities for research, and latterly educational materials for distance learning. These may be small and specialised, or have substantial collections and preservation programmes. Specialised or thematic archives concentrate on a particular format, subject-matter or locality, or relate to specific cultural groups.

Many examples could be cited, including the following: special events or periods in history; regional interests; specific cultural groups; academic and research disciplines; folklife collections; oral history; world music;

and specific organisations.

Many of these archives have developed within larger organisations. Production archives. Film companies, broadcasting companies and record companies maintain archives primarily for use and exploitation by the parent company. Many of these preserve and restore their materials for re-use, but the archives' main obligation is to the parent organisation rather than to preserving the cultural heritage.

This may be left to a national archive, which obtains a selection of the production company's material by deposit. Other institutions with archival responsibility include museums, cinematheques, videotheques and national libraries. Most of these are more concerned with maintaining stock for exhibition purposes, and originals may be deposited for long-term preservation in a national archive. There are also collections of last resort which attempt to conserve copies of material in usable condition, but seldom retain archival originals or masters.

Audiovisual materials result from a huge level of investment. Consider the costs of a television channel, or a film production or sound recording company. That the material is allowed to deteriorate through lack of funding for conservation is an unforgivable waste of financial resources and human talent. Considering the huge investment in production, the financial resources available for preservation of the material are ludicrously small.

Although some archives were established by private means, the ultimate responsibility for the protection and maintenance of a national heritage must lie with the nation itself, and this means government and granting bodies. It is incumbent upon government to ensure that the national heritage is protected for posterity. Archives in organisations such as broadcast associations or film production companies have commercial backing and motivation, and meet costs from their revenue. Once that commercial motive is fulfilled, however, it is generally acknowledged that, as with other records of the national cultural creativity, the cost of maintaining the collection reverts to government and granting bodies. Many valuable collections have disappeared for ever as a result of production company closures or changes in franchise when materials are not taken over by already overstretched archives.

The basic tasks of an audiovisual archive are collection, preservation, documentation and access provision. Methods of collection and acquisition vary, and include the legal or voluntary deposit of collections or individual items, the deposit of in-house productions, donations, special agreements for copying nationally produced materials, and purchase. Other archives collect their own materials in the form of oral or video history programmes, with the purpose of recording cultures, languages and music before they disappear.

Closely allied to acquisition are evaluation, selection and appraisal. The audiovisual archive acquires materials according to a particular remit, balancing new acquisitions against existing stock and the purpose and function of the archive. Storage space and resources being what they are, archives have to select material for preservation on the basis of relevance, uniqueness and quality. Wherever possible an archive should be dealing with original materials, but originals are hard to come by. There is strictly only one original film, video or master sound recording. Such originals seldom survive and there are various forms of tampering with the products - cut/uncut versions, director's/producer's cut, censored and unexpurgated versions. Owners of original material may be reluctant to deposit their master material in an archive until they have no further use for it, by which time the technical quality has deteriorated.

Three elements in audiovisual documents have to be

considered in the selection process: the artefact or carrier, the information content and the aesthetic content, particularly with film and sound recordings. The artefact or carrier will designate the form of the audiovisual and influence selection for technical reasons. Can this material be replayed in the collection which acquires it, or is the carrier so esoteric that it has only antique value? Is the carrier in good physical condition or will it need transfer and/or costly restoration before or on receipt, or indeed is the damage irreparable? There are also implications for damage and disaster to the rest of the collection; canker present in one item may spread to others if it is stored untreated and without inspection. Archives have very stringent selection policies. It is widely quoted that archives select less than 2% of the material presented.

Audiovisual archives, therefore, do not have a huge selection of material, but most of it has unique value, and such archives retain more material than many other archives. Some audiovisual collections will include several interpretations of the same work—for example, music recordings—or several records of the same event carried in different documents: a film, video or sound version. Guidelines for archival selection exist, but they are usually those of organisations with their own parameters. Selection of material is dependent upon the function of the archive, the quality of the material and the uniqueness or rarity of the content. Audiovisual archives should concentrate on recordings of national origin. To avoid duplication of effort, material should be offered back to the country of original production or to archives with a more relevant collection remit.

Preservation

The main function of any archive is to preserve the heritage and the artefacts which make up that heritage. These are the major concerns of audiovisual archives. Many of the difficulties encountered result from the fragility or the volatile nature of the materials. The carriers are the weak link and the materials have to be transferred to other carriers that are more stable, with a longer life expectancy or more up to date. Audiovisual materials are made of polymers, and all polymers decay! Progress is being made to slow this decay and prolong the life expectancy of the carriers and thus the source material, but preservation measures will simply retard deterioration, not prevent it. The life expectancy of audiovisual materials is dependent on chemistry and storage and handling conditions. After 100 years much early film has been lost, especially volatile nitrate. Sound and video recordings are subject to attack from many enemies. No universal panacea has been found and the new technologies of optical disks are as prone to damage as the old. For example, there have been problems with vinegar syndrome producing tape and laser rot affecting optical disks designed to act as storage media for tape materials. Archives must copy material from one format to another to save the content, to overcome the obsolescence of equipment and systems, and to provide copies for research and other uses. There are three steps in preservation work:

— Conservation;
— Preservation ; and
— Restoration.

Wherever possible the original data have to be preserved on the original format for future use by more advanced technologies of transfer and presentation. Guidelines and standards exist and can be adjusted to suit prevailing conditions—hot and humid climates call for different standards of storage and preservation than cold, temperate climates. The American National Standards Institute (ANSI), the International Standards Organisation (ISO) and the British Standards Institute (BSI) all publish standards for composition of tape, and for storage environments and conditions. The international audiovisual NGOs also issue guidelines. Digitisation is not yet the answer as there may be loss of quality in copying the original, even though clones will retain the quality of the copy. Digitisation is often associated with mass storage techniques, but data density techniques are not necessarily reversible—hence the caution of technicians in retaining originals whenever possible.

Access

If preservation is the primary concern of the audiovisual archive, access is the second. Audiovisual archiving is a culturally motivated activity, intent upon the preservation of the audiovisual heritage because of its intrinsic worth, regardless of commercial potential. Such values are still important, but most archives are now growing faster than the financial resources to support them. There is therefore a certain necessity for archives to generate some income; there is also the public service aspect—that is, to provide access to the people whose heritage is contained within the archive.

Copyright in archive material is usually vested in the owner and respected, but the archive itself requires rights to acquire, copy, use and provide access to the material. Acquisition of material is achieved by some countries through legal deposit arrangements, but this will only cover a small proportion of the material acquired by an archive—that which is published. Much of the material is unpublished. Archives have ad hoc agreements with donors for voluntary deposits but, in the case of some commercial producers, the archive's rights may be severely restricted. Archives are not in competition with producers or owners, and need some rights over material deposited with them, on which they may have spent considerable time, effort and money for preservation and storage.

Archives are not simply convenient storehouses, and have to maintain the integrity of the material. Most especially they need rights to copy the material for preservation, access and exhibition purposes, and some rights to retain the material once acquired. Once deposited, archive copies should not leave archive premises but should remain under archive control.

Detailed cataloguing of archive material is essential to provide a permanent, accurate record, especially of the unedited, unpublished material which abounds. Many archives developed their own rules, but an international initiative is now under way to produce ground rules for all audiovisual materials. Ground rules are necessary for the exchange of information in electronic databases—if everyone uses different criteria, then confusion will result and information exchange be retarded. Accurate and rapid information retrieval is the goal of indexing, and essential data elements have to be devised to make this possible, even though each kind of material will have its own set of data elements. Retrieval by subject has been made easier by the introduction of computer techniques and free-text searching—but the terms for description of subject content have to be carefully chosen, based on international thesauri, or data and material will be lost.

As electronic technology develops so the means of transmitting information—printed and audiovisual— are advanced. In a world of incompatible systems (computers are no exception), the search continues for a system capable of access by as wide a public as possible. Work has started to find the lowest common denominator for the transmission of information with the highest common quality, a sort of 'ASCII' code for all information. In addition to information retrieval, archives have to keep detailed technical records—what has happened to the material, its current format, has it been restored, if so on what system, how and why to assist future technicians.

The technical record is usually kept separate from the information record. There are many published information tools ranging from catalogues of holdings to discographies and filmographies, but national discographies and filmographies are compiled independently of the archives, because the latter's stock is not comprehensive, even when legal deposit exists, and seldom up to date. Other discographies and filmographies are selective and cover directors, performers or composers.

Audio, film and video archives was carried out by the Library of Congress on behalf of Eastman Kodak. The figures are alarming. Even with the most stringent selection criteria and limited collection resources, the holdings of just 500 archives amounted to 11,175 million feet of film, 8.5 million hours of video, and 44.5 million hours of audio, and there are many more archives than this. A recent studies of audiovisual archives in Europe alone, Map-TV - Film and Television Collections in Europe, identified some additional 1,900 archives and collections for film and television. There are approximately 40,000 radio and television stations around the world, many of which have archives; film archives exist in over eighty countries, and sound archives in fifty countries at a conservative estimate. A large part of audiovisual production will be lost for future generations without greater efforts from the international community to support the establishment and development of audiovisual archives worldwide.

Personnel working in audiovisual archives come from many different professions and scientific disciplines, and have long professional experience and on-the-job training. There is a serious gap, however, between the growing importance of audiovisual archives and the provision of professional education, a gap no less wide in developed than in developing countries. Audiovisual archivists need to be specialists with a thorough knowledge of archival principles and the special characteristics of audiovisual materials. There are two main types of audiovisual archivist:

a) collection managers, documentalists and selectors and
b) technical staff, who have to be of a high standard with thorough knowledge of their disciplines.

There are few courses available; most are summer schools and seminars, but some longer courses can be found in existing schools of library and archival studies.

The UNESCO Memory of the World Programme is an attempt to save the cultural heritage, and audiovisual materials cannot be excluded. These materials, however, are among the most vulnerable to destruction. Lost collections are a sad reminder of the ravages of time, chemistry, natural and man-made disasters, wars and conflicts, but fortunately endangered collections are currently being identified by this programme.

Audiovisual archives have set up their own federations: the International Federation of Film Archives (FIAF) was established sixty-eight years ago, the International Association of Sound Archives (IASA) in 1969 and the International Federation of Television Archives (IFTA) in 1977. All have NGO status within UNESCO. Although each has its own constituency and membership structures, the audiovisual NGOs, ICA and the International Federation of Library Associations and Institutions (IFLA) have collaborated since 1979 in a Round Table on Audiovisual Records under the auspices of UNESCO. The Round Table has been responsible for many activities including publications, the development of guidelines and training. It provides an arena for audiovisual organisations to address common issues and improve the recognition and status of audiovisual archives as vital components in safeguarding the cultural heritage. The Round Table has an important subcommittee—the Technical Co-ordinating

Committee—which organises Joint Technical Symposia across its spectrum of interests and provides technical advice and expertise.

In addition to the international NGOs there are several national and regional associations: the Association of Recorded Sound Collections (ARSC) in the United States, the Association of Moving Image Archives (AMIA), with its network of interests in North America and beyond, and the recently formed South-East Asia-Pacific Audiovisual Archives Association (SEAPAVAA). Other closely allied associations include the International Council on Museums (ICOM) and the International Council on Traditional Music (ICTM). Thus many associations are willing to assist if one knows where to look.

Accessing Unique Library Materials

The period from 1988 to 1994 has been one of dramatic change and rapid but uneven development. The growth and spread of consensus on the general principles of access to archival and primary documentary materials have been remarkable. In contrast, the state of affairs in different countries and regions varies significantly, and there are enormous resource problems to be faced. Nevertheless, the outlines, or at least the principles, of a generally agreed system for access to primary documentation and the dissemination of information from it are now beginning to emerge. Technological change and the emergence of international electronic highways have begun to affect the way we see the situation, but from a worldwide point of view have not yet begun to influence seriously the way access to archival and manuscript material is provided.

The potential for change here is very great, and will probably be the most obvious development during the next decade. All archival and unique documents are, and always have been, subject to some kind of appraisal, and this appraisal process has, of course, been fundamental in determining what information would survive and what would be provided for use. In the past, much appraisal has been haphazard and completely or substantially a matter of chance or, in some cases, subject to political control. From the beginning, archivists have sought to establish a general set of rules by which appraisal should be carried out. At times this has been seen as an attempt to delineate a science of appraisal. Probably few would still make the claim that selection procedures can be so objective and so exactly based on an analysis of the information world that they can be regarded as scientific in the full sense. Nevertheless, there is a consensus, expressed in most new archival legislation, that general lines of approach can be laid down.

That a wide spectrum of human activity is worthy of being included in appraisal at the national or international levels - hence the documentation of areas such as literature and scholarship (the work of individual authors), politics (personal, central and local), government (central, regional, municipal), science and medicine (research and implementation), banking, insurance and commercial activities generally, and manufacturing industry are all to be included in appraisal and collection programmes. One result of this understanding is that the process of appraisal is no longer seen as being essentially the preserve of government agencies or of large corporate bodies. Although no longer claimed as a science, the principles on which appraisal is conducted have been developed in important new ways over the last decade or so.

Traditional ways of approaching the task of appraisal were centred upon structural analysis: archivists would examine the surviving documentation and apply tests to it. These tests were to establish the value of the material in terms of its evidential or informational quality. More recently there has been a tendency to include appraisal tests based upon functional analysis. Here the archivists would be attempting to judge whether the documentation available did or did not present a true overall picture of the relevant field of activity; where it did not, they would seek to fill in the missing bits by alternative means.

Another development of increasing importance has been the tendency of archivists to take into consideration the costs (both financial and in terms of informational value) of retention or disposal of the material being appraised. These changes in the principles of appraisal have not yet been disseminated to all parts of the world, nor are they universally accepted, as yet, by the archival profession; but they are well established in the most advanced areas. Overall, it is probably true that everywhere in the world it is accepted that appraisal and collection policies should cover a very wide range of activities. The effective implementation of this perception varies greatly, of course, from country to country. In 1995-96 the International Council on Archives (ICA) published the text of recent new archival legislation in two volumes of its main journal, Archivum.

This reveals that in the period 1981-94, ninety-seven countries introduced new laws, or revisions of earlier laws, on the management of archives, and at least ten international, quasi-governmental institutions did so too. The weight of this legislation varied considerably, but there is no doubt that most of it incorporated generally agreed international principles of archival operation. Differences mostly concentrated upon the degree of centralisation within a state structure and on the detailed control of government materials. Several features are worth reporting. New laws in Australia, Canada, the Netherlands and the United States show the application of new principles, advancing to new levels of activity and new quality standards.

The most advanced of the new laws explicitly define the right of citizens to access materials held in archival institutions, redefine the range of materials that fall within the purview of these services, and make provision for systematic appraisal. The most striking changes were in the legislation introduced by states created by the break-up of former imperial groupings. The most important of these were the republics of the former USSR. During the communist period, the archival system of the USSR had been extremely centralised. By 1994 the central structure (Glavarkiv) had been dismantled and replaced by new controlling authorities at the level of the constituent republics, and in some cases at lower levels as well. The reconstitution of the central archival training facility as a new University of the Humanities will doubtless have an effect on user services and on access to archives generally.

The Russian Federation, under its own new legislation, is in the process of giving up the central control of archival services; the new legislation in Belarus, Latvia, Lithuania and Ukraine provides these countries with their own national legal framework. The states of the former Yugoslav federation show a rather similar situation. New laws in Albania, Croatia, the Czech Republic, Hungary, Poland, Romania and Slovakia are all intended to bring their respective national systems in line with accepted international standards by allowing clearly defined rights of access not only to their own citizens but also to researchers from abroad. The new archival law in Germany reflects the union of the country after 1989, and provides for a centrally organised federal archives service, with state archives services in each of the Länder, within which a network of city and specialised archives and libraries exists.

The changes that have made this possible involved an enormous upheaval in established practices and services on both sides of the former dividing line, but have been carried out with professionalism and thoroughness. The official policy of the old regimes in all the former communist countries had allowed access to archival sources for approved researchers but there had been no clear delineation of the principle on which access was based, nor on what finding aids should be open.

The new legislation has sought to change this. Most countries now seem to have adopted some variant of the thirty-year rule (the delay between the storage of archival material and its accessibility to the public), which now can be regarded as an international norm. Interesting new developments in archival regulation can also be seen in South Africa, where the regime established after the fall of the apartheid system has begun organising the archives to support its attempt to resolve past enmities and open its society. This has led to the re-establishment, in professional terms, of the country's leadership of the Central and Southern Africa region, a leadership that had been impossible to exercise during the apartheid years. Bibliographic control, finding aids and descriptive standards It is clear that whatever the law may say, users cannot have access to either archival or unique library materials unless there are adequate finding aids, and unless these finding aids are openly available.

It is, and always has been, a difficult and slow job to provide these aids, and it is probable that completely satisfactory finding aids will never be available for all the documentation that has to be covered. Even in countries and sites where archivists and librarians have been steadily working at the completion of catalogues, there remain substantial backlogs, and there are cases, sometimes notorious, where access cannot be given because lists are not ready or not divulged. These cases are not always confined to countries that have suffered from political control. A notable example is provided by the papers of Eamon De Valera, founding President of Ireland, which are nominally open to access but in practice are largely closed because of the lack of finding aids. Archivists and librarians continue everywhere to work at backlogs, and there are signs that eventually a substantial investment in computer equipment may improve the rate of progress.

There is a particular problem in the countries of the former USSR, and to a lesser extent in the countries of the former Eastern bloc in Europe. Under the previous regimes finding aids were either secret or restricted to internal use. Under the liberalised regimes that have been established since 1989, these internal lists are now being progressively released for use by researchers, but their coverage and adequacy as catalogues have often been questioned.

In these countries, enormous quantities of new archival materials, previously secret, have now been transferred to the archives services or have been released for consultation. It is clear that the task of drawing up adequate finding aids for all this documentation is so massive that even if there were no resourcing difficulties, the job would take a very long time. Microfilming and other external projects do little to attack the main core of the problem. An additional problem is that government bodies are tempted to sell access rights to their archive materials, or even the materials themselves, in order to obtain hard currency. This has led to a patchwork of uncoordinated releases, often through American universities.

ICA, with funding from UNESCO, has begun to follow the example set many years ago by the International Federation of Library Associations and Institutions (IFLA) for the library community, in establishing description standards for the international exchange of data about archival holdings. The basic document is the International Standard Archival Description ISAD(G), adopted by the International Congress on Archives in Montreal in 1992. ISAD(G) has now been translated into French, Italian, Japanese, Spanish and probably other languages. Training courses and workshops in its use have also been held in different parts of the world. The standard is minimal, but is serving as a skeleton upon which national or subject-based finding aids can be structured. For many countries and traditions this is an innovation, the first such standard that has had any degree of penetration from the outside world.

ICA is now working on the development of a standard for authority files covering the names of creators of archival holdings, whether official or corporate bodies, private individuals or families. This standard is not as yet fully accepted by the archival community - it will be debated at the ·International Congress on Archives in Beijing in 1996 - but it also follows in the footsteps of the library community. Another standard for the description of archives and manuscripts was developed in North America in the early 1980s: the Archives and Manuscripts Control (AMC) version of the longestablished Machine-Readable Record (MARC) bibliographic exchange format. AMC became wellestablished in the United States because it was a required format for the large public online catalogue systems, Online Computer Library Center (OCLC) and Research Libraries Information Network (RLIN), both of which have extensive but partial outreach capabilities in other parts of the world.

It has since become more important because of its use in the project to catalogue the Vatican Secret Archives, undertaken by the University of Michigan in 1988. The opening of the Vatican Archives almost coincided with the opening of the Communist Party archives in the former USSR and its satellites. The Vatican case has a broader and more technical signifi-cance, however, because of its use of the MARC AMC standard: this standard has allowed the great mass of this historic archive to be structured and managed in a way that conforms to best modern practice.

Significantly, this also marked the first international use of a previously purely American standard. A standard for the archival use of SGML (Standard Generalised Markup Language) is being developed at the University of California. If successfully completed and adopted by the archival community this standard will be of great use in under-pinning the use of the Internet for archival interchange. There will probably continue to be a need for international data exchange for two categories of archival and unique library materials: full text (in which the content of the documents can be displayed) and bibliographic (giving information about the existence and whereabouts of archival holdings). There have been interesting innovations in both these areas.

The imaging project at the Archivo de Indias in Seville, Spain, is making available the images of original documents from the Spanish discovery and administration of America from 1492 onwards. Some 10% of the holdings of this major archive are covered by the project. The images are retrieved by a separate but linked indexing system, and can be accessed remotely (although this aspect of the project still remains for the most part unexecuted). In the United Kingdom, large databases containing full abstracts of the personal papers of the first Duke of Wellington (a general in the Napoleonic wars and subsequently Prime Minister of Britain in the early nineteenth century) and the personal papers of Lord Mountbatten have both been made available electronically, giving access to full or almost full text. British universities also have provided bibliographic descriptions of other archives.

Unfortunately, none of these have been based upon any descriptive standard or format, nor have they yet been assimilated into the new formats required by the Internet. The wide-area bibliographic networks, OCLC and RLIN, both hold large quantities of bibliographic descriptions of archival and unique library materials. Although based in the United States, these databases also contain materials relating to other countries and, of course, can be accessed from anywhere in the world. Since American universities and other institutions hold much important material relating to other regions, the ability of users to consult them is an important enlargement of the world's information resources. During the late 1980s it appeared likely that these databases, or others like them, would expand to include comparable materials from other countries. This promise has not, for the most part, been realised. The failure of these projects to expand fully over the world was probably caused by a lack of resources, but also by the development of alternative, and less restrictive, media of communication, and more generally by the backlog of descriptions that could be made available.

The idea that archives and unique documents are kept primarily so that users may have access to them spread only slowly through the world. Certain countries, such as Sweden and France, accepted early the principle of public access to materials held in archival or library institutions. By the middle of the twentieth century a consensus had developed that there should be statutorily supported rights of (or at least facilities for) access. The spread of this principle received an enormous boost in the late 1980s and early 1990s, when most countries, in all parts of the world, set about revising the relevant legislation. Practical implementation of the new approach has been slower and less predictable than the acceptance of the principle. However, it is probably true that researchers now expect to be able to gain access to a wide range of documentation, and there is a growing body of literature that reports on the success or failure of such expectations.

Several nations that can be regarded as being in the vanguard of the modern information movement have enacted Freedom of Information legislation. These laws give the public rights of access to government documents, irrespective of date or of whether they have been transferred to archival institutions. The most notable of these countries are Sweden (where the legislation has historic roots), the United States, Canada, Australia and the Netherlands. The International Archive Round Table Conference held at Austin, Texas, in 1985, and one of the recommendations from that meeting was that archivists should be professionally charged with the duty of advising their governments on questions of freedom of information and of privacy.

Since then, although the principle of freedom of information is still gaining ground (especially, of course, in the countries of the former communist bloc), the privacy side of the equation has come into more prominence. At the Austin meeting the areas in which privacy should be ensured were set out: personal registration details (birth, marriage, death); the health of individuals; income; criminal proceedings; professional life; political, religious or philosophical opinions; the basic documents providing statistical information (for example, census returns); questions of family honour; police matters; and information gained under promise of confidentiality.

Methods used to ensure privacy include control both by regulating the transfer of relevant documents to the archives and by the operation of a phased closed period. Most countries now have data protection legislation that applies these principles to databases held on computer systems. Important principles are involved. One is that under data protection legislation it is usual to give subjects the right to insist that erroneous information about themselves should be changed. Archivists, however, must argue that there is a broader historical interest: data that are erroneous in terms of the current situation are not necessarily erroneous as a historical historical record. In some notorious cases a conflict of interest has come to the fore, for example, where persons who have changed sex during their lifetime have demanded the right to have their birth certificates altered.

Although desirable for their current rights as citizens, it is clear that to alter the certificate would be historically a falsification. It is likely that there will be further controversy on these issues in the future. Similarly, if personal information is rendered anonymous in order to promote rapid current use, this process damages its long-term historical value. There is a need to ensure that information supplied under conditions of confidentiality is preserved archivally without being rendered anonymous. In some countries, for example Australia, this question has become politically sensitive and has led to the destruction of important census material. The major event of the last decade must surely be the actual and promised release of the enormous and detailed archives previously closed because of the nature for the regimes that generated them.

The release of this material has been accompanied by important upheavals in the archival administrations and library services of these countries. The attention of the world has been drawn to these events, which indeed have had considerable significance for everybody. In Germany the process of unifying the two previous republics into a federal structure included a radical reorganisation of the federal archival system.

The two archive administrations were brought together, with a considerable change of senior personnel. The older archival holdings had been scattered by the occupation of Germany in 1945, and these were now reassembled. The enormous archives accumulated by the apparatus of state control of the former German Democratic Republic, including secret dossiers on large numbers of individuals, were brought under archival administration and a start made on making them available for consultation. A particular problem in these countries was what to do with the archives of the Communist Party.

Theoretically these belonged to a private organisation, but in practice they contained material relating to the entire range of government activity, and reached deeply into the affairs of many citizens. For the most part, these archives have now been brought under the control of the national archives system, though the problems of creating and making available the necessary finding aids remain formidable.

Interestingly, this resolution of the question of the Party archives has brought into relief the parallel problem of the archives of the Church in these countries. While the state had taken over from the churches the responsibility for civil registration, church archives still contain important demographic information, and access to them is a subject of broad interest. One particular aspect of this issue concerns the recovery of confiscated Church property, the re-establishment of monastic institutions and the specific ownership (as between different ecclesiastical groups) of buildings. There have been bilateral projects intended to assist in the preservation and accessibility of archival holdings in the former communist states.

For example, the Hoover Institute at Stanford University in the United States had an agreement between 1992 and 1995 to microfilm some of the state archives in the Russian Federation. This project was very controversial and recalls similar projects in the past, such as that of Syracuse University and the archives of Kenya in the 1960s. Though they help to preserve and make accessible parts of the world's archival heritage, it is not clear that the best way to achieve this is to remove control from the country of origin. China, echoing its importance in world affairs, is now strengthening its impact on international archival matters, and in 1996 assumed the presidency of ICA. Despite the damage and setbacks of the Cultural Revolution in the 1960s, the country has made considerable new investment in the management of archives and unique documents, and has begun to attack the problems posed by a tradition of secretiveness.

Archives for the period up to 1949 were opened by legislation in 1980, and there has been increasing international co-operation in archival training since then. When discussing archive collections in terms of human rights, the development of archival services in international bodies and the coming together of archival services in the countries of the European Union are both significant. The latter has been marked by a determination to recall the importance of proper archives services for democratic regimes and the rule of law, and to implement such services. An important statement made by the countries of the Council of Europe as a result of a conference in Strasbourg in 1994 included plans for the computerisation of finding aids and publications, microfilming, and improving access facilities as an underpinning to the concept of a common European heritage.

A particular programme was announced for the management and opening of the archives of the Comintern (the Third Communist International), and for aid to currently disadvantaged countries - a specific programme is proposed for Albania. This European statement applies principally to archives held in traditional form. Similar problems exist in connection with appraisal, preservation and access to archival material in audiovisual form. These have been the subject of international discussion and agreement in specialist forums. The importance of computers for library cataloguing and for archive administration is clear, and several projects and events have underlined this potential in the world arena. The project for an extended international catalogue of eighteenth-century books has now been virtually completed, and is another example of the effective use of agreed formats and cataloguing standards.

After long delays and hesitations, the Manuscripts Division of the British Library adopted a system for computer cataloguing which has, in effect, eliminated the notorious thirtyyear backlog between the acquisition of materials and the publication of the finding aids to them. This achievement alone should give cause for optimism that in the following decades similar backlogs can be removed. The arrival of the Internet has caused a flurry of activity, and it is now possible to find on it descriptions of archive and manuscript holdings in many countries. One reason for the rush to put homepages on the World Wide Web is that, once access has been gained to the Internet by way of a provider agency (usually the archive's parent institution), archivists and librarians are not impeded by the need to learn and adapt to detailed formats and cataloguing rules.

It is a simple matter to put descriptions on the Web as free text, embellished by graphics and digital images. Comparing the structure of MARC records with pages entered using the standard Internet format, HTML, shows immediately how relatively quick and easy the latter method is, both in the technicalities of data entry and in the presentation of the material to users. The Web is itself, moreover, directly a user interface. Nevertheless, it should be added that from a worldwide point of view the computer age has hardly hardly begun for manuscripts and archives. In many of the most important regions it is not easy for archivists and librarians to get access to hardware or software, or to keep their equipment maintained to a reliable standard. When equipment is obtained, there is a shortage of relevant training.

Software may have to be adapted to local conditions, and there is little or no standardisation in either the developed or developing world. In some developed countries, such as Italy, Germany or the United Kingdom, archivists and related communities have attempted to develop specialised software, only to find that they do not have the resources to compete with the constantly upgraded commercial packages. In less developed areas, UNESCO's CDS/ISIS software has been used to good effect, but here again the absence of pre-designed applications or of general standards has prevented rapid development of databases, and this despite the devoted efforts of a few trainers to extend the body of expertise. In other developed areas, for example Japan, archivists and manuscript librarians have not yet generally come into contact with computer systems.

Even in the most highly developed countries there are many smaller, local, specialised or poorly supported archives and manuscript collections that have not yet seriously begun to use automated methods. ICA is now actively establishing a presence on the World Wide Web, and is supporting a project under which the national archives of key countries in the developing world will be enabled to join the Internet community. Appraising, preserving and giving access to electronic records and data sets has been an increasing preoccupation in many countries. Most progress towards a technological solution to these problems has been made in North America, and from there the expertise has been disseminated. In November 1994 an important conference in Australia, 'Playing for Keeps', assembled a body of authoritative papers which is likely to serve as a structure for action in this field. These papers deal with the management of electronic archives.

In the case of unique but nonarchival documents in electronic form, a body of expertise has already been developed, under the general aegis of the International Association for Social Science Information Service and Technology (IASSIST), operating through electronic data archives. One or more of these institutions can be found in most developed countries, and there is now a regular system for identifying, appraising, acquiring and making available data sets in electronic form. In some countries, such as Sweden, this operation is strongly co-ordinated with the national archives service. In others, such as the United Kingdom, the operation is separate. Access to this material is increasingly provided remotely by way of the Internet or other networks.

The Memory of the World Programme, initiated by UNESCO, aimed at preservation of and access to the documentary heritage of the world. As stated in its initial document, 'access facilitates protection and preservation ensures access'. The seven introductory projects include digitisation of manuscripts from the cities of Prague, St Petersburg and Moscow, and from Bulgaria and the Yemen, a newspaper project in Latin America and a programme for scientific manuscripts in Turkey. A Memory of the World national committee now exists in ten countries, and it is clear that the programme will have important effects in preserving and making available specific sets of unique materials. So far these materials appear to have been chosen because they are considered particularly valuable and attractive; the real problem lies with the vast masses of undescribed and unmanageable archives, bearing intimately on the life of people, that have suddenly, in the last few years, been thrust upon the world stage. Documentary heritage reflects the diversity of languages, peoples and cultures. It is the mirror of the world and its memory. But that memory is fragile.

Every day, fragments, if not entire sections, of the documentary heritage disappear for ever. To guard against collective amnesia, it must remain our aim and hope to preserve manuscripts and other rare and valuable archive and library material existing in any form, whether written, audiovisual or electronic, and to ensure their wider dissemination.

For this reason, UNESCO has launched a vast and ambitious programme entitled 'Memory of the World'. The twofold purpose of the UNESCO 'Memory of the World' Programme is to safeguard and promote the endangered world documentary heritage. The scale and structure of the programme are such that intellectual, technical and financial partnerships will be required. In this programme, UNESCO intends to act as a co-ordinator and catalyst.

An International Advisory Committee guides the overall implementation of the programme and determines the award of the 'Memory of the World' label to the projects selected. At the national level, a committee is responsible for project selection and follow-up. A world list of endangered library and archive holdings will be a cornerstone of the programme. Preservation by means of the most appropriate techniques, ease of access and wide dissemination must be the hallmarks of this programme, which is to include not only rare manuscripts and documents from libraries and archives, but also audiovisual and computerised recorded material. The 'Memory of the World' Programme has aroused great interest from the time it was launched, and requests for assistance are regularly being received by UNESCO.

The well-ordered world of the university library is giving way to a new era of promise and uncertainty, of technology, of new forms of engagement and redefined roles in learning. The assumptions and rationales that have been relied on in the past are inadequate as a guide to future developments. To be successful in this new environment those responsible for academic libraries need to understand:

— the changing expectations faced by universities,
— how universities are responding to these new expectations,
— how this affects the library's mission,
— how libraries can develop a strategy to be a central part of the university's response, and
— how the Association of Research Libraries can assist its members to take on new roles.

This concept of learning requires a shift in focus from the teacher's knowledge to the student's understandings and capabilities. This shift in focus leads to a new perspective on the development of quality in the academic enterprise. More than anything, it requires the faculty to bring the strength of the research paradigm into the learning process. The high quality of research in American universities is, in part, the result of the central role of assessment in the research process. With an understanding of student learning objectives, the scholarship of teaching and learning identifies critical issues, uses research methods, and applies results to understand and improve learning outcomes.

For over a decade, institutional and professional accreditation bodies have been shifting their attention from input measures (faculty, courses, books) to outcomes measures (what students learn). Universities and colleges are required to develop and implement a student outcomes assessment program. Assessment requires academic organisations (departments, colleges, universities) to:

- make expectations and standards for quality explicit and public
- systematically gather evidence on how well performance matches those expectations and standards
- analyse and interpret the evidence
- use the resulting information to document, explain and improve performance.

The focus on learning involves looking at the academic program not from the perspective of its subject matter content but from the perspective of the competencies to be developed by students. These competencies include knowledge, skills and abilities, and attitudes and values that are important to a graduate's future success. It is easy to treat these new expectations as one more example of a demand for accountability in higher education.

A closer examination leads me to conclude that they represent a recognition of the changing needs of graduates to be successful in an increasingly complex knowledge economy. Faculty have always assessed the performance of individual students within their individual courses. The focus of outcomes assessment is on the collective success of the program in developing the competencies of the students in the program.

The faculty is being asked to accept responsibility for a broader set of outcomes. To a significant extent this represents a new challenge because while faculty are knowledge experts, they are not necessarily learning experts. Students will also be required to approach the learning experience differently.

They are being asked to become more actively involved in the learning process. While they have mastered the passive accumulation of knowledge, they are less comfortable with the responsibility to demonstrate their ability to use knowledge in unstructured situations. They must become proficient as members of teams, in communicating their solutions, and effectively taking advantage of access to information and the use of technology.

Finally, they must begin to develop and demonstrate maturity in how they approach their work. The focus on learning outcomes leads to a consideration of the learning process and the learning community. From the University's perspective, they are achieved as a result of a total experience over a four (or more) year period. Each element of the educational program contributes, directly or indirectly, to their achievement. Looking at the learning process allows us to recognise the various activities that contribute to learning.

On the far left of the figure we see how foundational courses (math, composition, etc), general education courses and special prerequisite service.courses prepare the student for the major. The requirements for the major are designed to produce the learning outcomes necessary for the graduate to be successful. Across the bottom of the figure we see how the program offerings of the library, student life and technical services can contribute to the learning outcomes of the graduate. Looking at the learning community allows us to consider how faculty, students and other learning professionals can contribute to learning outcomes. The faculty responsible for the major is in the best position to develop the complete set of learning outcomes, since those outcomes will depend on the specific objectives for the degree program. The American Association for Higher Education's Principles of Good Practice for Assessing Student Learning recognise that "student learning is a campus-wide responsibility, and assessment is a way of enacting that responsibility.

Faculty play an especially important role, but assessment questions can't be fully addressed without participation by student affairs educators, librarians, administrators, and students. ...assessment is not a task for a small group of experts but a collaborative activity; its aim is wider, better informed attention to student learning by all parties with a stake in its improvement." The University is made up of various communities, each of which has a direct and/or indirect view of student learning outcomes.

Faculty with responsibility for designing and delivering a general education program must define outcomes that assure students across the University will have a common foundation and also contribute to the learning outcomes that are important in many degree programs. An academic department has a direct interest in the learning outcomes for students in their majors. A department with an important course that serves a critical role in preparing students in another department's degree program has an indirect interest in the learning outcomes for students in that major. For example, physics is an important service course for students in an engineering program. The Physics faculty can not be effective unless they are working with the Engineering faculty to produce a clear set of learning outcomes for their service courses that will help achieve the outcomes desired for the engineering students.

Within the new environment, we need to measure the ways in which the library is contributing to the learning that the University values. Like the general education program, the library has a direct and an indirect interest in the learning outcomes for all the students at the University. Like the Physics Department, the Library should be able to contribute to the achievement of learning outcomes for various academic programs across the University. Developing a set of learning outcomes will allow libraries to determine the extent to which their interests are aligned with the expectations of other academic communities in the University. They will find that faculty responsible for the general education program as well as those responsible for many of the academic degree programs also are interested in critical thinking, the effective use of information and technology, the search process and collaborative reasoning.

The library can build on a shared view of what are important student learning outcomes. All the individual communities are being asked to prepare students in ways that go.beyond their expertise in their fields. It is this shared need to go beyond our traditional focus on what students need to know that creates an opportunity for the library. Consider for a moment the way in which a department faculty might look at the learning outcomes for their degree program and how they are achieved through the course requirements.

Having agreed on what outcomes they believe are important to their graduate's future success, they can ask the faculty responsible for each course to identify the extent to which each outcome is a focus of the course. Collectively, across the curriculum, they can determine which outcomes are covered to a major, moderate or minor extent. At this point, while they haven't yet assessed how well their students have developed on each learning outcome, they can evaluate whether enough attention is being paid to individual outcomes.

The library must take the initiative in determining what the library has to offer that will help the department achieve greater success in achieving their learning outcomes. Libraries have developed organisational strategies to serve the various academic communities. But the focus to date is primarily on making information more and more accessible rather that addressing specifically the learning outcomes important to student success.

The library needs to ask what kind of expertise is required to be actively engaged in the learning process and an effective partner in achieving learning outcomes. It then will be in a position to adapt roles and responsibilities of its professionals to take full advantage of the opportunity.

Collaborative Digital Reference Service (CDRS)

In United Kingdom the Collaborative Digital Reference Service (CDRS) provides professional reference service to researchers anytime, anywhere, through an international, online network of libraries and related institutions. Launched by the Library of Congress in June 2000, CDRS now includes more than 200 member libraries—academic, public, special, and national—worldwide and that number is growing weekly.

The collaboration has been very beneficial in that each library brings its professional experience, knowledge of user behavior and needs, and subject expertise to bear on the project. CDRS uses technology to provide the best answers in the best context, by taking advantage not only of the millions of Internet resources but also of the many more millions of resources that are not online and that are held by libraries around the world.

CDRS supports libraries by providing them additional choices for the services they offer their patrons. Libraries can more ably assist their patrons by sending questions that are best answered by the expert staff and collections of CDRS member institutions from around the world. An advisory board, comprised of representatives from CDRS member institutions, meets to discuss policy and future directions of the program. Business meetings with member representatives are also regularly held to get feedback, report on and solve workflow problems, discuss training and performance measures, and build esprit de corps.

The CDRS homepage posts general information and news links, information for members, and project milestones. An electronic mailing list allows members to communicate frequently with one another, get technical questions addressed, and comment on the efficacy of the network.

At no other time in history has the emergence of technology affected so significantly the core mission of a library. These technological advances have created new service opportunities for libraries and library patrons. For information to have relevance, it must be up-to-date and receive the hands-on touch of the skilled reference librarian to provide context and added value.

Through the CDRS network, LC and its partner libraries can serve researchers everywhere and, in so doing, bring control, context, greater choice, and timeliness to the world of information. CDRS includes two component parts: submission of a question and answer, and archiving the answer for future use. The workflow looks like this: An end user requests information through a CDRS member institution.

The member institution sends the query to the online Request Manager (RM) software for processing and assigning. The RM searches a database of CDRS member institution profiles looking for the institution best suited to answer the question. Once a match on an institution has been made, the query is sent to that institution for answering.

After the query has been answered, it is routed back to the original CDRS requesting library via the RM to allow for closing out the case and completing other administrative tasks. The library profile is the core of the routing and assignment activity, and each institution can "code" itself as broadly or as narrowly as it chooses.

Library profiles contain basic information about the library, including hours of service, collection strengths, staff strengths, education levels served, languages covered, geographic location of users served, whether there are special services provided and what they are--as many as 28 data fields. This information is captured in a table, where it is used by the online RM to sort, assign, and track incoming questions and to deliver answers to the end user.

Further, the profile tool is flexible enough to allow for regular updating to reflect staffing changes or special circumstances that would affect the automatic routing by the RM. For example, if the astronomy specialist is on sabbatical for several months and no back-up is available, the library might choose to remove that subject strength from its profile until the staff member returns.

Answers are edited and stored in a separately searchable knowledge base of information. The knowledge base, to be populated with the diverse and authentic information provided by CDRS librarians, will ultimately serve as a front end to CDRS, designed to "catch" and answer incoming questions if there is a ready match. If there is no match on the knowledge base, the question will be routed through the RM and assigned to a library.

There are no restrictions on the types of libraries that can participate. Size of a library or collection is not a factor in determining whether a library can become a member. The aforementioned Service Level Agreement defines the nature of the member library's relationship to the CDRS and that agreement is codified in the library profiles. Many types of agreements are possible and are limited or expanded depending upon the strengths (e.g., subject) or limitations of the individual library.

A library may agree to ask and answer questions; only ask questions; ask or answer questions only during specified periods; serve as an editor for the knowledge base; or serve as the on-call library if the automatic Request Manager function is inoperable.

In addition, many libraries have local collections that are unique to them. These local, specialised collections make a potent contribution to CDRS overall, filling special niches that larger research institutions may not be able to fill. In addition to defining roles and responsibilities among the partner libraries, the SLAs will ultimately be used to determine what it will cost a library to be a member of CDRS.

We have encouraged maximum flexibility in developing the many component parts of CDRS. For a library to want to participate, CDRS has to be perceived to have value. Just as there are no "one size fits all" libraries, so too are there no "one size fits all" arrangements with CDRS. Libraries are structured and organised differently, they have different local audiences, and they have different policies and procedures for ensuring quality control.

To be useful to a library, CDRS must fill an unmet need and offer something that the library does not already have, e.g., adequate staff, a subject strength, or a special collection unique to a participating library that the whole collaboration then has access to. When the participating library defines the terms of that value, that library will have greater incentive to make the arrangement work, for itself and for CDRS.

Currently, libraries participating in CDRS connect with other libraries on behalf of patrons so that the libraries can conduct the reference interview before sending the question, define the parameters of the service, determine what works and what does not work, and create a service that is scalable and maximally responsive to user needs. From the beginning, however, we have envisioned that CDRS will become a service that is available directly to patrons, recognising that many individuals never go to their local library but still need information. In January 2001, the Online Computer Library Center (OCLC) and the Library of Congress, on behalf of CDRS member libraries, signed a cooperative agreement to guide CDRS through its next phase of development.

OCLC will provide technical and development support to CDRS by building and maintaining a database of participating institution profiles that will route questions and answers through CDRS; building and maintaining a question-and-answer database system that will enable CDRS participants to catalog answers and store them in a searchable and browsable database; and providing administrative support for CDRS, including marketing the service, registering new members, and providing training and user support.

Together, the Library of Congress and OCLC will develop a viable model for a self-sustaining digital reference service and promote CDRS in the library community. The major factors that influence the level of investment an institution can make are software and hardware costs (including laptops for telecommuting librarians), staffing/hours issues, and training.

Some libraries are offering experimental services that are open only a couple of hours a day and use inexpensive software, while others are committed to 24/7 service, delivered via sophisticated call center software from the corporate sector.

When choosing software, there are a large number of chat software programs and services on the market to choose from. Libraries also have the option of installing the software on their own computer networks or having it hosted by a commercial vendor or by a free service such as Yahoo! Chat. Each approach has its associated challenges, including response time, maintenance issues, and control over the user interface.

5

Network Infrastructure

The Internet is a worldwide, publicly accessible network of interconnected computer networks that transmit data by packet switching using the standard Internet Protocol (IP). It is a "network of networks" that consists of millions of smaller domestic, academic, business, and government networks, which together carry various information and services, such as electronic mail, online chat, file transfer, and the interlinked Web pages and other documents of the World Wide Web.

The implementation of a technology infrastructure should be fully integrated with the creation of content that people will want to use, with the National Grid for Learning, with training and development programmes inside the library service, and with coaching programmes for users. The funding proposals presented here attempt to provide the means for such an holistic approach to implementation. These proposals provide the means to encourage innovation across the library networks. When implemented, they will make networked information and learning resources available to every UK citizen in all communities, linking individual learners - adults and children - and their teachers to a panoply of institutions and organisations.

At the same time this network can make UK public libraries' services available worldwide, and give UK citizens access to global information sources. The largest libraries will need forty or more terminals for users, plus those for librarians'. If we estimate that an additional 40,000 terminals are required - together with printers, other ancillary equipment and installation on a suitable LAN (local area network) - then a spend of around £120 million is likely. To ensure people have fast access to networked services, every library should be connected by ISDN (Integrated Services Digital Network) where available. Where this is not currently possible, a negotiation with the network providers will be required to plan and agree the provision and financing. As the number of terminals and user sessions increases, higher bandwidths will be required.

Sufficient bandwidth (i.e. capacity) will be required to deliver distance learning and real-time interactive visual services, as applications become available. The whole of the system should be linked by a UK-wide network that ensures that individuals in any area can enter into and interact with resources and learning programmes available outside their immediate area. Technology is available to help do all this, but the best, most advanced and highest capacity is not available everywhere.

As a start, the core requirements for information and learning can be delivered everywhere, and it will be possible to go beyond this in many places. Main sites in all authorities can be connected to the proposed UK-wide network. Within authorities, technical and cost constraints will prevent all of the requirements being delivered to every single place from the start - it should be possible to reach all locations as the project continues.

Right from the start, funding and contractual arrangements should be created that enable remoter places to have services otherwise unaffordable. The costs of the network technology are difficult to estimate at this stage, before a full audit and design study. In round terms, a gross budget of £36 million is proposed for connections and £48 million annual rentals should be made available for local library systems. This would provide for a mix of network capabilities designed to fit local requirements.

A budget of around £10 million for connection and £36 million annual rentals for UK networking would also be required. For local networking, an important point to consider is the possibility of libraries being connected into a local branch of an education network such as that being considered by government. An ICT project of this scale will also create opportunities for efficiency savings, as well as new revenue-earning services, including payment from central government for the delivery of electronic services. It is proposed that the network should consists of two main components:

a) the library authority networks;

b) the UK Public Library Network.

The objective here is to assist library authorities to continue to develop their networks with maximum flexibility, responsiveness to local needs, and sensitivity to existing infrastructure. It is proposed that library authorities should be assisted with funding which could be bid for according to agreed criteria and could cover the cost of:

a) connectivity;

b) hardware;

c) Web sites/servers;

d) maintenance;

e) upgrading;

f) staffing/training;

g) special needs;

h) convenient and extended opening hours.

Allowing a choice of how funds are allocated between these areas would ensure local flexibility and sensitivity. There should be minimum standards of connectivity for all locations, providing for:

a) fast connection to the Internet;

b) interactive sessions using videoconferencing and multimedia tools with locations inside and outside the libraries network.

The capability (subject to demand) for higher-quality real-time services should also be considered. A mixture of network provision dependent on local conditions is envisaged, including ISDN and higher-bandwidth networks. We also recognise that some digitally recorded material could be more cheaply and efficiently provided by increasing the availability of CD-roms.

It is also proposed that minimum standards of hardware provision (terminals for users) should be set out, to ensure wide availability to library users. These standards should be specified in detail by the Public Library Networking Agency when established. This would interconnect all public library authority networks at a guaranteed level of bandwidth. This capacity would allow a universal availability of multimedia to reasonable level.

The UK network would enable higher-quality connections to other similar networks, and permit the creation of services for delivery across the whole of the network. It is recommended that a managed network service be purchased for the UK public library service. There should be a UK-wide funding programme in which there are two pools of funding:

a) for the library authority networks - funded by a procurement process through a managing agent. Funds should be available for regional consortia where library authorities choose to have cooperative arrangements. Compliance with the minimum standards will be required. The managing agent should be capable of managing an allocation process when required.

b) for the UK network - the network to be specified and awarded to an operator or operators after a tender process.

It is widely recognised that the Internet will continue to be the principal driving force for the development of the information society. The Internet is a versatile and pervasive digital network capable of supporting a wide range of applications and providing access to a diverse and rapidly expanding range of information services. The Internet also provides a dynamic development environment that is pioneering a wide range of new technologies, applications and services.

Connecting the UK public libraries to the Internet will therefore enable them to extend their services to a wider user community and to participate fully in the development of the information society. The Internet is formed by the interconnection of thousands of separate networks in different management domains. Within a single management domain there may be several networks, and the management domains cover both private and public network services.

The component networks exploit numerous telecommunication technologies, ranging from the dial-up telephone network to state-of-the-art broadband switching technologies. The objective of the Internet is to integrate this complexity and diversity into a single unified network from the user's point of view. The Internet approach offers considerable flexibility for networking the public libraries, allowing a solution that matches the organisational and funding characteristics of the sector, that can take advantage of specific UK opportunities and developments in telecommunications at both UK and regional levels, and that can embrace a variety of network technologies -

including new technologies that will help the networking programme to evolve in the future.

Furthermore, the Internet is associated with a rich and diverse development programme that is pioneering new applications and addressing major issues such as privacy, security, copyright, etc. The public libraries will be able to participate in the benefit from this programme. However, the Internet alone cannot provide the level of service required by the UK's public libraries. The Internet has bottlenecks of information flow which cannot be managed, and it is a complex environment in which undesirable material cannot easily be controlled. It is therefore proposed that the library service adopts a model which allows management of these and other important issues. The proposed model for networking the public libraries has two levels:

a) the provision of local networks to interconnect the libraries associated with each library authority;

b) the interconnection of the library authority networks and their connection to the Internet and to other UK and international networks, including the National Grid for Learning and the University for Industry.

In UK, library authority networks project is directed at the public library service, implementation has to be through the library authority structures and funding mechanisms. In referring to library networks, it is recognised that these are sometimes part of a wider integrated local network. The following assumptions have been made about the nature of local networked public library services:

a) Every local public library service can be represented as:

   i) clusters of users;

   ii) a provider and publisher of content and services;

   iii) a provider of expert guidance through information channels and sources, and in content publishing.

b) Users are in a variety of contexts, combining location, need and service level:

   i) in major lending and reference libraries;

   ii) in local community libraries, where (for example) after-school and student use should intensify from late afternoons, particularly when stimulated by homework clubs;

   iii) in mobile libraries;

   iv) in schools and other educational institutions;

   v) at other community information and service access points - such as information kiosks in rural post offices or in hospitals;

   vi) at home and at work (thereby impacting on the remote dial-in services offered by public libraries), from where users should be able to access a range of free and chargeable services, via the Internet;

   vii) in prisons.

c) Users will be presented with a range of services and advice, and these should be matched to users' ability to make use of the systems and software available. The principle of access to increasingly sophisticated systems, software and advice should be built into the services presented. Expert assistance and guidance will be integrated with the services, and this expertise will be available online and on-site, and will include an extended-hours service.

d) All publicly provided locations will benefit from full multimedia access to services - text, audio and graphics and simple video services as a minimum, but ranging to higher-quality video and other services, dependent on demand - and for the purposes of costing there will be a minimum standard of terminals provided for users, to comply with the overall UK framework.

e) Library authorities will continue to plan and purchase systems independently, but public library development will be in line with the UK-wide policy being developed here.

f) Individual local public library systems will be interconnected (using agreed UK standards) to provide a UK Public Library Network service that provides interactive communication with:

   i) other public-sector online services;

   ii) commercial online and Internet services;

   iii) services running on SuperJANET and other similar networks in the higher education sector.

g) The purpose is to provide:

   i) guaranteed high-quality levels of service for users;

   ii) cost-effective purchase for the public sector of the infrastructure and content.

Each library authority will be responsible for managing an Internet-compatible network connecting all the libraries within its jurisdiction. These networks could exploit specific regional initiatives and opportunities where they exist - including collaborative ventures with local industry, schools, colleges, universities, etc., and local telecommunications opportunities. Each local network will exploit a mix of network technologies to meet its specific requirements.

These technologies include the standard telephone network, higher-bandwidth services available on public and private networks, leased lines, and cable/modem, radio and satellite solutions. It is expected that responsibility for each of these networks will be a local matter, but they should be supported via a UK programme that pump-primes and stimulates development and offers technical support and coordination. An appropriate UK-wide support programme will help to ensure local network compatibility, will encourage sharing of resources and experience, and will help to ensure that complete coverage of all libraries can be achieved within a time-scale to be defined. Two basic approaches have been considered:

a) a managed approach, under which there would be coordinated procurement and management of the network;

b) a totally decentralised approach, under which library authorities would separately negotiate and procure their own Internet connections.

Each library network would independently connect to the Internet, using an appropriate Internet service provider (ISP). It is likely that several ISPs would be involved in covering the full set of library networks. These connections could be procured either independently by each authority or by a central procurement initiative covering all networks, though this would carry with it the problem of reconciling dispersed funding with strategic direction.

Central procurement would have the advantage of bulk purchasing on a UK scale, which should attract considerable interest from the ISPs and yield reduced costs compared with independent procurements. The central procurement would identify the best ISP for each library network, and the library authorities would then individually contract with the appropriate ISP. It is strongly recommended that option (a) - the managed approach - is taken, on the grounds that it offers advantages of:

a) economy;

b) technical resilience;

c) guaranteed service levels;

d) realisation of a UK-wide strategy.

Electronic Sholarly Information

Archiving is sometimes taken to mean preservation or

conservation in perpetuity. A more utilitarian approach sees the objective of archiving as 'to ensure that information survives in a usable form as long as it is wanted' or 'retention for a period of continuing value'. There is also potential for confusion between digital preservation and digitisation for preservation.

In the latter case, back issues of rare or important serials are often digitised and made available over networks, both to improve accessibility as well as sometimes to aid the preservation of the original item. Examples of this type of operation are the Journal Storage Project (JSTOR), described in more detail below, and the Internet Library of Early Journals (ILEJ) funded by the UK Electronic Libraries Programme (eLib). Digital preservation, on the other hand, embraces both the preservation of the information embodied in a document (the informational content) and the conservation of the information carrier itself (the physical object).

Archiving is problematic in a further sense. Use of the term suggests a distinct activity in the publishing value chain, but in reality archiving is part of a continuum in which there is overlap with storage and distribution of current electronic journals. There is no functional distinction between these activities but rather different cultural practices and attitudes towards the intellectual and commercial value of scholarly material. Subject areas will vary in where they draw the boundary between a current collection and an archived collection.

Archiving implies a change in status of the information: it is likely to be associated with different licence agreements, different access conditions and different retrieval mechanisms.In the short term, the interests of publishers, librarians and scholars are being served by a strategy of parallel publishing, with print and digital versions of substantial numbers of key journals. This has provided all parties with a 'transitional space' to explore the potential value of networked information and to work through the implications of the digital paradigm. At a time of intense pressure on library budgets, however, it is proving increasingly difficult to maintain subscription levels for digital and print versions, particularly where access to both formats carries a significant additional premium. Furthermore, there are organisational as well as physical costs in maintaining a dual holdings and access strategy for journal acquisitions and collection management, which libraries can ill afford. Faced with this situation, university libraries are looking to make their budgets go further through the use of a range of options such as consortium purchasing, subscribing to the online version only of serials, whilst also exploiting the capabilities of networked information for the benefit of the academic end users.

Although direct subscription prices may still go up in some cases, the university may reduce costs by trimming technical and public services, saving space, and achieving organisational efficiencies for the electronic version. There are, however, some major impediments to the more widespread uptake of networked online serials.

One serious impediment concerns the archiving of electronic scholarly information. Libraries have traditionally played an archival role to their communities through acquiring and storing journals for long term use. In the case of electronic serials, the continued existence of electronic information cannot be guaranteed in the same way, and the preservation role in a digital world appears to sit more logically with the producers or the aggregators of information. There is a real challenge here for the academic library community. Historically, the archiving/preservation role has been theirs.

The economics of the electronic production paradigm suggest this function might be better undertaken elsewhere in the publishing value chain. Archiving of journals in a digital age is far more complex than the preservation of print collections and likely to become increasingly so. Although often presented as a primarily technological issue, there are more intractable dimensions relating to organisational, social and legal issues. This is not surprising, given the highly systemic nature of electronic publishing and the dynamic tension which surrounds the entire scholarly communication process.

Digital archiving of networked journals has become an issue because there is no easy solution. There are problems associated with three aspects of digital information technology: the digital storage medium itself, the hardware configuration, and format or software dependence. Whereas in the 1980s, media longevity was often seen as the key technological problem, this is now overshadowed by hardware obsolescence and software dependence.Digital information comes in a variety of physical formats (media) which differ widely in their longevity and fragility.

Among the common formats are floppy disks, magnetic tape and cartridges, WORM optical storage and CD-ROM disks. New media appear all the time, although not all survive for long in the marketplace. Digital media, both magnetic and optical, have short lifetimes in comparison with media like paper and microfilm. CD-ROM and optical WORM seem very durable, with lifetimes of 100 years. Fragility is important, in that some media are sensitive to the number of times they are used, or have stringent storage requirements.The technological response to media longevity is known as 'digital refreshing' - the periodic recopying of the data onto a new medium. Refreshing only lengthens lifespan if the storage format is independent of any particular technology. ASCII text is about the only format that can be currently considered independent of technology.

Much more important than fragility or longevity is the technological obsolescence of the equipment to read the media. The most popular technologies of the 1960s, punched cards and 9-track tape, are almost gone today. Even if the equipment were available, the storage and handling capacity of new media are so much greater than earlier ones that it is very unlikely that libraries would want to hang on to old technologies, even if they were to have the chance (Lesk).

Digital information is increasingly stored in formats which are dependent upon particular software to interpret them correctly. There are a great many more formats than there are media, and this is likely to get worse in the future as delivery mechanisms and formats change and increase in complexity. A migration strategy for preserving digital information involves the periodic transfer of digital materials from one hardware/software configuration to another, or from one generation of computer technology to a subsequent generation.

The purpose of migration is to preserve the integrity of digital objects and to retain the ability for clients to retrieve, display, and otherwise use them in the face of constantly changing technology. Migration is a much more complex task than refreshing in that it takes account of the hardware and software obsolescence problem. While refreshing has been attempted for some years and is known, migration is new and mostly unknown. The migration strategy has two facets:

1) preserving the integrity of the objects (journals, abstracts, and indexing) themselves, and
2) migrating the system to provide convenient ongoing access to those objects

Migration strategies for simple digital objects exist but those for more complex digital objects are still to be developed. For migration purposes, the content of a digital object may be preserved whole, or in part, or as a surrogate. The different levels of preservation relate in part to the complexity of the digital objects being preserved.

Issues in Copy right and Ownership

The legal issues relating to copyright and ownership of information are, if anything, more challenging than the technical ones. This stems in large part from existing copyright laws which have not yet been amended to take account of a digital environment. Publishers and vendors have been able to take commercial advantage of the uncertainties in this area by using contract law rather than copyright law. With print journals, information is purchased through subscriptions and under the terms of 'fair dealing' so libraries have quite a lot of control over how information is used, distributed and stored.

The organisation retains physical custody of an artefact - a volume or an issue - for as long as it is required. The situation for online serials is very different. Publishers and vendors license specific rights of use over a journal or group of journals for a limited period of time. There is no physical artefact, unless it is like a CD-ROM, and the terms of licence may specifically exclude copying, distributing and storage for long term use. Some of the rights libraries have in the print environment are being challenged by publishers. The long term future of the intellectual property rights held for digital objects is uncertain.

The enormous variety of agencies publishing and distributing digital objects, and the numerous and ill-defined roles of the creators of digital objects make legal responsibility unclear. There is as yet no legal deposit for digital objects, so there is no impartial source for such rights.There are two distinct organisational or management issues that surround long term archiving. The first relates to decisions about who should preserve and what should be preserved.

The second concerns the potential loss of librarians' preservation role and whether they would wish to reclaim this. In many countries, including Australia, decisions about who should preserve have been dealt with under the legal deposit legislation which has ensured that all relevant published works are collected and preserved. This legislation does not usually cover electronic publications.

Although efforts are being made by some national libraries (examples discussed below) to archive online scholarly serials, there is a growing consensus that the physical transfer of online publications to central repositories is not going to be a cost-effective solution although no economic case has yet been established either way. The Task Force on the Archiving of Digital Information has proposed that digital information creators, providers and owners should have the initial responsibility for archiving while certified digital archives should be given the right and duty to exercise an aggressive fail-safe rescue function.

The crucial time will come when publishers no longer have any interest in keeping a journal going. It is at that time that fail-safe mechanisms should be activated. One danger in the digital world is that some librarians believe that they should save everything, and very often fail to recognise the associated costs of cataloguing and archiving the material.

Having a fail-safe mechanism does not imply that all scholarly journals need to be permanently archived. The same kind of principles that applied in the past can be used, although adapted to the new modes of communications. The second issue relates to the librarian role. Duranceau questions whether librarians should allow the preservation role to slip from underneath them into the hands of commercial entities - the vendors, aggregators and publishers.

Whilst it might be expedient in the short term for these parties to step into the archiving breach, she suggests that in a library that is re-engineered with efficient workflows for electronic serials, it might be feasible for serials acquisitions departments to be central players in archiving key resources.

The social dimension to long term archiving concerns the matter of trust. Scholarly publishing, with its economic perversities, is a fertile ground for mistrust and relationships between publishers and university librarians. 'Solutions' to long term archiving of journal collections which leave university librarians in an unequal negotiating position vis-a-vis publishers, or which run the risk of entrenching monopoly power, are unlikely to gain library support.

Future Trends

Archiving is integral to the value-adding publishing chain. Where it sits in this chain among the various functions from authoring through to utilisation, and which party or parties assume responsibility for it, is bound up with the economics of journal publishing.

Many observers of the journal marketplace have noted the significant increase in electronic scholarly publishing activity. The number of mainstream titles appearing in parallel print and electronic formats is steadily rising, although licence agreements and pricing models have not yet stabilised and the market remains immature.

Print-only journals still constitute the large majority of journal titles, both in absolute terms as well as proportionately for most publishing houses. However, the situation is changing and most commentators expect this trend to accelerate once market uncertainty is reduced. It is difficult to obtain up-to-date and reliable data, not least because there is so much activity in this area and much of it is small scale and incremental.

In Odlyzko's view, electronic journals will become almost universal but most of them will be versions of established print journals and will be equally expensive. Free or inexpensive electronic journals will grow, but probably not too rapidly. However, this situation is not likely to persist for long. A longer time frame is predicted for the real paradigm shift from print to electronic with corresponding transformation of the scholarly communications process.

Meantime, the numbers of online serials available only in electronic version is increasing rapidly from a low base. Some are commercial operations by publishers using the new electronic medium; others are non-profit ventures undertaken by professional scholarly bodies seeking to reappropriate the scholarly publishing function; and yet others are state-of-the-art feasibility or pilot publishing activities funded from foundation or public monies. Many of the major publishers are exploring the marketplace to see what pricing models makes sense and how to protect their revenue streams from declining print sales.

The frustrating area for libraries and consumers is that these varying pricing algorithms are more often than not linked to the print product, whether one wants to receive it or not. Conditions imposed by publishers commonly include restrictions on storage and access to distributed information as well as non-cancellation clauses. These inhibit the functioning of an open market for information services. Several publishers are however permitting university libraries, within the terms of licensing agreements for electronic journals, to download and archive their publications if they so wish.

There is continuing uncertainty as to whether libraries in these instances will have long term low cost or no cost access to archived journals, or only for so long as they maintain subscriptions at existing levels.

The transition to global markets has seen some repositioning within the scholarly publishing industry, parallelling restructuring in the global information services market more generally. A characteristic feature of the industry hitherto has been its highly diversified nature: multiple stakeholders with a diversity of visions and interests; large and small players co-inhabiting a competitive 'space' through product differentiation.

Recent trends have seen a consolidation at the top end, with mergers among the large publishing houses to create vertically integrated companies that have a global reach. Another nascent trend is the severing of the association between publishers and scholarly professional associations in their joint publishing endeavours.

The market shake out is likely to see non-commercial operations such as low volume scholarly journal publication discontinued by publishers, leaving the professional associations to take on a solo publishing role. Significant changes are underway in the distribution of journals. Some of the larger or more progressive publishers have decided to offer their journals through the Internet directly by themselves and to refuse to offer any of their full-text electronic journal titles to any aggregator.

Publishers can thus avoid costs associated with intermediaries at the same time as adding value through additional features so as to gain a competitive edge for their particular products and services. The longer term effectiveness of this strategy may depend on whether they have clusters of journals in given disciplines that can compete with the integrated databases.

Developments of this kind possibly presage an even more fundamental collapse of the value chain, with publishers looking ultimately to relate directly with end user scholars, bypassing the librarians as a stakeholder group. One way to do this would be for publishers to establish their own digital distribution function by creating a Universal Resource Locator (URL) for each title.

The important point about the trend to vertical integration among the large players is the potential for strengthening their monopoly position, allowing more total control over the publishing process. At the same time, a smaller trend appears to be the strengthening of the hand of the aggregators. Many publishers have decided to offer their electronic services through an intermediary service which aggregates the titles from many different publishers under one interface or search system. From an institutional perspective, this trend holds out the prospect for a real service paradigm, in which a small number of aggregators between them are able to provide the necessary institutional coverage and seamless access that has so far proved elusive. Blackwell Science, the largest publisher of scholarly society journals in the world, is an example of a publishing company that has decided not to offer their own online service but to offer their titles through many other aggregators.

Consortium Developments

A noticeable trend on the demand side has been an increase in collaborative activity between libraries, including newly established library consortia. A main reason behind this development has been a recognition that libraries need to act globally and nationally to strengthen their ability to influence pricing and other terms and conditions related to the purchase of that information. The International Coalition of Library Consortia (ICOLC), for example, has formulated a statement of preferred practices to guide negotiations with electronic information providers which includes access, archiving, systems and licences among the items. In particular, ICOLC is seeking licence agreements which (1) permit member libraries to take reasonable steps to archive content that they purchase or lease (eg. to make back-up copies) and (2) obligate the provider to guarantee perpetual availability of the content (although not realtime access).

Nationally, the Consortium of Australian University Libraries has also sought to increase its market position through negotiating licence agreements for networked information at a system level, and archiving rights and responsibilities are likely increasingly to figure in such negotiations with database vendors.

There is a great deal of national and international activity relating to the archiving of electronic scholarly information. Much of it was initiated post-1995, in the aftermath of the Task Force on Digital Archiving in the US which recommended the development of a national system of digital archives to act as repositories for digital information. Large scale preservation initiatives and projects, found in many countries, are aimed at raising awareness of the issues, fostering collaboration among libraries and allied organisations to take responsibility for preservation and access, building archives, and supporting the development of frameworks and standards for long term preservation of digital information electronic records.

The focus of these efforts is the nation's archival heritage in the broadest sense, including the Internet as a cultural repository. Developments of this kind include the US National Commission on Preservation and Archiving, the National Library of Australia PANDORA project, the Internet Archive (US) and the European Preservation Information Centre, to name but a few from a long list.

Other bodies (some national, some international) have assumed a responsibility for digital preservation in a specific field of scholarly endeavour, such as the arts and humanities, the natural environment, and political and social research. Their concern is with both digital preservation as well as preservation of digital data. Whilst important for establishing models for managing archiving facilities and setting frameworks for national preservation strategies, initiatives of this kind have little to say about how archiving is to be funded long term.

For scholarly electronic journals publishing, this means developing archiving strategies that 1) make a profit and 2) can be sustainable over the long term. A number of developments in the archiving of scholarly electronic journals are to be found. A few of these are close to real market conditions, others are pilot activities supported by R&D funds although with a view to longer term sustainability. They involve various key stakeholder groups in the publishing process, sometimes as single actors but more often as multi-party collaborators.

Publishers are not generally taking a proactive stance on long term archiving, beyond in some cases relaxing licence requirements that allow libraries to store and distribute electronic data through inter-library loan or consortia arrangements. Publishers (and learned societies) may see some strategic advantage in the short to medium term for taking on an archiving role in order to preserve the concept of the journal and the collection. As a cultural product of the print paradigm, the journal is potentially under threat in a networked information environment where users may get more value from linked information via gateways and integrated databases.

Vendors are searching for and creating their own new roles in the digital environment. Some are committed to archiving at least some titles, as is the case for a subset of the Blackwell's Electronic Journals Navigator. The most substantial proposal on long term archiving has been put forward by the aggregator, OCLC.

OCLC is positioning FirstSearch Electronic Collections Online as a substitute for print collections of scholarly journals. One of its principal strategies for competitive advantage in this field is to provide an assurance of ongoing access to an archival copy that will enable the library to discharge its responsibility as a repository. In its contractual agreements with publishers, OCLC will obtain the right to mount all content at OCLC and create a permanent electronic archive.

As a digital library, the service will select, obtain, store and provide access to academic journals, on behalf of participating institutions. As a digital archive, the service will 'ensure the integrity and long term accessibility' of these journals. When a library subscribes to Electronic Collections Online, OCLC proposes to establish an access account on its behalf.

OCLC intends to work with publishers to provide data in a single, widely used format, and to migrate journal backfile to new data formats as current formats become outmoded. Where it does not migrate backfile to emerging data formats, it will ensure access through adequate and available mechanisms. OCLC is not making access to archival material dependent on continuing use of the electronic journals service, nor seeking exclusive agreements with publishers that limit their choice of online distribution channels for their content. However, it will not provide libraries that discontinue the service with digital copies of their journal subscriptions for local mounting and storage.

Many initiatives have been taken by libraries to develop digital collections of scholarly materials. They are mostly based on a preservation model, with no involvement of major commercial publishers. Although these developments have little direct relevance for archiving of electronic journal collections in the commercial arena, they are pointers to archiving expertise and systems that could possibly be harnessed in any distributed journal archiving model.

5

Challenges of Information Revolution

Networking Revolution is opening new "digital opportunities" for developing countries. They can significantly benefit from investments in modern information infrastructure in a pro-competitive regulatory environment, and leapfrog stages of development in terms of networking roll-out. In one of the most significant developments ever to emerge in the communications industry, the Internet is redrawing the economy of communication networks and creating incentives for the expansion of connectivity at a dizzying pace.

The resulting "Networking Revolution" is seeing the introduction of large-scale data communications networks that promise broadband access and substantially lower costs to all consumers. These developments are already having a significant impact on the global economy. Between 1995 and 1998, the global telecommunications markets worldwide connected 200 million telephone lines, 263 million mobile subscribers, and 10 million leased lines. 1 And while only 15 million Internet connections were made in 1991-1994, this number exploded to 88 million in 1995-1998, nearly a sixfold increase in network growth. While it took the telephone close to 75 years to reach 50 million users, it took the World Wide Web (WWW) only 4 years to reach the same number. The forces of technological advance and competition are driving this infrastructure revolution and fostering the growth of a global networked economy.

When the first transatlantic cables for telephony were laid in the 1950s, a minute of voice communication cost US$2.44; by 1996, operating costs per minute were just over a cent. The costs of many other key networking components (cellular handsets, computers, switching equipment, etc.) are also falling sharply. Some of the main technological innovations driving this process are: The move from copper to fibber optics in telecommunications backbones. This has increased exponentially the amount of information that can be transmitted over cables. Transmission speeds that used to be clocked in kilobits per second have now reached the terabits-per-second range. More information is now carried at higher speed and lower cost, making connections more affordable and promoting content development. New mobile wireless technologies have increased the ubiquity of communications services, allowing users to stay connected irrespective of location, while new fixed wireless technologies have increased the capacity of the airwaves to transmit information at very high data rates.

Cables and wireless systems can now be connected by fast electronic switching components that cost a fraction of the price of old analog switches, making possible real-time networking through Internet and wireless communications. And perhaps most central to the explosion of the Internet has been the huge increase in affordable computing power made possible through inventions including integrated circuits, miniaturisation, and large data storage devices.

The widespread adoption of digital packet-switched technology has spurred a convergence of voice, data, and multimedia applications, enabling all communications traffic to be managed and delivered over multipurpose platforms. Together, these changes have made possible the emergence of new technological and communication paradigms. The Internet, personal computers, and wireless telephony foster an increasingly dynamic network of individuals, firms, schools, and governments communicating and interacting with each other. And since the value of a network increases as its number of users grows, by accessing the global information network each additional user not only benefits from a new ability to communicate and trade, but also adds value to the rest of the connected world.

Digital technology allows significant savings to be achieved in the provision of communication services networks. In turn, this is driving a change in the economics of information and communications, allowing competition between cable TV providers, cellular companies, and fixed-line telephone systems over Internet service provision. Continued technological advance will allow for both greater competition and improved functionality of the Internet, through real-time interactive communications, faster data exchange rates, and the ability to build entirely new service concepts and applications.

Technological advance has facilitated the contestability of incumbent communications providers. This has in turn been further stimulated by the policy drive toward liberalisation (elimination of regulatory barriers to entry), competition (particularly, via efforts to constrain abuses of market power by incumbent companies) and privatisation that over the last two decades has characterised the sector all over the world. Rather than a move toward laissez-faire, regulatory reform in most countries has been characterised by a shift in the focus of regulation from one of control of "natural monopolies" toward the elimination of barriers among the sectors of the communications field (to facilitate convergence), re-regulation and support for public-private partnerships.

In the United States, government support for design and early operation of the Internet was critical. Equally critical for the Internet's success, however, was the government's decision in the early 1990s to privatise operation of the Internet backbone-while continuing reform of the telecommunications marketplace to expand competition. At the same time, regulation of content and commerce over the Internet has been kept to a minimum during this period. Elsewhere, not only have many national governments acted decisively to liberalise the telecommunication sector, but also negotiated under the World Trade Organisation (WTO) a groundbreaking effort to reach a general agreement on basic telecommunications, to further extend this process.

A number of positive feedback mechanisms, driven by technological change and regulatory reform, further promote the dynamism of the networking revolution. As the unit costs of many key networking technologies fall, this further stimulates increased demand and higher production volumes-the evolution of cellular handsets being a good illustration. In the information-carrying business, the decreasing profit margin per bit carried implies the necessity to operate on larger and larger volumes.

The Internet is complying, due to both a rapidly evolving technology and greater and greater volumes of information exchanged within a denser and denser network of users. The 1990s were also characterised by the emergence of new approaches to standardisation. Until then network standardisation was the preserve of highly specialised technicians, who cajoled networking and IT corporations towards laboriously negotiated standards.

The explosion of the Internet has entirely transformed the dynamics of standardisation, making the quick establishment of standards an essential prerequisite for the continued dynamism of the market. Incentives to move faster in establishing such standards via public-private partnerships and industry negotiations are increasing significantly. In the developing world, the combined impact of liberalisation and ownership reform has been substantial.

Telecommunication and networking possibilities are no longer limited to narrowband wireline telephony and analog wireless telephony. The range of choice is expanding significantly, although still in a limited number of -mostly urban- areas, by the successful deployment of state-of-the-art mobile networks, broadband metropolitan area networks and paging networks.

And, of course, the World Wide Web allows each connected user to access a dynamic global information space. The Internet is providing a platform for a global marketplace, supporting-among other things-electronic commerce, where as more suppliers and customers enter the arena, the benefits of participation grow, and the penalties for non-participation also increase. The global economy has already been profoundly affected by these developments. In 1999, global e-commerce transactions amounted to US$150 billion. Continuing developments in the ICT sector are expected to further compound the impact of the networking revolution on world economic activity.

The remarkable reduction in the cost-and enhancement of functions-of communications networks, made possible by the forces of change described above, are fostering the emergence of new businesses with potential to drive economic growth and to transform the social environment in the developing world. However, these businesses are often quite different in profile from the traditional telecommunications service providers. Moreover, their success requires not only appropriate economic conditions and regulatory environment, but also innovative business models. ICTs are potent tools whose power lies in their ability to support integrated development with long-term social and economic benefits. There is cross-country evidence that telecommunications rollout facilitates economic growth.

The Internet's power to leverage a network connection suggests that this link will only become stronger. Moreover, the Internet presents numerous opportunities to increase the efficiency and equity of government services and improve the lives of the poorest. The ongoing Networking Revolution may augur a closer and more productive integration of affluent and developing nations.

A number of economic research papers indicate that economic growth is being increasingly influenced by the availability of efficient telecommunications and informatics infrastructure. Recent econometric studies have found evidence of a causal link between telecommunications development and economic growth; others provide evidence of high returns on investment in telecommunications equipment and, more generally, in the telecommunications sector. Other studies have extended these correlations to a range of development indicators, such as social development, cost savings for industry, and increased transport efficiency.

The Internet, by leveraging the potential value of a telephone connection suggests that the economic effects of networking will be far greater in the future. At the micro-level, the Internet is an unprecedented opportunity for firms to reduce costs and increase market coverage (both home and abroad), facilitating the achievement of economies of scale and scope. In the next few years, a growing share of the world population could become customers or suppliers, not just of globalised industries, but also of any firm or individual who can connect to modern information infrastructures and benefit from modern logistics of technology-facilitated international trade.

The Internet thus offers immense opportunities to developing countries. Following are several ways that the Internet is revolutionising business:

— *Reach*: The "death of distance" brought about by the Internet and other innovations in telecommunications opens a variety of opportunities in marketing, purchasing, and collaboration with large numbers of potential suppliers and customers-over a limitless geographic area. This phenomenon increases the potential for businesses to link into global supply chains, and to exploit local comparative advantages in language skills, trained human resources, or complementary time zones. These opportunities exist in both manufacturing and service industries.

— *Information-based products*: The Internet expands prospects for trade in information-based products and services. The reach of the Internet allows professional services (such as software, engineering, architecture, education/ training, medicine, and law) to be provided remotely-increasing opportunities for highly skilled individuals to find well-compensated employment in their home countries. Developing and transition economies gain new opportunities to export services. The new business environment created by the Internet offers the chance for countries to "leapfrog" to high-skill, high-wage industries.

— *Rich information flow*: Theories of the firm have long emphasized that the set of activities undertaken by a firm are determined by the relative cost of intra-firm versus inter-firm transactions. By dramatically reducing the cost of inter-firm transactions, the Internet increases the potential for outsourcing of business functions. Firms provide the newly outsourced function to a larger partner, or they themselves can gain advantage by outsourcing functions previously done (expensively or poorly) inside the firm.

— *Disintermediation*: The increased reach and richness of communication possible via the Internet has had a big impact on traditional market intermediaries, which previously have been able to exploit inefficiencies in information flows. The result is dis-intermediation, as traditional go-between functions are eliminated. Internet-based procurement systems, auctions, and business-to-business exchanges are quickly gaining in use. Supply chains become more efficient due to the richer and more direct interaction with customers and suppliers. Cutting out middlemen might increase the portion of the value chain that firms in developing countries can capture.

— *New intermediaries*: Although traditional intermediaries are under attack, new firms help navigate the vast information now available and bring buyer groups with a mutual interest closer together. The greater ease of comparing costs across large numbers of suppliers, assisted by these new intermediaries, gives small firms access to an unprecedented variety of sources for purchasing inputs, and allows them to sell their products more broadly due to the penetration of these new Internet-based intermediaries. New intermediaries serving the needs of a particular industry or group of firms/individuals offer access to news and information, links to vendors, and other ways to maximise value from bundling of services for the group (e.g., group health insurance, purchasing alliances, marketing, and order fulfillment).

Entrepreneurship therefore plays a particularly critical role during periods of rapid economic change, as small, agile firms increase the ability of an economy to quickly respond to new challenges. Unfortunately, most developing countries have a poor environment for entrepreneurship. Beyond the obvious legal/regulatory and financial constraints, early-stage firms lack a network of experienced mentors/advisers, specialised legal or accounting services, and basic IT infrastructure and facilities.

Thus, although the Internet offers increased opportunities for economic development, it also offers the risk of exclusion for those economies that do not adjust. In particular, countries with inadequate infrastructure might be disadvantaged. In the same way that a weak port infrastructure reduces the attractiveness of all merchandise trade with a country, it might be that a weak information infrastructure will reduce the trade attractiveness of an even wider. range of goods and services, thus acting as a bottleneck to development.

There is already growing evidence that a range of ICTs is vital for taking part in global exchange. One recent estimate suggested that as much as one-half of the difference between Africa's manufactured exports as a share of GDP and East Asia's share could be accounted for by the weak state of communications networks in Africa.

ICTs present particular opportunities to the disadvantaged to help themselves, seize advantages and demand services or control over their lives that they previously lacked. In Brazil's urban slums, the Committee to Democratise Information Technology (CDI) in four years has created 110 sustainable and self-managed community-based "Computer Science and Citizenship Schools," using recycled technology, volunteer assistance, and very limited funds.

CDI schools train more than 25,000 young students per year in ICT skills that give them better opportunities for jobs and education. CDI also provides social education on human rights, non-violence, environmental issues, health, and sexuality. The Association for Progressive Communications and Partner Networks implemented a Gender and Information program.

The program gave women in Africa, Asia, and Latin America the necessary technical skills, computers, hardware, and networking to plan the UN's Fourth World Conference on Women and to disseminate the results. Such examples are multiplying, as collaborative approaches and partnerships between the public and private sectors are demonstrating the broader value of advanced communications services.

Many commentators have asserted that the potential for networking to make an impact on the public sector matches or even exceeds the potential in the commercial sector, although it may take longer to see major impacts. First, networking may allow greater access to decision-making. The global transition towards pluralist forms of government relies on adequate social capacity to understand complex policy issues and communicate information. Through ICTs, non-governmental organisations (NGOs) are helping to give a voice to marginalised segments of the population, raising awareness of economic, social and environmental issues, and directly influencing local, national, and multilateral decision-making.

For example, in Mexico City, the NGO Women to Women used e-mail connections with women's groups in California to obtain information on the business practices, profit structures, and ownership information of a textile company that had announced plans to build a new plant in their community.

As a result, they were better prepared for discussions with local government and plant management. Second, through automation and software applications, ICTs reduce administration costs, reduce the cost of service provision, and open the workings of government to public oversight and accountability. In Morocco, the Ministries of Finance and Planning have used ICTs to greatly increase the efficiency of the budget process, for example. They have created a common platform to share their data on tax revenues, auditing, and expenditure management.

As a result, the time required to prepare the budget has been cut in half, and budgets better reflect actual income and spending trends. An example of how new networking can help subnational governments to become more responsive and transparent is the case of the state of Andhra Pradesh in India. There, ICTs have provided opportunities for government to redefine its relationship with citizens by encouraging (1) economies resulting in efficient government, (2) personalised service, (3) equal access to government for all, (4) speed and responsiveness, and (5) responsible and measurable government.

Andhra Pradesh was the first state in India to design a statewide computerisation program covering all levels of the administrative spectrum from the smallest—the Mandal Revenue Offices—to the largest. The statewide Multi-Purpose Household Survey was launched in 1995 to store large volumes of citizen data and information exchange through networking, and Land registration offices throughout the state are now equipped with computerised counters under the Computer-aided Administration of Registration Department (CARD) project.

Before the computerisation program, tedious bureaucracy, and lack of transparency in property valuation resulted in a flourishing business of brokers and middlemen who exploited citizens selling property, since a premium was usually attached to speedy delivery of services.The Government of Andhra Pradesh has recently launched another high profile IT initiative, the Twin Cities Network Services (TWINS) pilot project. It is designed to provide citizens of Hyderabad and Secunderabad with access to computerised, one-stop Integrated Citizen Services Centers (ICSCs) to handle a variety of services, including (a) payment of utility bills (electricity, water, and sewerage) and property taxes; (b) issuing certificates (birth, death, caste, and income); (c) issuing permits and licenses (trade, driver's, vehicle registration); (d) providing information (building permits, transport procedures, property registration); and (e) facilitating common transactions (change of addresses, transfer of vehicle ownership).

ICTs also offer a range of opportunities in the provision of public services, particularly education, environmental monitoring and health care. Education-Putting ICTs into schools is an important first step to developing computer-related literacy. Distance education also offers a variety of educational and training opportunities to support lifelong learning.

Chile has been a leader in using advanced ICTs to improve educational outcomes. The Enlaces Project, which is funded by the national government with assistance from the World Bank and the private sector, has linked almost all secondary schools and more than half of all primary schools to the Internet. Schools are provided with computers and technical support, as well as extensive technical training in order to make the program equipment self-sustaining.

The goals of the program include: ensuring equal access to information regardless of geography; modernising curricula and administration; development of collaborative projects across different schools; and enhanced teacher training and education. Environmental monitoring-inherently data-intensive, is more effective using ICTs, particularly geographic information systems. These systems are already practical and increasingly inexpensive, providing effective tools for regional planning based on dynamic modeling, early warning of natural hazards, and small-scale, community data for local capacity building. But environmental management requires more than the analysis and publication of environmental threats.

Communication between governments, business, and citizens is vital if environmental remediation programs are to meet their objectives in an efficient and equitable fashion. In Indonesia, for example, government officials discouraged by the weak enforcement of water pollution standards developed a public access information database rating the degree of firm compliance with pollution discharges. In Mexico, satellite-generated images are dramatically improving the capacity of the government to fight fires in the wilderness. By helping the administration focus their resources on the most critical incidents, the technology has contributed to a decline of more than 50 percent in the geographical area impacted by fires over the last year.

Healthcare-Electronically based support systems are now being deployed to support health care workers, providing support tools that allow them to reduce time spent doing paperwork, and increase the accuracy of the data flowing up and down through the healthcare reporting structure. These ICT tools also provide a means for getting healthcare data at the village level in an electronic form, and can provide healthcare workers with information to help them to provide more-effective service to the villages within their responsibility.

In Rajasthan, India, for example, an innovative ICT pilot application substituted manual registers with client data stored on hand-held computers accessible through a variety of icons. The pilot reduced the paperwork burden of the village health care workers, empowering them to provide more timely care and information. However, as with the economic advantages of the Internet, the risks of exclusion are also growing in terms of empowerment and access to quality government service provision.

If the poor are discriminated against having access to government services online, they will fall yet further behind in relative terms. For developing countries, the potential benefits from advances in information and communications technologies (ICTs) could mean an acceleration of economic and social development and greater inclusion of isolated-particularly rural-populations into the mainstream of society and economic activity. Fears do exist, however, that countries lacking in education, infrastructure and institutions-the resources most needed to fully benefit from ICTs-would be further marginalised by the networking revolution. This is referred as the "digital divide"-that is, the gap between those with access to new digital technologies and networks and those without.

There are two types of inequality that merit special attention: cross-country and within-country. The growth of ICTs in developing countries has been impressive. In 1995-1998 the developing countries connected more than 155 million telephone lines, 105 million mobile subscribers, and

4 million leased lines. The growth statistics are even more impressive. From 1991 to 1998, in countries outside the Organisation for Economic Cooperation and Development (OECD), average annual growth levels of telephone lines, mobile subscribers, and leased lines were 14 percent, 83 percent, and 27 percent, respectively.

Technology is also reshaping the flow of investment, goods, and services around the world economy. In 1995-1998 investments nearly doubled from the 1991-1994 period to US$304 billion. Service revenues grew to US$200 billion in 1998. Even faster growth is expected in the near future. This growth hides a wide disparity between rich and poor in provision, however. In Africa, with 739 million people, there are only 14 million phone lines-fewer than in Manhattan or Tokyo. 80 percent of those lines are in only six countries. Moreover, according to the latest UN Human Development Report, industrialised countries, with only 15 percent of the world's population, are home to 88 percent of all Internet users.

The geographical distribution of Internet hosts (see Figure 4-1) further illustrates the wide.differences in connectivity between industrialised and developing countries. There were only one million Internet subscribers on the entire African continent compared with 15 million in the UK in 1999. The average OECD country has roughly 40 times the per capita number of computers of a Sub-Saharan African country, 110 times as many mobile phones, and 1,600 times as many Internet hosts. The rate of investment supporting rapid technological development and deployment is also highly skewed toward the developed world. Recent data developed for infoDev by Pyramid Research reveals that in per capita terms OECD countries spend as much as 11 times the amount spent in Sub-Saharan Africa on information infrastructure.

Several of the most important measures of technological inputs-the investment necessary to produce high-technology goods-are also substantially higher in developed economies than in developing economies. OECD economies invest nine times as much of their income in Research and Development-that is, in creative, systematic activities intended to increase the stock of knowledge and on the use of this knowledge to devise new applications-and have roughly 17 times as many technicians and eight times as many scientists per capita as the economies of Sub-Saharan Africa.

These "soft infrastructures" are as essential for successful ICT diffusion as are the "hard" technologies. The availability of local language content is a further pointer to the dominance of developed countries. Spanish and Portuguese which combined have a larger population of native speakers than is the case for English, appear only four percent of the web pages. The unbalanced access to ICTs is also visible inside countries. The findings in a spate of recent survey studies in both developed and developing countries underscore these inequalities:

— *By income*: The Living Standard Measurement Survey (LSMS) at the World Bank shows that in Panama and South Africa, households in the wealthiest quintile are respectively 43 and 125 times more likely to have private telephones than those in the poorest quintile. In Nepal, 11 percent of the wealthiest households have access to a phone, compared with 0.5 percent of the households in the previous quintile.

— *By education*: An Australian study shows that more than 34 percent of people with a university degree or other tertiary qualification can access the Internet from home, compared with just over 12 percent for those with secondary school as their highest educational qualification. A recent study of Capacity Building for Electronic Communication in Africa (CABECA, 1998) found that 87 percent of Zimbabwean and 98 percent of Ethiopian Internet users had a university degree.

— *By geographic region*: 10.4 percent of homes in urban Nepal had private phone access compared with 0.11 percent in rural areas, a 100 to 1 ratio. The ratio is the same in South Africa and 6 to 1 in Panama. There are almost 4 times as many telephone lines per 100 in the largest city of lower middle-income countries as in their rural areas, and more than 5 times as many lines per 100 in the largest city of low-income countries as in their rural areas. These gaps are even more significant given the fact that more than 50 percent-and as many as 80 percent-of the population in poorest countries, live in rural areas.

— *By race*: ICT penetration also varies by race. In the United States, according to the 1998 Current Population Survey, Blacks and Hispanics lagged by more than 7 percentage points behind Whites for telephone access in 1998. Moreover, their households are roughly one-half as likely to own a computer as white households and nearly 2.5 times less likely to use the Internet.

— *By gender*: The Wall Street Journal reports that only 38 percent of the population polled in urban Latin America who use a computer and Internet are women. The numbers are even more skewed in Africa. The CABECA survey of African users found that 86, 83, and 64 percent of Internet users in Ethiopia, Senegal, and Zambia, respectively, were male.

— *By age*: As reported in the UNDP's Human Development Report 1999, the average Internet user in the United States is 36 years old, while in China and the United Kingdom the average user is under 30.

Information and Digital Divide

It is important to stress that some of the trends in ICT provision around the world have been toward convergence. ITU figures, for example, suggest that, since 1960, the poorest one-fifth of countries have expanded telephone lines per capita about fifteenfold, compared to a threefold increase in the richest one-fifth of countries. This trend has continued in basic service provision over the last two years. In 1997-99 the number of telephones per capita in Sub-Saharan Africa increased 17 percent, compared to a four percent increase in the OECD countries. The picture is different for advanced services, however.

The number of Internet hosts per capita increased 29 percent in Sub Saharan Africa in 1997-99, compared to 87 percent in OECD countries. And this divergence continues from an already huge gap in the provision of services, as we have seen. A recent study by Rodriguez and Wilson finds that an "Index of Technological Progress" - a comprehensive proxy of the status of a country's information infrastructure-indicates significant divergence in this measure across countries. The mere existence of a gap in levels of ICT services between rich and poor across and within countries is not an automatic reason to argue that ICTs should be placed near the top of the development agenda.

After all, poor countries have fewer factories, fewer cars, fewer doctors and nurses, and a lower calorie intake per capita than wealthy countries. The gap in provision is large-much larger than income disparities for some regions. In particular, the gap is growing in provision of advanced services. All of this is occurring at a time when the trends in other determinants of development (e.g., levels of education, health, and access to transport) are converging.

There is a significant threat of less developed regions being forced into an ICT-related poverty trap. Countries that do not have sufficient access will be increasingly excluded from the international trading system. Similar bottleneck effects apply within countries, too: if the rural poor have no access, they might fall further behind.

Within-country gaps in service provision raise the issue of equity. This will become even more important as government service provision moves on to the Internet. Without low-income access, those who need such services the most will be excluded.

The opportunity costs of development impact and the risks of economic exclusion presented by a lack of ICTs suggest that it is important that policymakers- governments acting in consultation with civil society, the private sector (and donors when appropriate) -act now and determine the appropriate priorities for their countries.

Besides, adjustment to a networked economy is not an overnight process: it takes education, widespread legal reform and significant investments on infrastructure. For many developing countries, limited access to basic telecommunications networks still remains a major handicap. For these countries, the goal is to hasten the pace with which their economies can embark upon a convergent path vis-à-vis the leading countries in the networking revolution. Failure to address the related challenges and opportunities is not an option. Inaction today will only prolong the period of divergence.

A Policy Agenda

In developing a policy agenda for the networked economy, some useful lessons can be drawn from the experience with telecommunications reform over the last two decades. First, governments must commit to sector reform, setting up credible independent regulatory authorities and allowing for active competition. Second, the market, acting alone, will not be enough to ensure that the digital divide will be bridged. By engaging in partnerships with grassroots NGOs, donors, the private sector, and multilateral agencies, governments in developing countries can help bridge the digital divide.

In what follows, elements of a pro-active "networking policy" are discussed encompassing not only the regulatory front, but also specific programs that can accelerate the take-off of the networking revolution in developing economies. A modern information infrastructure is the first building block of the "new economy." In this context, a proper telecommunications regulatory environment is fundamental. In order, however, to fully engage in the networking revolution, countries have to go beyond traditional regulatory reform, addressing the challenges of convergence and setting the rules needed for the expansion of e-commerce.

The importance of privatisation and competition in promoting the development of modern information infrastructure is now widely accepted. A recent study suggests that privatisation, good regulation, and a competitive mobile market could double the number of lines per capita in some of the poorer markets in Africa. Competition also can dramatically improve the quality of service and lower the costs of provision: in several competitive markets the average price of a call from a Global System for Mobile Communications (GSM) handset is 40 to 50 percent lower than in markets with a single provider; and a recent study of Internet access pricing in Africa found that countries with the least liberal markets had access charges 700 percent higher than countries with the most liberal telecommunications regimes on the continent.

The privatisation of telephone services in Peru provides another example of how reform can also increase access for the poor. Given the impact of privatisation and competition on access, it is encouraging that in developing countries, a significant number of reforms along these lines have taken place in the 1990s. More than 90 developing economies opened their telecommunications sector to private participation between 1990 and 1998, with US$214 billion in new investments committed. However, the new operators were often given monopolistic protection for an extended period following privatisation.

Competition has come more slowly and has so far been concentrated in mobile telephony. Sixty-four countries had at least two mobile service providers by 1998. Only in recent years have developing countries become more aggressive in promoting competition in fixed-line telephony, and still only 15 countries allowed long distance and local competition by 1998.

Overall, ITU data from 1998 suggests that only ·12 percent of local markets in developing countries are liberalised. A lack of awareness of the ultimate benefits of privatisation and competition often means that governments promoting these policies suffer in popularity, increasing the difficulty of having such policies rapidly adopted. Within a state-owned or quasi-public monopoly the existing conditions may be highly beneficial to existing managers, workers, unions, suppliers, and politicians, or the fear of change and/or loss of employment can be a serious obstacle. Policies designed to promote private investment and competition may also bring short-term adjustment costs.

Loss of the tax revenue and dividends derived from a former monopoly PTT, decline in foreign exchange revenues from reduced settlement payments, and lower revenues from reformed tariffs may have an initial negative impact on strained public budgets.

Access to information about the international experience in this area and the long-term net benefits of reform - provided by institutions, like the World Bank Group, that can play the role of "honest-brokers" can help governments in addressing these concerns. In addition to traditional regulatory reform, focusing on the promotion of liberalisation, competition and ownership reform within the telecommunications sector and the establishment of an independent regulatory authority, it is increasingly important to pay attention to the elimination of regulatory barriers among communications sectors.

Such reforms are essential for a country to explore the convergence opportunities of the networking revolution. For the effective take-off of e-commerce, however, a country has also to address a number of elements in its broader legal/ regulatory environment. Most governments have taken a cautious approach in imposing new regulations on the Internet.

Initiatives promoting self-regulation and alternative dispute resolution mechanisms suggest that the private sector may be able to cope with at least some of these policy questions without direct government intervention. Yet, there is a growing need for governments to address the many difficult issues associated with on-line transactions as e-commerce is mainstreamed into a country's economy. Special attention should be given to issues such as:

— adoption of non-discriminatory taxation policies;
— management of intellectual property rights in "cyberspace";
— adoption of effective privacy and consumer protection policies;
— well defined content policies;
— access to encryption technologies; and
— adoption of technologically-neutral authentication and certification rules.

There is also a need to define: (1) how trading partners, service providers, and networks should divide risks for errors among themselves; (2) how governments should apply record-storage and control requirements for electronic communications; and (3) what replaces the hard-copy audit trail.

It is clear that outside the field of communications itself, there is also need for broader reform in areas such as investment policies and trade controls to encourage investment in and use of both basic infrastructure and advanced services. Financial systems in many countries also require significant upgrading and regulatory changes in order to meet the demands of e-commerce.

The same applies to the availability of supporting services, in particular, the postal system. Although market-oriented sector reforms are fundamental in helping bridge the digital divide, there are a number of reasons why a pro-active engagement of governments in networking activities remains vital. The market alone is likely to under-provide levels of access to infrastructure and content, from the point of view of both economic efficiency and equality of opportunity. And in order to fully utilise that access and content, users must have the necessary skills and education. Finally, market reforms do not guarantee that the government itself will use ICTs effectively in the full range of services that it provides.

Market Under-Provision: A user in an area of low demand density (attributable either to sparse population, low spending on communications, or a combination thereof) will tend to have proportionately higher communications costs and lower available functionality. This phenomenon is firmly rooted in the basic economics of networks, which encompass both high fixed costs and related economies of scale. Similar market barriers face Internet content providers.

Locally relevant, local language content makes the Internet far more attractive to users. More users increase the attractiveness of local content provision to Internet entrepreneurs. But this virtuous cycle will never begin if the high fixed costs of content creation deter local investors, leaving countries in a low-use, low-utility equilibrium. Market failures such as these present significant barriers to growth in access and content, barriers that are highest for poor and rural populations. This suggests that intervention to overcome them is not just an issue of efficiency but also a vital concern of equity.

More fundamentally, however, it underscores the challenges faced by most educational systems in addressing the issue of "digital literacy." In short, there is a significant need not only to expose students to the Internet (e.g., via programs that support school connectivity), but also to ensure proper training of teachers in the use of modern ICTs tools.

ICTs can play a significant role in improving the efficiency, transparency and responsiveness of government services. Reform of the legal and regulatory and legal environment for the ICT sector alone is no guarantee that the technologies will be adopted for more widespread use in government, however. The history of the introduction of information technologies into government services suggests that while the potential benefits are large, the process is highly complex, time and resource-consuming, and frequently unpopular with stakeholders. Thus, without a strong commitment to well-designed programs of reform that incorporate appropriate rollout of ICTs, it is likely that government use of the new technologies will remain limited.

In order to address these challenges a number of countries have embarked on creating national information infrastructure strategies. Such strategies, when designed with a clear focus on consultation, public-private partnerships, and public access can play an important role in building consensus for.reforms and programs designed to ensure equitable advantage from the new ICTs.

National information strategies often encompass:

— "Knowledge Assessments" - a comparative review of the educational and infrastructural underpinnings of ICT use. Knowledge Assessments often also study broader educational resources, and the legal environment for investment, labor and e-commerce. Such assessments frequently review current uses of ICTs in both the private and government sectors. These analyses can help policy makers to determine where the country could learn from global best practices, and what opportunities are available to the country from the networking revolution. A forthcoming joint World Bank-OECD report on the knowledge economy in Korea might provide a model here.

— Improving Access to the Tools of the Knowledge Economy - efforts in this area typically include programs to widen access to the range of ICTs, from community radio and posts to broadband Internet. Infrastructure strategies also encompass regulatory and subsidy programs to ensure access to both infrastructure and content for the poorest (discussed in detail below), as well as education reform programs focusing on ICT-based training in literacy, language and technical skills.

— Expanding e-government - innovative use of ICTs in areas such as online government contract bidding, customs and tax administration. Moreover, by setting an example, e-government initiatives can be a powerful catalyst for dissemination of relevant ICTs applications. In what follows, two areas in which new initiatives have the potential to promote important digital opportunities, while addressing digital divide concerns, are discussed: promoting public access and e-entrepreneurship.

Policies and institutions to promote public access to communications services are a central element of "universal access" (or universal service) policies. By focusing on providing public access, be it to a telephone line or to an Internet terminal, countries can aggregate demand and thus a large number of people can benefit from one or a few connections.

Broadly speaking, in high-income countries, with residential telephone penetration typically above 75%, households without a telephone are considered to be disadvantaged. Hence advanced country governments and regulators are concerned with policy instruments for achieving universal telephone service.

The "universal service" objectives are defined as a minimum set of services of specified quality that must be available to all users regardless of where they live and at a price affordable to all. They vary with the level of network development and are likely to change as market boundaries are pushed outward.

Larger and more modern networks make it easier and less costly to extend service to outlying areas. In low-income countries, however, the focus should be on providing public access to services. The only realistic objective in the short term is therefore to achieve "universal access", whereby everyone would be able to access a public booth in every town, village or vicinity or within "reasonable" distance. What "reasonable" distance actually means, what services are to be provided at every public booth (telephone, e-mail, real-time Internet), and which of these services are appropriate at what level in the hierarchy of towns and villages, will very much vary from one country to another, depending on potential demand and ability to pay for these services.

The scale at present runs from access to 2mbps high-speed Internet lines for every home in Korea to a telephone within (distant) walking distance in some African countries. Broadly speaking, in high-income countries, with residential telephone penetration typically above 75%, households without a telephone are considered to be disadvantaged. Hence advanced country governments and regulators are concerned with policy instruments for achieving universal telephone service.

The "universal service" objectives are defined as a minimum set of services of specified quality that must be available to all users regardless of where they live and at a price affordable to all. They vary with the level of network development and are likely to change as market boundaries are pushed outward.

Larger and more modern networks make it easier and less costly to extend service to outlying areas. In low-income countries, however, the focus should be on providing public access to services. The only realistic objective in the short term is therefore to achieve "universal access", whereby everyone would be able to access a public booth in every town, village or vicinity or within "reasonable" distance.

What "reasonable" distance actually means, what services are to be provided at every public booth (telephone, e-mail, real-time Internet), and which of these services are appropriate at what level in the hierarchy of towns and villages, will very much vary from one country to another, depending on potential demand and ability to pay for these services. Public access policies also include so-called "virtual telephony", which has been an innovative step introduced in a number of countries to promote increased access to telecommunications services for the poor. Virtual telephony gives a subscriber a telephone number and a voice mailbox, enabling him or her to receive messages and access them from any phone, in particular from a public phone.

An upgraded but still economical service, radio paging, would alert the subscriber when new messages arrive. Public access policies do not have to limit themselves to improving access to telephones. Indeed, many countries are using similar principles to support the provision of more advanced ICTs, ranging from fax to Internet access. A model that is receiving increasing attention is the multipurpose community telecenter (MCT).

An MCT is a facility that provides public access to a variety of information and communication technologies and services. These centers may vary from single rooms with a telephone or two-way radio to facilities with full Internet access and other value-added services. Users may include local government and church leaders, traders, teachers and schoolmasters, students, agricultural and health extension workers, hospital staff, NGOs, and donor agencies.

An increasing number of MCT services are commercial in nature, and are being offered around the world by private sector providers on a cost recovery basis. South Africa, for example, has shown that for-profit public Internet access can work outside the Internet cafes present in many African capitals.

The majority use the telephone alone-but increasing numbers are turning to the two Internet-connected computers. Many successful models have relied both on some level of external support (at least to cover initial costs) and collaborative and participatory assessment programs both before and during the creation of MCTs. It should be noted that the MCT movement is still in its infancy in many countries, and it has faced some setbacks. One study of a pilot program of the Ministry of Environment, Natural Resources, and Fisheries in Mexico, for example, found that of 23 telecenters set up in rural areas around the country, only five remained functional after two years. Problems encountered included insufficient maintenance funding, inadequate political interest and will, and cultural constraints which hampered community interest in the projects.

Without appropriate content, the relevance of the networking revolution for developing countries will remain in doubt. Unless the private sector - particularly, small and medium enterprises - fully engages in exploring digital opportunities, the impact of the networking revolution on societies will be uneven at best.

However, entrepreneurs in developing countries face a number of difficulties in their efforts to provide locally relevant content. In general, there is a lack of knowledge with respect to the new business models that characterise

Internet-centered businesses. And people that combine skills and creativity in Internet site creation, business know-how, access to finance and knowledge of local community needs are rare worldwide, but particularly in developing countries.

In the past, governments have often assisted the private sector to overcome initial barriers to creating software both for local use and export-oriented activities. Teleports, free economic zones, and aggressive marketing and promotion were used to jump start informatics export growth in Mauritius, for example. In Taiwan, China, the Small and Medium Enterprises Bureau subsidizes software development for small businesses from laundries to bicycle shops. Similarly, government support for Internet incubators could encourage development of innovative web-based applications by helping local entrepreneurs overcome financing and knowledge gaps. There are a range of Internet incubators emerging around the world. In addition to capital, these incubators provide a full range of resources to infuse startup companies with the development strategies and financial support needed to rapidly introduce innovative products and services.

Resources include office space and the accompanying network infrastructure, consulting and services relating to development and technology, graphic design, marketing, competitive research, legal, accounting and business development support and services. Incubators can also provide advice on strategy, branding and corporate structure.

World Summit on the Information Society

Library and information services are key actors in providing unhindered access to essential resources for economic and cultural advance. In doing so, they contribute effectively to the development and maintenance of intellectual freedom, safeguarding democratic values and universal civil rights.

They encourage social inclusion, by striving to serve all those in their user communities regardless of age, gender, economic or employment status, literacy or technical skills, cultural or ethnic origin, religious or political beliefs, sexual orientation, and physical or mental ability. The communities they serve may be geographically based or, increasingly, linked only by technology and shared interests.

A library is a means of access to information, ideas and works of imagination. The library experience may be the key to understanding your place in the world, the pleasure of a children's story, advice on securing a safe water supply, or the record of the healing wisdom of an elder.

The publicly-funded library is one of the most democratic of institutions, serving the needs of the community it serves As a public space it helps define a sense of that community, providing a safe meeting point. At different points in their lives, people see libraries as a:

— place of wide-eyed discovery
— tool for life-long learning
— support for political and social enquiry
— bank of ideas and inspiration
— source of answers to factual questions
— place to acquire new skills
— community centre
— local studies resource
— a place of sheer pleasure and enjoyment.

Libraries take many physical forms, ranging from large purpose-built buildings, to rooms in parent institutions, and small temporary structures. Mobile examples include road vehicles, boats, trains, trams and even donkeys and camels. Many libraries are now 'hybrid', combining both physical space and collections with a virtual library of electronic materials and services.

The term "library" is often taken to equate to "public library". However, there is a huge variety of other kinds of libraries, fulfilling different purposes and serving different client groups. They exist in every country of the world, including the Least Developed Countries.

Most countries have a national library, which often has the role of coordinating the network of other kinds of libraries throughout that country, in addition to collecting materials and making them available. Countries which are federal in structure often have state or provincial libraries which perform a role similar to that of national libraries in their area.

Most countries also have a large network of public libraries. In some countries, notably in Africa, the national library acts the coordinator of the network of public libraries. Public libraries range in size from large central libraries to small village centres and mobile libraries. Educational institutions, such as universities, colleges and schools all have libraries, serving the educational objectives of their parent bodies. In some countries, it is common for them to be open to the general public. In a small number of countries, notably in Eastern Europe, a large university library also acts as the national library.

Libraries also provide vital services in government departments, research institutes, museums, and in many different environments in the private sector. These are sometimes referred to as special libraries or workplace libraries. Libraries are needed more than ever in an age in which people and communities desperately need to consider alternative points of view and information, to challenge the spin doctors and the mass media, to take control of their own destinies and make up their own minds.

In European Union, there are 90,000 libraries. On that basis there must be well over 250,000 around the world. A network of libraries large and small is therefore already available. They are in a good position to contribute positively to bridging the digital divide, because they are staffed by people whose business it is to help users obtain the information they need.

A relatively modest investment in technology, capacity building and the acquisition of print and electronic materials could dramatically transform the degree of access to information and knowledge. Studies suggest that where this investment has been made, use has increased substantially especially attracting people who otherwise would not have such access. Traditionally libraries have acquired print-based materials, including newspapers, maps, pamphlets, illustrations and many other items as well as books.

Despite the popular misconception, they have never confined themselves to books. Indeed, libraries pre-dated the invention of the book, collecting papyrus scrolls (the original Alexandria library was a good example) and manuscripts (the mediaeval monastery libraries, for instance). It was therefore no great leap forward to collect new information media as they emerged. All forms of sound and visual recording quickly joined the collections in many kinds of libraries as they became available.

Computer based sources of information were quickly added to the portfolios and there are now many libraries around the world which have very substantial collections of CD ROMs and electronic journals. Many publications are now "born digital" and a good proportion never appear in print form. Where they do, the digital and print versions are increasingly different in content.

As a result, there are some libraries which, to the first-time visitor, do not look like the conventional idea of a "library" at all. It should be noted that there has been a long-term trend towards the creation of global media corporations embracing publications in many different media, created in different countries. Content is much more important than the medium which contains the content.

On the other hand for many kinds of media, especially those in the Scientific, Technical and Medical (STM) fields, libraries are a hugely important market segment. An advantage of the application of new technologies recently emerging is the ability to introduce differential pricing in favour of libraries in the developing world. However, there remains substantial cause for concern in the growing concentration of media ownership into fewer, larger corporations. It is increasingly important that libraries collect and make available the output of smaller, more local and specialist publishers.

Libraries have an important role in encouraging local and regional publishing and in collecting and preserving oral history and indigenous traditional knowledge. This depends very much on the kind of library and the client group or groups it serves. National libraries, for example, usually are required to collect and preserve the national publishing output of the country it serves, making sure that it is available not only for current users, but also for future generations.

Typically they also compile the national bibliography of publications, and act as the library of last resort for items, which other libraries in the national library network cannot provide. They are usually assisted in their task of collecting by a legal deposit system, whereby publishers have to make copies of their publications available to them free of charge. They frequently have sophisticated preservation and conservation programmes.

Electronic publishing provides many challenges to this aspect of their role. They are developing methods of collecting, archiving and making available electronic publications. National libraries also often take on the role of making available material published in other countries, especially scientific and technical publications. Public libraries typically provide services free of charge to anyone who wishes to use them, although lending is often restricted to residents of the locality. Many provide literacy programmes, reader development promotions and act as an information point for the availability of local public services. Typically they collect and preserve a wide range of materials relating to the history and development of the locality. Special services have been developed to serve the needs of particular groups such as children, housebound people, and the visually impaired.

Public libraries in particular strive to serve all sections of their communities without discrimination. Libraries in education institutions have developed a wide range of services to meet the educational objectives of their parent institutions.

School libraries clearly need to support the curriculum, but they also collect books and other materials to encourage reading and spirit of enquiry, as well as to meet the needs of the teachers and administrative staff. University libraries are usually among the most advanced in terms of developing electronic based services. Many have large collections of electronic journals, as well as sophisticated searching tools available both to students and faculty. Teaching hospitals are often attached to universities. They require sophisticated library services to make available the latest medical research published in a variety of media.

Libraries in the corporate sector have been in the forefront of developing services tailored to meet the needs of individuals or small groups of clients. They profile their users (the employees of the firm) and package information and provide alerting systems to ensure they are aware of the latest information relating to their current research or project. Increasingly they are involved in knowledge management, harnessing the totality of the knowledge available in their company. National and State Libraries are typically funded by the government from taxes. But in common with most public services around the world, they need to supplement these funds with money raised from a range of sources, including sponsorship, charging for some services, sales of publications, etc.

Public libraries typically rely on a combination of national and local government funding, increasingly supplemented by charges for some services and sponsorship or project money. Educational libraries often rely primarily on income from their parent institution. But they too are usually encouraged to raise income from a variety of sources. Those in the corporate sector are usually regarded as cost centres contributing to company objectives. Libraries have a long tradition of networking both within countries and across national boundaries.

Most countries have inter-library lending systems whereby books and other documents not in stock may be borrowed to satisfy the needs of a local user. These systems expanded into document delivery systems once photocopying became generally available and electronic document delivery is becoming the norm in some subject areas. Libraries also collaborate in such areas as collection development to avoid the duplication of expensive works and to ensure comprehensive collections in a region, and in staff training.

Libraries have grasped the opportunities presented by the application of new technologies to revolutionise the technical processes required to deliver services. Examples include shared cataloguing, whereby many libraries share the task of preparing catalogue records so that duplication of effort is avoided. Other examples include self-issue and return systems, and security measures. The most dramatic impacts have been in the expansion of the range of materials collected and made available, together with the ability to reach users regardless of geography. The 'Library without Walls', once a dream is now emerging as a reality.

The role of the library as a place for people to gain ICT skills in a welcoming atmosphere is becoming a decisive element in capacity building. Technology is gradually transforming the lives of library users who have been largely excluded from using traditional library materials, for example the visually impaired.

A recent trend is the convergence of the so-called memory institutions, including some kinds of libraries, archives and museums. One objective is to take advantage of new technologies to make available the collection of all three types of institutions to users in one of them, or indeed remotely from all of them. In most countries librarians are educated in universities in what used to be called "library schools" at undergraduate, masters and doctorate level, depending largely on the overall educational tradition in the country or region. This is supplemented by periods of practical training and experience.

In some countries this leads to a licence to practise. In others, the courses themselves are accredited by the professional body. The curriculum includes studies of information science, computer based information systems, electronic publishing, legal considerations, including intellectual property laws and understanding user needs, as well as the more traditional subjects such as reference sources, cataloguing, indexing and classification. Specialist, optional programmes treat serving user groups such as children, the visually impaired, those with learning disabilities, and specific industries, etc.

The rapid application of technology in libraries emphasise the urgent need for continuing professional development of library staff to enable them to help their users exploit the facilities available. In many countries the training of technical and para-professional library staff is now carried out on a systematic basis. A combination of college-based courses and in-service training is usually employed. Web-based education and training and other forms of.7 distance learning are increasingly being used both for professional and para-professional staff.

IFLA Internet Manifesto

Unhindered access to information is essential to freedom, equality, global understanding and peace. Therefore, the International Federation of Library Associations (IFLA) asserts that:

— Intellectual freedom is the right of every individual both to hold and express opinions and to seek and receive information; it is the basis of democracy; and it is at the core of library service.
— Freedom of access to information, regardless of medium and frontiers, is a central responsibility of the library and information profession.
— The provision of unhindered access to the Internet by libraries and information services supports communities and individuals to attain freedom, prosperity and development.
— Barriers to the flow of information should be removed, especially those that promote inequality, poverty, and despair.

Libraries and Information Services

Libraries and information services are vibrant institutions that connect people with global information resources and the ideas and creative works they seek. Libraries and information services make available the richness of human expression and cultural diversity in all media.

The global Internet enables individuals and communities throughout the world, whether in the smallest and most remote villages or the largest cities, to have equality of access to information for personal development, education, stimulation, cultural enrichment, economic activity and informed participation in democracy.

All can present their interests, knowledge and culture for the world to visit. Libraries and information services provide essential gateways to the Internet. For some they offer convenience, guidance, and assistance, while for others they are the only available access points. They provide a mechanism to overcome the barriers created by differences in resources, technology, and training. Access to the Internet and all of its resources should be consistent with the United Nations Universal Declaration of Human Rights and especially Article 19: Everyone has the right to freedom of opinion and expression; this right includes freedom to hold opinions without interference and to seek, receive and impart information and ideas through any media and regardless of frontiers.

The global interconnectedness of the Internet provides a medium through which this right may be enjoyed by all. Consequently, access should neither be subject to any form of ideological, political or religious censorship, nor to economic barriers. Libraries and information services also have a responsibility to serve all of the members of their communities, regardless of age, race, nationality, religion, culture, political affiliation, physical or other disabilities, gender or sexual orientation, or any other status.

Libraries and information services should support the right of users to seek information of their choice. Libraries and information services should respect the privacy of their users and recognise that the resources they use should remain confidential. Libraries and information services have a responsibility to facilitate and promote public access to quality information and communication. Users should be assisted with the necessary skills and a suitable environment in which to use their chosen information sources and services freely and confidently. In addition to the many valuable resources available on the Internet, some are incorrect, misleading and may be offensive.

Librarians should provide the information and resources for library users to learn to use the Internet and electronic information efficiently and effectively. They should proactively promote and facilitate responsible access to quality networked information for all their users, including children and young people. In common with other core services, access to the Internet in libraries and information services should be without charge. IFLA encourages the international community to support the development of Internet accessibility worldwide, and especially in developing countries, to thus obtain the global benefits of information for all offered by the Internet.

Meeting in Glasgow on the occasion of the 75th anniversary of its formation, the International Federation of Library Associations and Institutions (IFLA) declares that: IFLA proclaims the fundamental right of human beings both to access and to express information without restriction.

IFLA and its worldwide membership support, defend and promote intellectual freedom as expressed in the United Nations Universal Declaration of Human Rights. This intellectual freedom encompasses the wealth of human knowledge, opinion, creative thought and intellectual activity. IFLA asserts that a commitment to intellectual freedom is a core responsibility of the library and information profession worldwide, expressed through codes of ethics and demonstrated through practice. IFLA affirms that: Libraries and information services provide access to information, ideas and works of imagination in any medium and regardless of frontiers. They serve as gateways to knowledge, thought and culture, offering essential support for independent decision-making, cultural development, research and lifelong learning by both individuals and groups.

Libraries and information services contribute to the development and maintenance of intellectual freedom and help to safeguard democratic values and universal civil rights. Consequently, they are committed to offering their clients access to relevant resources and services without restriction and to opposing any form of censorship.

Libraries and information services shall acquire, preserve and make available the widest variety of materials, reflecting the plurality and diversity of society. The selection and availability of library materials and services shall be governed by professional considerations and not by political, moral and religious views. Libraries and information services shall make materials, facilities and services equally accessible to all users.

There shall be no discrimination for any reason including race, national or ethnic origin, gender or sexual preference, age, disability, religion, or political beliefs. Libraries and information services shall protect each user's right to privacy and confidentiality with respect to information sought or received and resources consulted, borrowed, acquired or transmitted. IFLA therefore calls upon libraries and information services and their staff to uphold and promote the principles of intellectual freedom and to provide uninhibited access to information.

Information Technology programme

A programme aiming at the long-term provision of integrated library systems and information technology based services in all Afghan libraries, public as well as school and university. In the initial stages the programme should offer:

- Free Internet access for all in the premises of the University, school and public libraries.
- A local administrative library IT-system handling catalogue, loans and other administrative tasks.
- An electronic library network system giving all libraries access to a system for a national union catalogue, an

ordering system for inter-library lending and other networking facilities.

Professional training and development programme

A systematic programme should be implemented to establish professional education and training in Afghanistan. The long-term objective of the programme should secure the education of new young librarians, who can become the working force in Afghan libraries in the coming 20-30 years. In short term the programme should:

— Identify training opportunities for staff both in Afghanistan and abroad

— Investigate the possibilities to establish formal professional education within Afghanistan

— Open Afghan professional links to international professional communities, including memberships of international professional organisations

— Establish dialogue and co-operation between library professionals within Afghanistan and in neighbouring countries. Encourage and support Afghan staff attendance at international conferences

— Provide brush-up courses and continuing education for working professionals.

Cultural heritage programme

A dramatic consequence of war and conflicts is the damage and destruction of documents and objects of cultural heritage. Afghanistan has been especially affected by war and conflicts for a very long time. New conflicts may arise and it is urgent to safeguard the cultural heritage represented by books, documents and a large range of other objects are kept safely for the future.

Political, cultural and religious activities are dependent on memory and documentation. A programme aiming to preserve and safeguard Afghan cultural heritage should be initiated in order to:

— Compile inventories of cultural property at institutional, regional and national level
— Identify short term projects for emergency protection of property at risk
— Establish links and partnerships with relevant institutions abroad holding collections relating to Afghanistan
— Begin digitisation of printed or written cultural heritage
— Reassume the production of an Afghan national bibliography
— Establish emergency plans and training of staff in risk preparedness and recovery for relevant institutions

Women, children and youth programme

A library programme dedicated to women, children and young people providing educational, recreational and even psychosocial services should be established. Many Afghan children are supposed to suffer from post-traumatic stress and anxiety due to experiences they were exposed to during the war.

The programme should include various initiatives to create and strengthen reading habits in children at an early age and to stimulate the imagination and creativity of children and young people by:

— Developing adequate children's libraries or services in municipal libraries
— Encouraging the co-operation with local teachers of primary and secondary schools and lower high schools to address the needs of children and young people

— Providing children's books to such libraries both in foreign languages for immediate relief and by promoting translations into relevant languages

— Establishing smaller toy libraries, which could provide fairly cheap and efficient means for educational, psychosocial and recreational purposes in local Afghan communities, supporting other initiatives of more formal and structured nature.

— Providing cultural events, which can be performed in local libraries, e.g. theatrical or musical performances, smaller exhibitions, film shows or storytelling.

— Providing books and magazines in both local and foreign languages directed at young people

— Providing the venue and facilities for the development of clubs or associations

— Providing free Internet access, including support, guidance and training

Open access programme

The Open Access programme should promote, as comprehensively as possible, universal access and worldwide reference to both written heritage and the information contained in the new media. The programme should therefore investigate and offer solutions to security issues deriving from the changes in services.

Security measures must sometimes be taken in order to secure material and prevent theft or damages. The following measures should be taken:

— Collections should be opened to the public in libraries, where they are closed.

— Opening hours should be increased where this is possible.

— Children's and adults departments should be organised close to each other and not in separate premises.

— Suitable and sufficient reading rooms should be established.

— Extensive access to public information and information from political, social, ethnic and religious organisations should be given in the library premises as part of the democratisation process.

— Multicultural services should be offered.

— Internet access-points should be available for children and adults free-of-charge within the premises of the library.

Initiative Support Programme

A programme should be established to support local initiatives and participation. It should aim to establish bodies that could offer advice, guidance and consultancy, including international experience. Furthermore, it should both define, implement and run funds, that can provide financial support for local initiatives and initiatives serving common purposes.

Grants should be given on the basis of applications and the outcome monitored and documented. The aims are both to stimulate and further local initiatives and to provide incentives for co-operation, co-ordination and local participation in library policy matters and professional development.

6

Challenges of Internet Infrastructure

Infrastructure providers and users, the indicators play an increasingly important role in underpinning Internet self-governance and self-regulation. For each of the key reasons expressing why self-regulation is preferred by the Internet community, information to inform that process is essential.

If one Internet Service Providers (ISP) does the 'wrong thing', in terms of its inter-action with the Internet, it can impair the network and service performance for all ISPs. This can range from problems with day-to-day network quality management right up to, in the worst case, bringing traffic flows on the Internet to a standstill. Just as policy makers have needed indicators for regulation in traditional communication sectors, the Internet industry needs infrastructure indicators for self-regulation.

For policy makers familiarity with Internet infrastructure indicators is important in a number of areas. One aspect is the increasing number of regulatory issues being placed before governments, not only in relatively unfamiliar issues at the core of the Internet (e.g. the debate over domain names) but also in areas where the Internet is converging with other communication platforms (e.g. public switched telecommunication network and broadcasting regulation).

Moreover, a better understanding of Internet infrastructures is an important element underpinning wider issues bearing on electronic commerce. They can provide a better·understanding of the challenges for the private sector in upgrading infrastructure and of comparative national performance. They also provide an important input into a better understanding of how the Internet is becoming more critical for overall economic and social development in OECD countries.

The main criteria for inclusion of indicators in this document is that the data were generated by network surveys (e.g. queries of Internet Protocol network databases and objects connected to Internet Protocol networks) or by entities that play a role in administering core Internet infrastructure. In respect to the first criteria, online or electronic network measurements would qualify but an off-line survey or e-mail based surveys are not included.

The exclusions are not because such surveys may not provide valuable information but rather because the off-line survey methodologies used are generally well known. In addition, their exclusion assists to narrow the scope of this document to a manageable level and to focus on indicators that often rely on the policy maker to bring together data from different sources to generate the indicator.

The second criteria includes data that are collected by the managers of core infrastructure surrounding the Domain Name System (DNS), such as second and third level domain registration, Internet Protocol (IP) number assignment, Autonomous System Number (ASN) assignment. Some useful Internet Websites on this subject, with the summaries of attempts to draw together the results of official and commercial surveys, are those of HeadCount and NUA. How reliable the underlying results are for each country depends on the individual surveys and there is, of course, no harmonisation of methodologies.

At the same time some of the Internet's core administrative entities, in some countries, are collecting useful data from among their members. In this context a leading example is KRNIC, the organisation which administers domain names and IP addresses in Korea, which surveys Korean Internet Service providers (ISPs) to determine their number of business connections and dial-up subscribers. KRNIC is then able to publish national Internet subscriber statistics for Korea. IP addresses and autonomous system numbers. As appropriate, references are made to governance and regulatory issues where these indicators are being used to inform debate or form a tool used by industry for self-regulation.

Whereas surveys of hosts, servers and so forth are undertaken by the Internet's technical community, tools are available for policy makers to generate infrastructure indicators. These include the use of traceroutes to provide an indicator of market position and a better understanding of traffic exchange in backbone networks. In addition, the use of search engines to provide information on the implementation of webcasting technologies and the topography of Internet hyper-text links to leading electronic commerce sites.

By way of example, a matrix of all the hyper-text links between domains for the OECD area is made available. Accordingly, it is possible to see the emerging pathways of electronic commerce between OECD countries. Finally, readers may find the references to electronic glossaries at the end of this document a useful aid in respect to Internet terminology. The most common indicators used to measure Internet development are the surveys of Internet hosts undertaken by Network Wizards and RIPE (Reseaux IP Européens).

The Network Wizards survey includes all Top Level Domains (TLDs) and generic Top Level Domains (gTLDs) and is undertaken every six months. The RIPE survey is undertaken monthly but is limited to TLD registrations in their service area. While both surveys are much appreciated by the Internet community the results need to be qualified and have several limitations. The first qualification that needs to be made is that host data do not indicate the total number of users who can access the Internet.

The second caveat is that these surveys do not reach every host on the Internet, as access to some hosts is blocked by company fire-walls. Recognising the limitation of this second factor Network Wizards changed their methodology for the survey undertaken in January 1998 to enable access to a greater number of hosts. Notwithstanding this change, surveys of Internet hosts may only be interpreted as the minimum size of the 'public Internet', as it is impossible to determine the number of users accessing services via each host. The Netcraft Web Server Survey is a survey of web server software usage on computers connected to the Internet. Netcraft collect and collate as many hostnames providing an http-service as their survey can find, and systematically poll each one with an HyperText Transfer Protocol (HTTP) request for the server name. A host name is the first part of a hosts' domain name. In the July 1998 survey Netcraft received responses from 2 594 622 web servers. The growth rate for the first half of 1998 was 41 per cent. Some 96 per cent of these servers are in the OECD area.

By far the largest number of web servers are under .com which has 60 per cent of all web servers. As for Internet hosts, it is possible to provide penetration by domain and to weight this by the number of gTLD registrations. The country providing the most responses, on a per capita basis, is Denmark. This is because there are a lot of small virtually hosted sites in Denmark. Netcraft report, that while this is a characteristic of many countries, it is particularly so in Denmark and the Netherlands. TeleDanmark and Cybercity operate two of the largest virtual hosting sites in Denmark. Internet surveys of hosts and servers provide one indicator of Internet development and may be used as one potential indicator of comparative Internet development between countries.

The main limitations are not reaching all hosts or servers, and the structure of the domain name system being such that there is no guarantee that all hosts under a particular domain are located in a certain geographic location. That being said the OECD's observations, from an series of traceroutes to Websites under TLDs, are that by far the majority of hosts using TLDs are located in the country concerned. The availability of gTLD registrations by country presented the first possibility of redistributing Internet hosts under domain names such as .com to individual countries. The most simple option, used to prepare this report, was to weight the number of hosts under gTLDs according to the number of gTLD registrations from a particular country.

In other words if 5 per cent of the total gTLD registrations are from a particular country then 5 per cent of the total number of hosts surveyed under gTLDs are reallocated to that country. This methodology could, no doubt, be subject to a number of caveats. Nevertheless it seems reasonable to assume that this approach gives a more accurate distribution of Internet hosts, in OECD countries, than allocating all hosts under gTLD registrations to the United States.

Other countries recording significant increases at that time, albeit from smaller base numbers of hosts, were Turkey, Spain, Luxembourg and France. All these countries recorded a relatively large increase in the number of hosts relative to the average OECD increase of 21 per cent. The countries for which this made very little difference are those where users mainly rely on national TLD registrations, such as Iceland, the Czech Republic, New Zealand, Poland and Finland.

The Netcraft Server surveys also provide one of the best available indicators of the growth of electronic commerce on the Internet. Whereas the best known search engines only cover http sites, Netcraft also undertakes a secure socket layer (SSL) survey. The SSL protocol was developed by Netscape for encrypted transmission over TCP/IP networks. It sets up a secure end-to-end link over which http or any other application protocol can operate.

The most common application of SSL is https for ssl-encrypted http which enables electronic commerce to take place. In August 1998, Netcraft received responses from more than 424 000 web sites using encryption. However most of these responses are excluded, in terms of electronic commerce web sites, because they do not have third party certification. Sites without a third party certification are not expected to be engaging in electronic commerce because of the warning message that gets generated.

The key element for electronic commerce is third party certification with matching certificate. Netcraft say plausible reasons for the large number of responses, where the name in the certificate did not match the site's domain name, might include web sites run from virtual hosting configurations where the provider sets up all customers with https services, with customers buying certificates when they start to make use of the facilities. Netcraft adds that sites where the certificate issuer is not a known certificate authority, typically indicate that that site has generated and signed its own certificate, which is acceptable for prototyping, or where trust is not required outside a limited group of people, such as a company, or collaborative project. This is likely to be more commonplace on internal networks than on externally visible Internet sites.

The major electronic commerce uses of secure server software are for encrypted credit card transactions over the Internet. The most common non-retail use of SSL is subscription access to privileged information.

Domain Name System

The Domain Name System (DNS) maps Internet addresses. To function as part of the Internet a host needs a domain name that has an associated Internet Protocol (IP) address record. This includes any computer system connected to the Internet via full or part-time, direct or dial-up connections. DNS servers perform the necessary function of translating back and forth between names and numbers. These servers contain databases of IP addresses and corresponding domain names and they are interrogated each time a user wants to send an e-mail or request data over the World Wide Web.

A top-level domain name (TLD) can either be an ISO country code or one of the generic top level domains. To register a second level domain name or a third level domain name a user needs to apply to the domain name registry with the delegated authority for the TLD or gTLD. Some registries publish data on the number of registrations on a monthly basis while others publish intermittently. The Internet Hosts surveys undertaken by Network Wizards and RIPE also provide, as a by-product, an indicator of the number of registrations under each domain.

The main importance of DNS indicators are that they can be used to inform discussions over the different policies and prices of TLD and gTLD registries. Whether the registration process under a certain domain name is subject to industry self-regulation or government oversight, the availability of DNS data is important to ensure transparency in registration management for service providers, business users and consumers. This is particularly important in those cases where a monopoly or monopoly power exists in the registration of second and third level domain names.

These tools can provide useful information for constructing certain Internet indicators. While this information is not always reliable, and some users would like to see additional information or functionality included, the various 'Whois?' databases are valuable resources for the Internet community. The United States White Paper "A Proposal to Improve the Technical Management of Internet Domain Names and Addresses Discussion Draft", contained a number of suggestions for the type of information that should be included in domain registration databases and it will be up to the new DNS authority to work through guidelines in this area.

Internet Protocol (IP) addresses are the numbers used to identify computers, or other devices, on a TCP/IP network. Networks using the TCP/IP protocol route messages based on the IP address of the destination. The format of an IP address is a 32-bit numeric address written as four numbers separated by periods. Each number can be zero to 255.

The current version of IP (IP version 4 or IPv4), which was standardised in 1981, created a pool of 4 294 967 296 IPv4 addresses. Originally blocks of IP addresses were directly allocated by the Internet Assigned Numbers Authority (IANA). While in some cases the IANA still makes direct assignments to organisations most allocations are now made to three regional bodies-APNIC (Asia-Pacific Network Information Center), ARIN (American Registry for Internet Numbers) and RIPE NCC (Reseaux IP Européens Network Co-ordination Centre).

These organisations subsequently re-allocate or assign IP addresses to individual organisations, such as ISPs or national bodies co-ordinating IP address space for a certain country. As a general rule, end users receive IP assignments from their ISP. Notwithstanding this some ISPs receive addresses from upstream or backbone ISPs and some end users receive allocations directly from a registry or directly from the IANA. The question of the whether the institutions allocating IP addresses at various levels have monopolies, in terms of guiding their self-governance practices, is important. Reform to the IANA is ongoing at the time of writing which takes into account its monopoly position.

Whether the three regional registries have a total monopoly position is less clear because ISPs can, and do, apply to different registries. In addition, apart from convention, there may be nothing to stop an entity with a very large net block from reselling this resource in competition to the regional registries.

Certainly many entities at the sub-regional registry level 'resell' IP numbers. The best sources of data on IP addresses are the three regional IP address registries. However, the policies and practices of each organisation mean the dissemination of IP allocation and assignment is carried out in different forms. A further indicator to assist in the understanding of IP address allocations is work which has been undertaken by the Cooperative Association for Internet Data Analysis (CAIDA) to enable visualisation of IP address occupancy.

Such depictions of the address space can also provide inputs for analysis of public policy (equity) issues, as well as information for evaluating engineering and operational aspects of the commercial Internet. Some of the main self-governance issues, relating to infrastructure, facing the Internet community are in the management of the existing IPv4 address space. These include:

- co-ordination of the three existing IP address registries;
- proposals to create new regional registries;
- the criteria for allocation of IP addresses;.
- the pricing structure used by registries for this resource.

Issues such as these can generate vigorous discussion within the Internet community and raise governance questions of a similar nature to the controversial DNS debate. Perhaps the main differences with IP address issues are that the main players are ISPs, rather than the much larger community which took an interest in DNS, and the absence of intellectual property concerns associated with trademarks and domain registration.

Notwithstanding these differences, because the existing allocation of IP addresses are a monopoly, at least in one sense, the IANA and regional registries need to observe standards of openness, transparency and public accountability. An essential part of this process, and a pre-requisite for self-governance, is the publication of data and indicators in a readily accessible form to the Internet community. While the management of IP addresses is best done by the private sector, policy makers need to have an understanding of the IP address system because of its potential to spill over into matters placed before governments. The most significant case in point is the ongoing problem of IP address portability and the competition questions raised.

If a relatively small ISP can not get a direct allocation of IP address space from a registry they need to borrow numbers from upstream ISPs. If a small ISP then wishes to change its upstream (i.e. backbone provider), it has to return the borrowed IP numbers to the larger provider. In effect this means the smaller ISP has to renumber its network, which can be expensive and disruptive for its customers, if it wants to change backbone providers. This issue was raised in the context of the proposed merger of Worldcom and MCI which was considered by competition authorities in the United Sates and Europe.

The concern voiced by some relatively small ISPs, arguing against this merger, was that if a dominant player in the backbone market abused that position they would face a high cost to shift providers because of the lack of number portability. At the same time, the technical reasons for not encouraging portability for small address assignments and the attendant increase in the size of the routing table this would cause need to be borne in mind.

According to some experts the portability problem will not be solved by the introduction of IPv6.

Autonomous systems numbers acts as a label for a set of IP addresses and are used by ISPs to specify the global routing policy for those IP addresses. On the Internet packets of data are passed between devices known as routers. Part of this process involves consultation of the routing table to determine the best onward path. A routing policy indicates 'reachability information', and hence enables traffic to pass between the networks of different ISPs. If an ISP has two connections to 'the Internet', it is often useful to spread traffic out over those two links. This policy is then propagated in order to insure that traffic flows in the correct direction and that reachability of the addresses of an ISP providing services can be assured.In practice this means that most end users and small ISPs do not receive an individual AS number but instead use their upstream service provider's AS number.

If an ISP only has one connection to the Internet (i.e. it is singly homed), it only has one way in which traffic can flow, thus it does not need an AS number. However, the downstream ISP will still be exchanging traffic with the Internet, albeit under the AS number of their upstream provider. The distinction between being single-homed and multi-homed refers to the number of connections a small ISP, or content provider, has to the Internet via different backbone infrastructure providers.

If an organisation is connected to the Internet via one ISP it is single-homed, but if it receives connections from two, or more, ISPs it is multi-homed. Internet backbone routers need to maintain the complete routing information for the Internet. As the Internet has expanded, so too have the number of routes between AS numbers. This rapid growth has been a cause for concern among the Internet's technical community because it was felt that there was a limit to the amount of global routing information able to be accommodated by backbone routers.

In mid-1997 an accident occurred which demonstrated the 'high-watermark' for the 'core Internet' and the fragility of the Internet. This was due to one Autonomous System accidentally re-announcing the entire Internet through itself resulting in a sudden doubling in the number of global routes to just over 80,000. As a result backbone routers around the world were overloaded as they did not have enough memory to cope with the additional routes.

As these same routers tried to reboot, and establish peering, they once again received the information for more than 80 000 routes, and again ran out of memory. This problem recurred until filters were manually installed or the originator of the excess routes fixed the source of the problem. This accident demonstrated both the current upper limit of the routing resource and the need for industry to have information and indicators to assist in self-regulating Internet traffic exchange.

In other words, downstream ISPs, and smaller IP networks, used the AS number of their upstream backbone connection to the United States. However, the recent increase in allocation of AS numbers in the Asia Pacific has drawn some analysts to the conclusion that there is a corresponding increase in intra-national and intra-regional connectivity. In the Asia Pacific this process is believed to have been spurred by the devaluation of a number of currencies (increasing the cost of international bandwidth) and the desire to improve network performance via localised traffic exchange. Further analysis of the policies for the AS numbers in appropriate databases, such those of APNIC and routing registries, could provide a tool for better understanding the amount of intra-national and intra-regional connectivity.

Due to the nature of the Internet, measurement of performance across different networks can be much more difficult and controversial than the public switched telecommunication network (PSTN). Measuring the performance within one network is relatively straightforward and many ISPs are comfortable enough to place near real-time indicators on the World Wide Web. This strikes an immediate contrast to the PSTN where such information was generally reserved for engineering purposes, and only made public in regulatory filings or annual reports. Accordingly, it is possible to see in near real time how, for example, MCI's Internet backbone is performing or the performance of links to Singapore Telecom's Internet exchange point (STIX).

Measurements include the latency of round trip times over different parts of networks and the loss of packets during times of congestion. Where the problematic aspect of measurement arises, is in constructing indicators to measure performance across different ISP networks, core Internet infrastructure and the networks and sites of users. This can, of course, give rise to different interpretations of where the reasons for good and poor performance arise. There are several motivations for an increasing number of ISPs and Internet exchange points to put performance-related data on their Websites.

Publication of such data can be used for marketing purposes and to provide customers with an additional service. At the same time many of these indicators can be constructed by independent entities or by users themselves for their individual connections. As such there are a growing number of Websites that measure the "Internet Weather" from the perspective of their network or their Website. These are also companies that specialise in measuring the performance of particular backbone providers and ISPs, as well as services such as e-mail.

In large part initiatives in the area of Internet network performance measures are best done by the private sector, albeit some government funded basic research institutions are currently playing an important role. However if self-governance and industry co-operation evolves as the standard model for Internet traffic exchange, by contrast to the often heavily regulated interconnection in the PSTN, then the availability of performance indicators across different networks is essential.

One issue that may arise for competition authorities or regulators is the claim that if one ISP held a majority share of the backbone market it might downgrade performance to other ISPs to encourage their customers to directly connect to the dominant player's network. Where there is a strongly competitive backbone market this problem should not arise. However, in those countries where this is not the case, perhaps due to the existing or legacy effects of telecommunication monopolies, industry regulators may be called on to arbitrate very complex disputes between ISPs.

On the other hand, the more indicators make transparent the relative performance of different networks the less likely such problems are to occur.Traceroutes enable users to follow a path taken by packets of data via intermediate routers between IP addresses. A traceroute can be initiated from a user's PC, with a connection to the Internet, to a particular IP address. The second option is to use one of the many sites on the World Wide Web which enable a user to traceroute from that web-site to an IP address using their browser.

Boardwatch Magazine has compiled a comprehensive guide to traceroutes and how they work. Essentially traceroutes work by sending packets to an Internet address and getting intermediate routers to send a return message to the source. The return message identifies the IP address of each router and the round trip time, in milliseconds, between the original router and each intermediate router.

While the use of traceroutes as a tool for the Internet technical community to monitor the performance of peer networks is the leading application, traceroutes have also been used by some knowledgeable users to learn more about the performance of their ISP and their backbone provider.

For policy makers traceroutes also represent an important tool for better understanding and informing debates on national and international traffic exchange. For example, some traceroutes demonstrate that traffic follows a certain path not because it may be the most efficient but because of the legacy or existence of infrastructure monopolies. In other words traffic may travel a certain route because capacity on a more logical route to provide connectivity is either unavailable or priced at uncompetitive rates. In addition, traceroutes to the most accessed Internet sites in different countries can be used as an indicator to better understand the relative positions of players in backbone markets. Prior to consideration of this application, other interesting technical features, albeit sometimes erratic in terms of success, are:

— Traceroutes can indicate the capacity of a link between two routers either through the ISP incorporating this information (in the name of the router) or via traceroute software that endeavours to identify the capacity of each link.

— Traceroutes can be conducted between any two known hosts on some web sites.

— Some within the Internet community voluntarily incorporate latitude and longitude information in their routers and would like to see this practice generally adopted by all network managers.

— Users can employ traceroutes to provide an indication, or 'non-authoritative verification', of whether a Website is actually in the location specified on a Website or implied by a top level domain name or 'Whois? record'. In a number of cases bearing on electronic commerce or law enforcement and industry self-regulatory initiatives a user's first action is to use tools such as traceroutes to provide additional information about the source of data and possible recourse to ISPs or other authorities.

On the other hand critics of this view held that accurate data were not available either for the total Internet market or by relevant Internet market segment. Similarly, for policy makers considering the competition aspects of the merger, data were not available on Internet traffic such that an assessment of the market shares of various players could be constructed via that avenue. An alternative methodology is to use traceroutes to the most accessed Internet sites to gain a better understanding of backbone markets and Internet traffic exchange.

The basic idea is to undertake a series of traceroutes from a Website served by a certain backbone provider to the most sought after content and portals. It is then possible to see for how many of these sites a backbone provider can carry the traffic on an end-to-end basis and for how many of those sites they need to hand traffic to another provider.

Together, a merger of Worldcom and MCI's backbone networks would have meant the new entity could carry the traffic internally to 62 of the leading 100 sites. Worthy of note is that this market position paralleled many of the market share estimates forwarded by those opposed to the merger of Internet backbones of these companies. Yet, at the same time, the data also showed a high degree of multi-homing by major content providers in the United States with 53 of all sites being multi-homed and 35 of Worldcom customers being multi-homed.

Another factor could be that the Websites in the United States bear far high traffic flows, than counterparts in other countries, and therefore require a higher degree of multi-homing. It might also be simply a sign that the Internet market in the United States is more mature than in other OECD countries. One other potential indicator of the commercial maturity of the US Internet market relative to Australia, Germany, Sweden and the Netherlands is the high proportion of university Websites that figure in the top 100 Websites for these countries.

In other words, users in universities still account for a high proportion of Internet traffic and accordingly lift the ranking of university Websites relative to commercial Websites. One implication of this might be to bear in mind that academic backbone networks, while continuing to grow and provide important services, will either commercialise to capture mass market growth or form an increasingly smaller part of the total backbone market.

There are also interesting features that apply to the four individual countries, albeit in each market a variation on the methodology has been explored. In Sweden a series of traceroutes was also conducted from CERN in Switzerland to test the market positions from outside the country. The results were that SwipNet, owned by Tele-2 provided carriage for 41 per cent of the commercial sites (i.e. excluding Sunet the University network). Telia and Telenordia provided carriage for a further 39 per cent of commercial sites.

However, the most striking feature of this traceroute series was the amount of traffic between Denmark and Germany that traversed the United States. For one quarter of the traceroutes from TeleDanmark, to the leading sites in Germany, traffic was initially exchanged via MCI's network in the United States and then found its way back to Germany via the Netherlands or other European countries.

Whereas most large backbone providers which peer hand off traffic to another backbone network, as soon as the network determines they do not have a direct connection to the Website concerned and another path is available, Telstra's backbone network carries this traffic virtually the whole way.

Interestingly, this also leads to incoming international traffic being handed to Telstra, at an international exchange point, even if the ISP concerned has a direct backbone connection to Australia. Consider the series of traceroutes from CWIX (the Cable and Wireless US IP backbone network) which only carries traffic between CWIX and Optus (a Cable and Wireless Australian subsidiary), when it is to an Optus or Ozemail customer's Website. This international pattern of traffic is interesting in terms of Telstra's position on the financing of international infrastructure. If CWIX (and Optus) carried the traffic from the United States to Australia, Optus would have had to pay Telstra for the domestic traffic exchange to reach the Telstra customer's Website. The interesting point is that it may be less expensive for CWIX to pass the traffic to MCI, than carry it directly to Australia and have it exchanged locally by Optus.

There are a number of companies that seek to rank the most accessed sites on the World Wide Web. Lists of the most accessed web sites are of interest to a variety of different groups. For the companies wanting to advertise on the Internet it is useful to have an indication of the relative popularity of different Websites.

For users such rankings are sometimes used as a directory service in different categories. For policy makers the main interest in Website rankings is the indication they might give for the location of the most popular content and as an input to determining the leading players providing access infrastructure to that content. The OECD has used Web21's lists of the most accessed Websites in different categories both to highlight to location of popular content, and its impact on traffic patterns, as well as the benefits being generated for pluralism and cultural diversity at a national and global level.

Such lists have also been used to determine which ISPs have the most significant backbone networks in terms of carriage of traffic to these high volume sites. A number of companies undertake studies endeavouring to rank Websites by the amount of traffic or visits they generate. Web21 produces the "Hot100" in different categories (e.g. news, sport, business, overall) and by different countries.

Categories of content are useful when policy makers are endeavouring to better understand the location of popular content, such as webcasting radio stations and the potential impact on policy in respect to convergence between different communication platforms. Country categories are useful for examination of traffic exchange, via traceroutes, between major backbone providers in national markets and their relationships with major international backbone markets. By combining tools such as traceroutes and lists of the most popular Websites indications can be constructed for different markets in terms of infrastructure availability, competition policy and the extent of trends such as multi-homing.

Web21 collects data from a number of different sources but primarily use the logs from proxy servers and caches. These logs are sent on-line to Web21 on a daily basis and represent the surfing patterns of over 100 000 surfers world-wide. Approximately 60 per cent of these users are in North America and 40 per cent outside the United States.

Knowledge is another company which ranks web sites by getting users to download proprietary software via the Internet onto all computers they use to access the Web. These user's surfing patterns are then tracked by the company and made available on the net by different demographic categories. According to the Internet Advertising Bureau (IAB) the top 10 Websites receive 67 per cent of total Internet advertising expenditures. A portal is the term given to that part of a Website which acts as a gateway, or launch point, through which users navigate the World Wide Web.

A portal can be the page a user sees each time they log onto the World Wide Web, such as the home page of an ISP or AOL (America Online).

Accordingly, one measure of the usage of a portal is the number of subscribers served by a certain ISP, or other online service, although this is not precise as users can create their own portal or set their opening web page to another Website. These latter users will often define portals, such as Yahoo! or Excite, as their default Websites or use the default page of their browser (e.g. Netscape, Microsoft). These portals, which commenced service primary as search engines or directories have since moved to providing multiple applications designed to provide users with a variety of tools in one location.

Similarly, Netscape and Microsoft have incorporated an increasing number of portal-like functions into their browsers as well as selling hyper-text links and advertising space to other portals. Accordingly sites such as Yahoo and Excite are amongst the most accessed Websites on the Internet. It is this popularity, and the belief of many analysts that portals will become increasingly important to making the Internet more user friendly for electronic commerce, that has attracted increasing attention. Portals that were fairly recently in the preserve of sophisticated Internet users are now the best known sites on the Internet, a trend not missed by companies engaging in electronic commerce.

Another approach to investigating portals is to examine the number of hyper-text links to the gateway pages of these Websites and their origin. Many electronic commerce sites pay search engines, or other portals, a fee for each transaction referral. This can be done with, for example , 'click-through' banner advertising. In addition the total count of hyper-text links includes internal Website hyper-text links to a particular URL (e.g. back to main page hyper-text links, links to the web designer's page and so forth). It is also probable that if this measure became used as an indicator of popularity it would be relatively easy to distort. This is useful for examining hyper-text links between domains, including TLDs and gTLDs as discussed below, but in the context of an examination of portals it is interesting to link to the main URL of a company rather than its entire domain.

There is a vast difference in the number of hyper-text links to Websites needed to navigate the Internet (either via search and directory functions such as Yahoo! or equipment and software such as Netscape and Microsoft) for content and services than to the Websites of traditional print media. As an aside it is also possible to use this tool to get an indication of the amount of 'adult content' relative to all content on the World Wide Web.

Here it can be noted that the leading 100 Websites providing adult content make up only around 0.05 per cent of all content on the Internet. The proxy measure for content here is to count the number of outgoing URLs from these Websites relative to the total number of outgoing URLs from all domains. This does of course not deny the importance of using self regulatory tools, such as screening technologies, because of the ease with which adult material can be located intentionally or accidentally by children.

However it is interesting to compare this figure with the amount of content under .edu (used by institutions of higher education in the United States) which makes up more than 16 per cent of all Internet content. Taken together with the content under .us (used by schools in the United States) and the educational content under top level domains, the amount of educational content helps put a more balanced perspective on the different types of content available on the World Wide Web. It is also interesting to examine the number of hyper-text links to the traditional gatekeepers to the online world.

Significantly only AT&T and NTT exceed 10 000 hyper-text links to their main URLs. In the not too distant past telecommunication carriers with government mandated monopolies owned every 'portal' from the actual line connection to the PSTN, through to every piece of customer equipment and the cover and contents of telephone directories. Today, the majority of these markets have been liberalised in OECD countries, meaning that telecommunication carriers need to compete not only at the level of physical infrastructure but also for portals. Consider, for example, if as Internet telephony is increasingly incorporated into electronic commerce Websites, the additional communication revenue may accrue to the Internet telephony provider nominated by the owner of the portal.

Even for the telecommunication carrier that becomes an ISP, and therefore has the opportunity to create a portal via the launch point for subscribers, there is no guarantee that these users will not opt for portals like Yahoo! and Netscape. One indicator of the take up of different audio, video and other software tools on the World Wide Web is to use a search engine to count the number of applications.

As Internet searches can be conducted under a particular top level domain name, by using HotBot, it is possible to get an indication of the use of these technologies. By including objects found under gTLDs and the TLDs associated with OECD Member countries, there appeared to be around 600,000 audio and more than 200,000 video applications in July 1998. While the usual caveat applies, as to the allocations under gTLDs not being country specific, the data shown under TLDs might be taken to represent a very large sample for any given country. Accordingly by using search engines, analysts have one indication of the number of webcasting sites under a domain associated with a certain country. In future this may be an important source of information to assist policy makers dealing with convergence issues. This innovation created new pathways for electronic commerce and, by doing so, raised the question of whether indicators of the topography of linkages between domains could be useful for policy makers.

7

Electronic Information Resources

An "electronic resource" is defined as any work encoded and made available for access through the use of a computer. It includes both online data and electronic data in physical formats (e.g., CD-ROM). To avoid confusion with these terms as used in the copyright process, online will refer to intangible works; physical to a tangible work. The term "acquire" refers to any electronic resource, online or physical, which the Library receives though its various, typical acquisitions processes, or which the Library provides access to through official contractual, licensed, or other agreements; any of these electronic resources may or may not be owned by or housed at the Library. "Collect" refers to electronic resources owned by the Library and selected for the permanent collection, including works created by the Library.

It may also include works stored elsewhere for which the Library has permanent ownership rights. "Link" refers to pointers from the Library's internet resources or bibliographic records to the Library and non-Library electronic resources, created and maintained by Library staff for a variety of purposes; "link" is not an act of acquiring, and electronic resources linked do not necessarily constitute an acquisition by the Library. The Library collects materials in many formats to support its universal collections. This policy is intentionally general in order not to restrict the collecting of needed materials and to allow the Library to make these resources available as technology changes. It is the Library's policy with electronic works, as with all others, to obtain them through copyright unless they are not subject to deposit under sections 407 or 408 of the copyright law. Selection of works for the collection depends on the subject of the item as defined by the collections policy statement for the subject of the work, regardless of its format. Formats include home pages, Web sites, or internet sites required to support research in the subject covered.

The Recommending Officer responsible for the subject, language, or geographic area of the electronic resources is responsible for recommending these materials. Electronic editions of audio-visual materials, prints, photographs, maps, or related items are also covered by the Collections Policy Statements for their appropriate formats. The criteria used to evaluate electronic resources do not greatly differ from those used for books or materials in other formats. As with more traditional formats, the cost of the work and the requirements of serving, cataloging, storing, and preserving must be considered in the decision.

The Library selects electronic works for its permanent collections which rank high on the following list of criteria: usefulness in serving the current or future informational needs of Congress and researchers, reputation of the information provider, amount of unique information provided, scholarly content, currency of the information, frequency of updating, and ease of access. Priority is given to resources containing information not otherwise available. The Library will facilitate access to various kinds of electronic resources which it does not maintain in its own collections by means of bookmarked links, special catalog records, or index systems. The Library will not consider these resources part of its permanent collections and will not archive them.

Access to Electronic Resources

Electronic resources can be provided via different mechanisms and should be specified in the proposal based on the following:

1. Single workstation

a) Use will be limited to a small or specialised user community;

b) Search/retrieval capabilities may require staff assistance;

c) Space is not available on the LAN.

2. Library LAN

a) The product is needed by simultaneous users;

b) The license permits remote access;

c) Security is needed for disk products.

3. Remote or Gateway Systems (contract-based)

a) Access is limited to a gateway (e.g. Ingenta, Lexis/Nexis, etc.);

b) A gateway provides the most efficient access in terms of reducing computer and staff resources required to maintain the local system.

Just as the traditional library evolved to provide services to make its contents more accessible to its users, the effective digital library develops a range of services to assist its users in finding, understanding, and using its contents. In its digital form the library has the potential to not just emulate traditional libraries in the services it provides but to improve and extend them by capitalising on advantages inherent in the medium.

One important area where the digital library can extend the services it provides beyond that of the traditional library is in integrating and highlighting user contributions. With the exception of especially unique or noteworthy contributions, the traditional library is rarely eager to receive resource contributions outside of its usual channels, as the effort needed to catalog and integrate outside contributions into a physical library is substantial. Digital libraries, on the other hand, are more often willing to receive contributions.

It has been demonstrated that a combination of minimal submission data and basic verification procedures can result in high-quality digital library contributions with low rejection rates. Such contributions enhance the value of the digital library by increasing its size and diversity and the process of cataloging and integrating contributed resources into a digital library often requires less effort. However, the aspects that make digital libraries built from user contributions valuable-diversity of content, potential for large growth-also create potential drawbacks.

Search and browse facilities enable users to find resources based on features such as author, subject, and keywords, but as a digital library grows, finding specific resources of interest among the entire collection can become more difficult. At the same time, the prominence of a given contributor's contributions becomes diminished as the library grows. One way to help users find resources of interest in a digital library while ensuring that contributors receive recognition is to borrow a concept that has long been part of traditional libraries: the special collection. By defining and making available virtual collections believe the digital library can extend the special collection model and-at a modest cost-provide benefits to both its users and contributors that will encourage its own growth and viability. Traditional libraries often contain, in addition to their main holdings, special collections. In these settings a special collection is generally defined as a group of related materials that is given some form of special treatment.

The special treatment might be due to the rare or delicate nature of the materials, or because the library wants to highlight the materials in some way. In contrast to traditional libraries, the special or sub-collections of digital libraries can be much more fluid. Where the holdings of a traditional library are physically constrained to a single space and a single ordering, resources in a digital library can be distributed across many servers, can be owned by different organisations, and can be displayed in many different orderings and arrangements. This fluid nature makes defining collections and sub-collections in the digital environment less straightforward. Adhering closely to the traditional library definition, one could consider a digital library collection to be all those resources that reside on a single server, or alternatively, all those that can be accessed though a given library's interface, even if they are physically distributed.

As suggested in, however, even a broad definition of a collection in the context of digital libraries can be ambiguous. It can, for example, be influenced by the point of view of those making the definition. The people responsible for managing resources stored in separate databases might think of each as a distinct collection, while an end user with access to them all is more likely to consider them a single collection.

Defining sub-collections can be even more flexible as there are many possible factors that can suggest how sub-collections can be formed. A sub-collection can be defined by including all those resources that share a topic or other significant attribute, those contributed by a specific organisation, or those used for a specific purpose. These sub-collection examples are instances of collections that cannot be easily replicated in traditional libraries. They are made possible by exploiting advantages the digital environment inherently provides: objects can exist in multiple collections, collections with the same objects grouped in different ways can co-exist, collections can be created dynamically and exist for varying amounts of time. They become virtual collections and as such-in contrast to the traditional library-enable a digital library to provide a limitless number of sub-collections based on a wide range of features.

Although it is common for traditional libraries to create and maintain special collections, many digital libraries do not attempt to provide a similar service. Most digital libraries do create the most basic of virtual collections—the result set dynamically created from a search request or category browsing—but rarely do they explicitly create and promote the sort of virtual collections described above. Doing so, however, can benefit both the users of the digital library and those who contribute resources to it.

A digital library that contains virtual collections helps its users in several ways. A new user who may be intimidated by a digital library's search interface or the number of results returned by a query might be better introduced to the digital library through the more easily exploreable partitioned set of resources in a virtual collection. A directory of the virtual collections contained by a digital library, can provide a good introduction and overview of the library's contents to new or casual users. Associating resources with virtual collections enables those resources to be found more easily, either by browsing the contents of a highlighted virtual collection or through standard search and browse interfaces.

Looking at the use of the digital library from a "work-oriented perspective", other benefits to the user stem from a more productive use of time. In it is suggested that sub-collections can facilitate work by isolating a group of related content and enabling a user to focus on those resources. Defining virtual collections makes it easier for users to find and work with such groupings of related content, or by a "related resources" link based on virtual collection associations and tied to specific resources. Additionally, the virtual collection description might include links to related information outside the digital library, thus guiding users to more materials for their work.

Implemention of Virtual Collections

The benefits of virtual collections do not come without a price, of course. For a digital library to be able to easily create and remove virtual collections, to associate resources with different virtual collections in a flexible way, and to help users find and use the virtual collections, the library must have a structured approach to representing these collections. Moreover, to make creating such collections practical, this approach should also strive to minimise the costs associated with creating virtual collections. In the remainder of this matter describe an approach to implementing virtual collections based on work in creating collections for two different digital libraries. The current research related to representing collections in digital libraries and describe the costs and benefits of different types of metadata used to represent collections.

Collection-level metadata

Metadata is a key element of any library, traditional or digital. Metadata is used by libraries to describe and organise item-level resources and by users to search and browse the library. Collection-level metadata performs a similar function for collections and is used in traditional libraries for discovery across collections. Work on collection-level metadata from several fields including archives, museums, libraries, and the Internet is relevant to the design and implementation of virtual collections. As outlined in, each field defines collections differently and has different standards governing collection description. The past few years have seen a movement to create a standard for collection description that is informed by, yet transcends, the fields from which it is derived. Work in the UK and the US has resulted in the formulation of goals for collection-level metadata and the definition and development of schemas to describe collections.

Based on work with the eLib working group on Collection Level Descriptions, the RIDING Clump Project created a searchable database .of collection descriptions to provide information about what was available in its libraries. The purpose of its scheme was to describe any type of collection-physical or virtual (electronic), networked or otherwise. RIDING collection metadata should allow users to discover, locate and access collections, search across multiple collections and allow software to provide services based on user preferences. The Research Support Libraries Programme (RSLP) builds upon the RIDING goals above by requiring that collection metadata allow the refinement of distributed searching approaches based on the characteristics of collections.

The Alexandria Digital Library (ADL) is a research digital library focused on geo-referenced geo-spatial information. The goal of the ADL is to create a single model that supports the four roles ADL identified for collection metadata: collection registration, network discovery, user documentation, and management. Several themes emerge from this the requirements.

— It highlights the importance of establishing standardised collectionlevel metadata schemas that can effectively describe and manage a diverse set of collections and their metadata.

— It argues that the schemas must support a number of functional library services that enable users to access collections and items, to search for materials, and to comprehend and use them effectively.

One challenge to creating collection-level metadata noted in the literature is the potentially high cost of production.

Metadata can be automatically-generated or human-created with the latter clearly imposing more significant costs in terms of human effort and time. In the context of collections, describes two types of roughly corresponding metadata: inherent metadata, or information that can be extracted from the resource objects themselves, such as total number of objects or total file-size of the collection; and contextual metadata, or metadata which involves human judgment to create, such as a textual description of a collection of resources.

There are significant advantages to utilising inherent metadata as much as possible. Because it can be generated automatically, inherent metadata has minimal costs associated with its creation and maintenance and can be updated on a regular, automated schedule. In contrast, human-created metadata is time-consuming, error-prone, costly to create, and more likely to be inconsistent. A person assigned to create metadata may only perform this task on an occasional, as-needed basis, and it may be a lower priority task than others for which that person is also responsible.

Inconsistencies in metadata assigned to resources can arise due to variations in a given cataloger's judgment over time and because different catalogers may make varied judgements in cataloging resources. There are drawbacks to relying solely on inherent metadata to define virtual collections, however. A risk in complete automation is the loss of many of the benefits of creating a virtual collection. Contextual metadata is important because it enables us to give some character and cohesiveness to the virtual collection. A collection is likely to be more than an accretion of all it contains; it has been gathered for a purpose. Humancreated metadata is thus vital for articulating the scope, intent, and function of a particular collection-attributes that are likely to make the collection easier to locate, and easier to use.

The use of contextual metadata and human judgment in selecting resources to be included in a virtual collection has other benefits. Virtual collections can be described "in terms of expected use in addition to being characterised by the terms they actually contain". Resources can be more carefully chosen for inclusion in a virtual collection, with consideration of expected use, resulting in a more concise collection of high-quality resources that is easier to for the user to search or browse. It is important to recognise, however, that a collection-level schema that relies heavily on contextual metadata is relatively costly to implement and thus less likely to be maintained in the long term. A more viable approach is to define a schema for virtual collections that balances the costs and benefits of each type of metadata. In short, a cost-effective schema should include useful inherent metadata, supplemented by contextual metadata that captures human judgments of a collection's nature and the selection of criteria for inclusion in the collection.

Intellectual Property Rights

The educational community encompasses a broad range of public and private institutions whose primary missions include research, education, and the preservation of our scientific and cultural heritage. In the process of carrying out their missions, these institutions, which include research universities, colleges, university presses, libraries, scholarly societies, museums, and archives, among many others, are both creators and consumers of scholarly communication. These institutions participate in the full spectrum of activities regulated by the laws governing copyright and must be sensitive to the balance of interests embodied in them. While a degree of consensus has been reached concerning the rights of creators, copyright holders, and users of information in the print environment, new proposals for the copy rights of digital works are threatening to disrupt the balance between the rights of owners and public access in the electronic world.

As they revolutionise the means by which information is recorded, disseminated, accessed, and stored digital technologies are eliminating the technical limits that have supplemented the legal framework of balance between ownership and public dissemination: Unlimited technological capacity to disseminate transmission in ways that can violate the rights of copyright holders confronts equally unlimited technological capacity to prevent works from being used in ways contemplated by law. Carried to its logical extreme, either trend would destroy the balance, with results that would likely undermine core educational functions as well as radically transform the information marketplace.

The educational community is heavily invested in scholarly communication. This process includes such functions as exchange of cutting-edge discoveries and works-in-progress among scholars, scientists, curators; publication of new and synthetic works for the broad scholarly community; dissemination of new and existing knowledge to students through teaching; establishment of repositories to enable handing knowledge down from generation to generation; and transmission of knowledge beyond the educational community to the public. It requires the ability to cite and quote the work of others, regardless of format. Whereas quotations from text can be manually transcribed, quotations from digital objects may require machine mediation. Scholarly communication involves individuals, academic departments and research units, libraries, archives, university presses, museums, commercial publishers, external research sponsors, academic and industrial software developers, and others.

Because it carries information that ranges from complex graphical and sound data to plain text, and must reach an audience that ranges from Nobel scientists to freshmen in remedial courses to citizens visiting a local museum, scholarly communication must include the full range of content and take place in all media. It must flow back and forth between all of its participants and be capable of moving rapidly enough to contribute to the evolution of understanding and knowledge. It must be disseminated through an economically viable system, and it must not be overwhelmed by a permissions system so burdensome that it makes rapid movement impossible. Scholarly communication is based on an ethic of authorship that both compels publication and condemns plagiarism. It demands accurate attribution and respect for the integrity of works while asserting the importance of evaluating and interrogating sources for cumulative advance of knowledge. By promoting trust between authors, owners, and users, adherence to this ethic facilitates the rapid and broad dissemination of information.

Educational institutions have developed organisational structures that insulate faculty, curators, and students — the core, but not the only participants in scholarly communication — from direct dependence on economic returns from specific intellectual properties. Instead, they rely first on institutional rewards for their cumulative success in creation and dissemination. The institutions, however, function as both owners and consumers of the intellectual properties that circulate in the process of scholarly communication. As such, some of these institutions, such as museums, university presses, and scholarly societies, depend on the revenue from copyright ownership to support their educational, dissemination, and preservation missions.

New knowledge cannot be created without extensive reference to work already done by others and to the accumulated records of human and natural phenomena. or can the accumulated collective knowledge of a society be transmitted intact to succeeding generations without its preservation and organisation. Libraries, museums, and archives play crucial roles as custodians of knowledge and must continue to do so in order to carry out core educational missions. Faced with an exponential increase in the rate at which documentation is growing, libraries, museums, and archives increasingly seek to exploit the unprecedented storage capacities and facility for more effective access strategies of digital media.

Moreover, the increased data creation and storage capacities generate new pressures on systems for preservation, organisation, and access. Although the functionalities of digital technologies will continue to give rise to practices and relationships that bear little resemblance to those surrounding print, neither novel arrangements nor enhanced capabilities should obscure the fundamental continuity of purpose underlying preservation and organisation. The requirements of the academic mission and the accumulation of a cultural heritage do not cease when information and documentation cease to have commercial value and pass out of the marketplace.

Internationally, the WIPO treaties proved more supportive of the principle of balance between the rights of owners and the need for public use. But the treaties must now return to the U.S. for ratification and the possible development of implementing and related legislation. The educational community urges that changes in the law be carefully crafted to enhance rather than impede the rich and timely circulation of information as well as its preservation and organisation.

In preparation for the ongoing legislative debates on intellectual property in the digital environment. the educational community believes it necessary to develop its own consensus on a common set of broad principles which would provide standards against which coalitions and individual institutions can evaluate legislative proposals. Faced with the strong interests of the infotainment industry to maintain tight control of intellectual property in a global marketplace, the educational community may strengthen its more balanced position by speaking as one voice guided by the principles.

Risk Management

Digital information is produced in a wide variety of standard and proprietary formats. These formats continues to evolve, becoming more complex as revised software versions add new features or functionality. It is not uncommon for software enhancements to "orphan," or leave unreadable, files generated by earlier versions. The most pressing problems confronting managers of digital collections are not unstable media or obsolete hardware, but data format and software obsolescence. Migration is one of the major strategies for managing the later period of a digital lifecycle. A file format represents the arrangement of the structural and data elements in a unique and specific manner. In practice, migration is prone to generating errors. An obvious error occurs when the set of structural elements in the source format does not fully match the structural elements of the target format.

For instance, in a spreadsheet file a structural element defines a cell containing a numeric value. If a comparable element is missing from the format specifications of the target format, data will be lost. A more subtle error might occur if the data itself does not convert properly. Floating point numbers (numbers with fractions) are found in many numeric files. Some formats might allow a floating-point number of 16 digits while others might only allow 8 digits. With locally developed and commercial off-the-shelf data migration software available, migration could be tested, measured, and evaluated based on certain common criteria from which we could design a suite of risk assessment tools.

One way to minimise the risk associated with such uncertainty is to develop a risk management scheme that deconstructs the migration process into discrete steps that can be described and quantified. A risk assessment is simply a means of structuring the process of analysing risks. If the risk assessment methodology is well specified, different individuals, supplied with the same information about a digital file, should estimate similar risk values. Different methods or tools had to be developed to help quantify risk probability and impact in each of these risk categories.

Conversion process risks can be accomplished by examining a file before and after the migration process. A test file can be passed through the conversion software, migrating from source to target format. If the fields and field values of the original source file are properly reproduced in the target file, the risks incurred in migration are significantly reduced. If the fields or their values are not properly converted, the risk of migration is significantly increased. When the field tags and values in the test file are known, data changes associated with file conversion can be independently verified and characterised along a risk matrix.

Metadata

In an indefinitely large resource space, effective management of networked information will increasingly rely on effective management of metadata. Increased commercialisation and complexity of information resources makes this need all the greater. It is unlikely that some monolithic metadata format will be universally used. This is for a number of more or less well known reasons. There is a variety of types of metadata. There is traditional descriptive information of the kind found in library catalogues, which typically includes such attributes as author, title, some indication of intellectual content and so on. There is information that might help a client application make a decision based on format or on location.

There are different types of user: a user as customer wishes to know the terms under which an object is available; a user as researcher may wish to have some extended documentation about a particular resource, its provenance for example. There are different types of resource. Some resources may have a fugitive existence, existing to satisfy some temporary need and are only ever minimally described, if at all; some are important and valuable scholarly or commercial resources, where the value of extensive description is recognised. Some resources may be simple; some may be complex in various ways.

There will be many different information providers, some commercial 'yellow pages' type services, some scholarly or research oriented services, in different organisational configurations with different target audiences and products. Metadata may be closely coupled with the object it describes as an intrinsic part of its composition; or it may have no intrinsic link with it at all. At the same time, the technical and service environments in which metadata services are being deployed are the subject of rapid change and development. Thus, the nature of the problem to be solved suggests a variety of solutions.

It is helpful to consider a metadata spectrum, along which data becomes successively fuller, more structured, specialised, and expensive to create. This division into bands is presented for purposes of analysis only — as a way of presenting a view over an existing situation — and not as a set of fundamental distinctions. At one end is data used in services which currently support location and limited discovery. Terse metadata allows searching for known items, and for topics. This is the area inhabited by the webcrawlers which automatically extract data from resources. They currently provide web forms access onto proprietary databases.

There are moves to enhance the metadata on which they operate and to develop frameworks for interworking.

At the other end of the spectrum is metadata which supports much richer functionality. It is often associated with research or scholarly activity, requires specialised knowledge to create and maintain, and caters for specialist domain-specific requirements. Metadata formats being developed here can express a variety of formal and intellectual relationships, and are often part of a larger framework which provides for the encoding of the content they describe.

Typically, they are looking at the creation of a variety of SGML document type definitions to cater for metadata and 'content'. Such initiatives include the Inter-university Consortium for Political and Social Research (ICPSR) SGML codebook initiative to describe social science data sets, the Encoding Archival Description (EAD), Content Standards for Digital Geospatial Metadata (FGDC) and the Consortium for Interchange of Museum Information (CIMI). The Text Encoding Initiative can also be included here, and influenced some of these other developments.

There has been some interest in the Z39.50 profile for access to digital collections for search and retrieval of such metadata. This has been taken furthest with CIMI where a companion profile is being developed for specific use with museum data. The middle band contains services which contain full enough descriptions to allow a user to assess the potential utility or interest of a resource without actually having to retrieve it or connect to it, but not so full or complex as to require very specialist staff to create. Typically, but not essentially, these descriptions are manually created, or are manual enhancements of automatically extracted descriptions, and they include a variety of descriptive and other attributes. They may be created to be loaded directly into a discovery service or may be harvested.

Typically they are simple enough to be created by non-specialist users, or not to require significant discipline-specific knowledge. Descriptions tend to be of discrete objects and do not capture multiple relationships between objects. Again, typically, they involve some selectivity in what they describe and may have more or less explicit criteria for selection. An important motivation for such harvesting is to overcome some of the deficiencies of current crawlers without a provider incurring the cost of record creation.

At the same time, communities using the richer 'documentation' formats will wish to disclose information about their resources to a wider audience. How best to achieve this will have to be worked out: perhaps 'discovery' records will be exported into other systems. These directions suggest that the middle band will become more important as a general-purpose access route, maybe with links to richer domain-specific records in some cases.

Electronic Libraries Programme (eLib)

The Electronic Libraries Programme (eLib) is a three-year programme to modernise library services in the UK higher education community. The programme is spending approximately 15 million pounds over three years, and currently about 60 individual projects are in progress. Funding comes from the Joint Information Systems Committee of the Higher Education Funding Councils. UKOLN maintains the eLib information pages where further information about the programme and individual projects can be found. eLib is organised around a number of project areas. One of these is Access to Network Resources. A major focus of this area is metadata and resource discovery services.

Several subject-based information gateways have been funded, and are in various stages of start-up. They include:

— Social Science Information Gateway (SOSIG)

— Organising Medical Networked Information (OMNI)

— Edinburgh Engineering Virtual Library (EEVL)

— Art, Design, Architecture and Media Information Gateway (ADAM)

— Institute of Historical Research (IHR-info)

These are all organised in various ways but share certain characteristics. They are very much located in the middle band as outlined above: they aspire to provide discovery services to UK higher education. In some ways, they are rather like early abstracting and indexing services. They are developing databases of resource descriptions from which other services are derived. They are defining selection and quality criteria which determine which resources are included.

They are aiming to have comprehensive coverage of resources within UK higher education, but take different approaches to resources elsewhere. They are focusing on the server level — it is difficult to do otherwise and sustain this level of description — but aspire to move to the object level, however that might be achieved. Typically, their staff effort goes into management and administration, 'cataloguing', technical development, and promotion. Given the variety, volume, and volatility of relevant resources, it is likely that the subject services will consider how to lever their effort in a number of ways: by collaboration (with similar initiatives elsewhere, with commercial services, with a range of interested organisations), by more proactive use of gathering, discovery and alerting technologies, and so on. The services are considering various technical solutions to their services, and clearly have to make choices about metadata formats. The base service will have to provide web access to a searchable database of descriptions and some organised browsing facilities.

8

Automated Information Services

The term "automated digital library" can be used to describe a digital library where all tasks are carried out automatically. Computer programs substitute for the intellectually demanding tasks that are traditionally carried out by skilled professionals. These tasks include selection, cataloguing and indexing, seeking for information, reference services, and so on. The common theme is that these activities require considerable mental activity, the type of activity that people are skilled at and computers find difficult. Automated digital libraries should not be confused with library automation, which uses computing to reduce routine tasks in conventional libraries. In some ways, digital libraries are very different from traditional libraries, yet in others they are remarkably similar.

People do not change because new technology is invented. They still create information that has to be organised, stored, and distributed. They still need to find information that others have created, and use it for study, reference, or entertainment. However, the form in which the information is expressed and the methods that are used to manage it are greatly influenced by technology and this creates change. Every year, the quantity and variety of collections available in digital form grows, while the supporting technology continues to improve steadily. Uumulatively, these changes are stimulating fundamental alterations in how people create information and how they use it. To understand these forces requires an understanding of the people who are developing the libraries. Technology has dictated the pace at which digital libraries have been able to develop, but the manner in which the technology is used depends upon people.

Two important communities are the source of much of this innovation. One group is the information professionals. They include librarians, publishers, and a wide range of information providers, such as indexing and abstracting services. The other community contains the computer science researchers and their offspring, the Internet developers. Until recently, these two communities had disappointingly little interaction; even now it is commonplace to find a computer scientist who knows nothing of the basic tools of librarianship, or a librarian whose concepts of information retrieval are years out of date.

Over the past few years, however, there has been much more collaboration and understanding. Partly this is a consequence of digital libraries becoming a recognised field for research, but an even more important factor is greater involvement from the users themselves. Low-cost equipment and simple software have made electronic information directly available to everybody. Authors no longer need the services of a publisher to distribute their works. Readers can have direct access to information without going through an intermediary. Many exciting developments come from academic or professional groups who develop digital libraries for their own needs.

Medicine has a long tradition of creative developments; the pioneering legal information systems were developed by lawyers for lawyers; the web was initially developed by physicists, for their own use. Technology influences the economic and social aspects of information, and vice versa. The technology of digital libraries is developing fast and so are the financial, organisational, and social frameworks. The various groups that are developing digital libraries bring different social conventions and different attitudes to money. Publishers and libraries have a long tradition of managing physical objects, notably books, but also maps, photographs, sound recordings and other artifacts. They evolved economic and legal frameworks that are based on buying and selling these objects.

Their natural instinct is to transfer to digital libraries the concepts that have served them well for physical artifacts. Computer scientists and scientific users, such as physicists, have a different tradition. Their interest in digital information began in the days when computers were very expensive. Only a few well-funded researchers had computers on the first networks. They exchanged information informally and openly with colleagues, without payment. The networks have grown, but the tradition of open information remains. The economic framework that is developing for digital libraries shows a mixture of these two approaches.

Some digital libraries mimic traditional publishing by requiring a form of payment before users may access the collections and use the services. Other digital libraries use a different economic model. Their material is provided with open access to everybody. The costs of creating and distributing the information are borne by the producer, not the user of the information. Traditional libraries are a fundamental part of society, but they are not perfect. Can we do better? Enthusiasts for digital libraries point out that computers and networks have already changed the ways in which people communicate with each other.

In some disciplines, they argue, a professional or scholar is better served by sitting at a personal computer connected to a communications network than by making a visit to a library. Information that was previously available only to the professional is now directly available to all. From a personal computer, the user is able to consult materials that are stored on computers around the world. Conversely, all but the most diehard enthusiasts recognise that printed documents are so much part of civilisation that their dominant role cannot change except gradually.

Benefits of Digital Libraries

The final potential benefit of digital libraries is cost. This is a topic about which there has been a notable lack of hard data, but some of the underlying facts are clear. Conventional libraries are expensive. They occupy expensive buildings on prime sites. Big libraries employ hundreds of people - well-educated, though poorly paid. Libraries never have enough money to acquire and process all the materials they desire. Publishing is also expensive. Converting to electronic publishing adds new expenses. In order to recover the costs of developing new products, publishers sometimes even charge more for a digital version than the printed equivalent.

Today's digital libraries are also expensive, initially more expensive. However, digital libraries are made from components that are declining rapidly in price. As the cost of the underlying technology continues to fall, digital libraries become steadily less expensive. In particular, the costs of distribution and storage of digital information declines. The reduction in cost will not be uniform. Some things are already cheaper by computer than by traditional methods. Other costs will not decline at the same rate or may even increase. Overall, however, there is a great opportunity to lower the costs of publishing and libraries.

Lower long-term costs are not necessarily good news for existing libraries and publishers. In the short term, the pressure to support traditional media alongside new digital collections is a heavy burden on budgets. Because people and organisations appreciate the benefits of online access and online publishing, they are prepared to spend an increasing amount of their money on computing, networks, and digital information. Most of this money, however, is going not to traditional libraries, but to new areas: computers and networks, web sites and webmasters. Publishers face difficulties because the normal pricing model of selling individual items does not fit the cost structure of electronic publishing. Much of the cost of conventional publishing is in the production and distribution of individual copies of books, photographs, video tapes, or other artifacts.

Digital information is different. The fixed cost of creating the information and mounting it on a computer may be substantial, but the cost of using it is almost zero. Because the marginal cost is negligible, much of the information on the networks has been made openly available, with no access restrictions. Not everything on the world's networks is freely available, but a great deal is open to everybody, undermining revenue for the publishers.

These pressures are inevitably changing the economic decisions that are made by authors, users, publishers, and libraries. Early information services, such as shared cataloguing, legal information systems, and the National Library of Medicine's Medline service, used the technology that existed when they were developed. Small quantities of information were mounted on a large central computer. Users sat at a dedicated terminal, connected by a low-speed communications link, which was either a telephone line or a special purpose network. These systems required a trained user who would accept a cryptic user interface in return for faster searching than could be carried out manually and access to information that was not available locally.

Such systems were no threat to the printed document. All that could be displayed was unformatted text, usually in a fixed spaced font, without diagrams, mathematics, or the graphic quality that is essential for easy reading. When these weaknesses were added to the inherent defects of early computer screens - poor contrast and low resolution - it is hardly surprising that most people were convinced that users would never willingly read from a screen. The past thirty years have steadily eroded these technical barriers. During the early 1990s, a series of technical developments took place that removed the last fundamental barriers to building digital libraries.

Accessing Digital Libraries

Traditional libraries usually require that the user be a member of an organisation that maintains expensive physical collections. In the United States, universities and some other organisations have excellent libraries, but most people do not belong to such an organisation. In theory, much of the Library of Congress is open to anybody over the age of eighteen, and a few cities have excellent public libraries, but in practice, most people are restricted to the small collections held by their local public library. Even scientists often have poor library facilities. Doctors in large medical centers have excellent libraries, but those in remote locations typically have nothing.

One of the motives that led the Institute of Electrical and Electronics Engineers (IEEE) to its early interest in electronic publishing was the fact that most engineers do not have access to an engineering library. Users of digital libraries need a computer attached to the Internet. In the United States, many organisations provide every member of staff with a computer. Some have done so for many years. Across the nation, there are programs to bring computers to schools and to install them in pubic libraries. For individuals who must provide their own computing, adequate access to the Internet requires less than $2,000 worth of equipment, perhaps $20 per month for a dial-up connection, and a modicum of skill.

Increase the costs a little and very attractive services can be obtained, with a powerful computer and a dedicated, higher speed connection. These are small investments for a prosperous professional, but can be a barrier for others. In 1998 it was estimated that 95 percent of people in the United States live in areas where there is reasonable access to the Internet. This percentage is growing rapidly.

Outside the United States, the situation varies. In most countries of the world, library services are worse than in the United States. Some nations are well-supplied with computers and networks, but in most places equipment costs are higher than in the United States, people are less wealthy, monopolies keep communications costs high, and the support infrastructure is lacking.

Digital libraries do bring information to many people who lack traditional libraries, but the Internet is far from being conveniently accessible world-wide. A factor that must be considered in planning digital libraries is that the quality of the technology available to users varies greatly. A favored few have the latest personal computers on their desks, high-speed connections to the Internet, and the most recent release of software; they are supported by skilled staff who can configure and tune the equipment, solve problems, and keep the software up to date.

Most people, however, have to make do with less. Their equipment may be old, their software out of date, their Internet connection troublesome, and their technical support from staff who are under-trained and over-worked. One of the great challenges in developing digital libraries is to build systems that take advantage of modern technology, yet perform adequately in less perfect situations.

Terminology

Terminology often proves to be a barrier in discussing digital libraries. The people who build digital libraries come from many disciplines and bring the terminology of those disciplines with them. Some words have such strong social, professional, legal, or technical connotations that they obstruct discussion between people of varying backgrounds. Simple words mean different things to different people.

Some words cause such misunderstandings that it is tempting to ban them from any discussion of digital libraries. In addition to "copy" and "publish", the list includes "document", "object", and "work". At the very least, such words must be used carefully and their exact meaning made clear whenever they are used.

Data and Metadata

The information stored in a digital library can be divided into data and metadata. Data is a general term to describe information that is encoded in digital form. Whether the word "data" is singular or plural is a source of contention. Metadata is data about other data. Many people dislike the word "metadata", but it is widely used. Common categories of metadata include descriptive metadata, such as bibliographic information, structural metadata about formats and structures, and administrative metadata, which includes, rights, permissions, and other information that is used to manage access. One item of metadata is the identifier, which identifies an item to the outside world. The distinction between data and metadata often depends upon the context. Catalog records or abstracts are usually considered to be metadata, because they describe other data, but in an online catalog or a database of abstracts they are the data.

Library Objects

The term library object is useful for the user's view of what is stored in a library. Consider an article in an online periodical. The reader thinks of it as a single entity, a library object, but the article is probably stored on a computer as several separate objects. They contain pages of digitised text, graphics, perhaps even computer programs, or linked items stored on remote computers. From the user's viewpoint, this is one library object made up of several digital objects. This example shows that library objects have internal structure. They usually have both data and associated metadata. Structural metadata is used to describe the formats and the relationship of the parts.

The form in which information is stored in a digital library may be very different from the form in which it is used. A simulator used to train airplane pilots might be stored as several computer programs, data structures, digitised images, and other data. This is called the stored form of the object. The user is provided with a series of images, synthesized sound, and control sequences. Some people use the term presentation for what is presented to the user and in many contexts this is appropriate terminology.

A more general term is dissemination, which emphasizes that the transformation from the stored form to the user requires the execution of some computer program. When digital information is received by a user's computer, it must be converted into the form that is provided to the user, typically by displaying on the computer screen, possibly augmented by a sound track or other presentation. This conversion is called rendering.

Works and Content

Finding terminology to describe content is especially complicated. Part of the problem is that the English language is very flexible. Words have varying meanings depending upon the context. Consider, the example, "the song Simple Gifts". Depending on the context, that phrase could refer to the song as a work with words and music, the score of the song, a performance of somebody singing it, a recording of the performance, an edition of music on compact disk, a specific compact disc, the act of playing the music from the recording, the performance encoded in a digital library, and various other aspects of the song. Such distinctions are important to the music industry, because they determine who receives money that is paid for a musical performance or recording.

Several digital library researchers have attempted to define a general hierarchy of terms that can be applied to all works and library objects. This is a bold and useful objective, but fraught with difficulties. The problem is that library materials have so much variety that a classification may match some types of material well but fail to describe others adequately. Despite these problems, the words work and content are useful words.

Most people use the word content loosely. The word is used in any context when the emphasis is on library materials, not as bits and bytes to be processed by a computer but as information that is of interest to a user. To misquote a famous judge, we can not define "content", but we know it when we see it. While the word content is used as a loosely defined, general term, the word work is used more specifically. The term "literary work" is carefully defined in U. S. copyright law as the abstract content, the sequence of words or music independent of any particular stored representation, presentation, or performance.

Role of ***Computers and networks***

Digital libraries consists of many computers united by a communications network. The dominant network is the Internet. The emergence of the Internet as a flexible, low-cost, world-wide network has been one of the key factors that has led to the growth of digital libraries. The computers have three main function: to help users interact with the library, to store collections of materials, and to provide services.

— In the terminology of computing, anybody who interacts with a computer is called a user or computer user. This is a broad term that covers creators, library users, information professionals, and anybody else who accesses the computer. To access a digital library, users normally use personal computers. These computers are given the general name clients. Sometimes, clients may interact with a digital library without no human user involved, such as the robots that automatically index library collections, and sensors that gather data, such as information about the weather, and supply it to digital libraries.

— The next major group of computers in digital libraries are repositories which store collections of information and provide access to them. An archive is a repository that is organised for long-term preservation of materials.

— There are two typical services which are provided by digital libraries: location systems and search systems. Search systems provide catalogs, indexes, and other services to help users find information. Location systems are used to identify and locate information.

— In some circumstances there may be other computers that sit between the clients and computers that store information. Mirrors and caches store duplicate copies of information, for faster performance and reliability. The distinction between them is that mirrors replicate large sets of information, while caches store recently used information only. Proxies and gateways provide bridges between different types of computer system. They are particularly useful in reconciling systems that have conflicting technical specifications.

The generic term server is used to describe any computer other than the user's personal computer. A single server may provide several of the functions listed above, perhaps acting as a repository, search system, and location system. Conversely, individual functions can be distributed across many servers. For example, the domain name system, which is a locator system for computers on the Internet, is a single, integrated service that runs on thousands of separate servers. In computing terminology, a distributed system is a group of computers that work as a team to provide services to users.

Digital libraries are some of the most complex and ambitious distributed systems ever built. The personal computers that users have on their desks have to exchange messages with the server computers; these computers are of every known type, managed by thousands of different organisations, running software that ranges from state-of-the art to antiquated.

The term interoperability refers to the task of building coherent services for users, when the individual components are technically different and managed by different organisations. Some people argue that all technical problems in digital libraries are aspects of this one problem, interoperability. This is probably an overstatement, but it is certainly true that interoperability is a fundamental challenge in all aspects of digital libraries.

Automation in Public Libraries

The arrival of the microcomputer, also known as a personal computer (PC) or desktop computer, changed the face of data processing and information management in organisations. For the first time computers became affordable both to individuals and institutions that could not previously afford the expensive minicomputers and mainframe computers.

The opportunities presented by microcomputers, coupled with their relative low price, led some libraries, especially university and special libraries, in developing countries to consider automating some of their functions and activities. In general, there is a paucity of literature documenting the status and use of information and communication technologies (ICTs) in public libraries in developing countries. Although some attempts to automate library processes, especially in university libraries, can be traced to the 1970s, successful implementation of most library automation projects in developing countries began in the early 1980s.

Computer Servers

While some libraries are using PCs as servers, mainly as Internet proxy servers (serving as an interface between the local Internet enabled PCs and the ISP's Internet server), others have installed purpose-built, brand-name servers to run their automated library systems. As public library services are among the most underfunded institutions, it is very difficult to imagine how some of them will be able to acquire the equipment indicated without donor assistance. In almost all cases, computers are distributed throughout the library systems, including branch libraries, with the central library or headquarters having a large share of them.

Software: Operating systems

Library services that have computer servers use different operating systems to run their servers. Many libraries use Windows 95/98 on its server. Although Windows 95/98 has some networking ability, it is not really a network management system, and lacks the advanced functions found in systems like UNIX and Windows NT. However, given that purpose-built network software systems require skilled manpower to manage, and are also expensive in terms of user licence fees, it is not surprising that this library has settled for Windows 95/98. Most public library services cannot afford to employ skilled IT staff, and therefore cannot even use free open-source UNIX systems like Linux.

Microsoft Windows, especially Windows 95/98, is the most common operating system installed on PCs and laptops. The wide use of Microsoft Windows operating systems is due mainly to the fact that it is bundled with new Intel-based PCs, which was not the case in the past when it was necessary to purchase the operating system separately. Regarding the large number of machines with Windows 95/98, this can be attributed to the fact that most of these machines were purchased in the 1990s when it was the most commonly pre-installed operating system on PCs. Nowadays, new computers purchased are more likely to have Windows XP as the pre-installed operating system.

Application Software

With regard to office application software, the public library services in developinmg countrries generally use the Microsoft Office. Libraries that have laptops also have Microsoft Office installed on them. Other application software installed on all the library services' computers are Microsoft Internet Explorer and Microsoft Outlook. The reason for this is easy to understand, as they are bundled with the Windows operating systems that are in use in all the libraries.

However, it should be noted that the availability of Microsoft Outlook does not necessarily mean that it is the most widely used electronic-mail client software. Because some of the library systems have only one official e-mail account provided by their Internet Service Provider (ISP), staff who require their own private or personal e-mail accounts have to use the free Webbased e-mail services of Yahoo!, Hotmail, Excite or others, resulting in their use of Web browsers rather than Outlook to access their accounts. The use of WordPerfect certainly restricts how the catalogues might be accessed if the library decided to make them available online. Use of a databasemanagement system would be more appropriate for the development of an online library catalogue. All the libraries that have not yet automated any of their functions, and those using computers on only a small scale, have plans to automate in future.

The reasons given for this are that their existing manual systems are adequate and automation would bring no significant service improvement to users; they have unreliable power supplies that could cripple the library's operations; and no funds are available to meet the high cost of initial software and future updates.

All the services that have automated all or most of their library functions have branch, regional or affiliated libraries. Some also have several service points, located in various places. Most of the libraries that form part of its system are using automated systems for most library functions. The library services that have branch or regional libraries are using automated systems either at the main library only or at the main library and only a few affiliated or branch libraries. The major reason given for automating functions only at the main or central library was a lack of funds to extend automation to all the libraries within the system.

CD-ROM services

The development of CD-ROM technology has had a huge and positive impact on the provision of access to online databases and other information resources in libraries. Instead of an advanced and sometimes complicated infrastructure to obtain access to online databases, CD-ROMs offer a simple but efficient alternative. The widespread availability of PCs with internal CD-ROM drives/readers also means that it has now became easy for libraries to provide their users with access to CD-ROM-based services. In developing countries, where it is generally impossible to access online databases via telecommunication infrastructures, CD-ROM databases have found their way easily into many libraries, especially into university and research libraries.Unfortunately, not all public library services seem to have taken advantage of CD-ROM technology.

Internet connectivity

Internet connectivity, especially access to electronic mail, is available in most of the public libraries. The lack of connectivity, especially for library users, in those that do not is attributed to the high costs involved. In spite of the large number of public library services indicating that they had access to Internet facilities, almost none are providing Web-based information services to library users.

Internet Access and Control

The introduction of Internet access into public libraries raised concerns among different groups of people around the world. A major concern was for parents, who feared that their children might access Web sites with harmful or objectionable material. This concern has also been expressed in developing countries. In the early days of Internet use, especially Web access, the major concern expressed by most people and governments in developing countries related to the amount of pornographic information said to be accessible on the Web.

As a result, many organisations, including governments, spoke out against the introduction of the Internet. Now that the Internet is slowly finding its way into public institutions such as public libraries, librarians are expected to place some form of control on the use of their Internet facilities. Among the controls put in place are restrictions on the length of time that staff or users are allowed to spend on the Internet and blocking sites deemed to be providing pornographic material.

The major reason for restricting the duration of staff use of the Internet was to reduce the cost of telephone bills associated with dial-up Internet access. However, in one case it was reported that the number of PCs available for Internet use was limited, so it was necessary to restrict the length of time spent on them to allow as many people as possible to use the Internet during the hours that the library was open.

Electronic-mail

The most commonly used Internet facility around the world is electronic mail, and all nineteen public library services that had access to the Internet were using e-mail. However, it should be noted that some libraries had only one electronic-mail account, which was used for official library communication. This account was generally accessed on a computer located in the office of the secretary to the director of the library service. Staff requiring privacy set up e-mail accounts with free Web-based e-mail systems such as Yahoo!, Hotmail and Excite. The use of Web-based e-mail accounts also has an impact on the use of the limited Internet bandwidth available. Many public library services have their own web sites.

Web Sites

A large number of public libraries in developed countries are using the Web to provide access to a wide variety of information resources and services, including online community information, access to databases, online reservation of library materials and many other services. Information provided on the these Web sites is mainly similar to that found in library brochures, such as the services offered, opening hours, general library information, and contact details.

The reasons for not providing value-added services via the Web are many, although a major one could be that most people who use the public libraries in developing countries do not have access to Internet facilities at home. Therefore, there is no need for the libraries to develop and provide online services when no one will make use of them. Other reasons include a lack of staff with appropriate skills to develop digital library services, and a lack of suitable ICT infrastructure. In most cases, access to the Internet is via dial-up access, which is not suitable for provision of dedicated 24-hour Web-based services.

9

Virtual Library and Information Retrieval

The document collection of a virtual library consists of digital documents and Internet resources. A Internet resource is a link to other digital documents which are stored elsewhere in the Internet. Thus, only the link is under control of the virtual library and not the document to which the link points. In addition, a virtual library provides digital catalogs, containing metadata about the document collection. A virtual library must accomplish as far as possible all necessary services of conventional libraries and must also exploit the advantages of the technology used.

Communiçation in Virtual LIbrary

There are always three components involved in communication: a source, one or several destinations, and a medium. The source forwards the information which is transmitted by a medium (e.g. text or sound) and finally received by the destinations.

Depending on the conditions and situations, communication can take various forms, and several different proposals exist to capture them.

a) Communication is synchronous and non-distributed, source and destination are communicating with each other at the same time in the same place, e.g. talk.

b) Communication is asynchronous and distributed, if source and destination are communicating with each other at the same time in different places, e.g. a phone call.

c) Communication is asynchronous and non-distributed, if source and destination are communicating with each other at different times in the same place, e.g. a notice board.

d) Communication is asynchronous and distributed, if source and destination are communicating with each other at different times in different places, e.g. e-mail.

In, a formal communication is always based on an arranged appointment while an informal communication is spontaneous and takes place accidentally. For instance, a real time video conference is mostly a formal communication which is synchronous and distributed. If a communication is asynchronous it cannot be classified as formal and informal with respect to initiation. Nevertheless, in some publications, e.g., the terms "asynchronous, formal" and "asynchronous, informal" communication are used to characterise the content of the information communicated. For instance, refers to users sharing their home page by allowing other users access to it as informal communication.

Conventional Libraries

Conventional libraries are meeting places where students and researchers meet each other either accidentally or by arrangement. Often conventional libraries have areas for collaboration where people can work jointly. Further, most of the services a library provides are highly interactive and are based on communication between the people involved.

— There is formal, synchronous and non-distributed communication in conventional libraries when librarians introduce patrons to the use of the library.

— Formal, synchronous and distributed communication is required if the document collection of a conventional library is distributed to several buildings. For instance, a phone conference system can be used for this kind of communication.

— Informal, synchronous and non-distributed communication is found in conventional libraries because students and researchers often meet each other accidentally in the library. This is probably the most common form of communication in conventional libraries.

— Informal, synchronous and distributed communication is common in the conventional library as well. For instance, patrons call librarians and ask for documents they have reserved.

— An example for a asynchronous and non-distributed communication is a notebook in which patrons can add suggestions to or complaints about the library. Once a suggestion or complaint is made, the library can comment on that in the same book.

— Finally, asynchronous and distributed communication is found in conventional libraries since researchers can communicate their research results to a broad community through publishing in journals or in books.

Forms of Communication

A conventional library which is defined as the building where its document collection is stored, there is no longer a library building for a virtual library. Instead, the document collection of a virtual library is distributed among several servers in different places. Thus, people cannot meet each other accidentally or by arrangement in the virtual library. Due to this, synchronous communication in virtual libraries is only possible if it is distributed.

One might argue that people can work jointly at a computer at the client side and communicate with each other in a non-distributed way. Even though this is a non-distributed and synchronous communication it is outside the scope of the virtual library and cannot be under its control. Normally, the document collection of a virtual library is distributed. This fact allows librarians to work in different places.

Nevertheless, to achieve a common aim, communication is still necessary for collaboration. Therefore, a virtual library should provide corresponding services. Shared workspaces similar to virtual office systems, or electronic meeting rooms should exist in virtual libraries. Apart from research prototypes, there are also communication tools that use the capabilities of the Internet and are normally available on the Internet. DigiPhone or VocalTec are prominent tools for phone conferencing on the Internet. Further, MBone and Cu-SeeMe are often used for video conferences. For instance, the use of MBone in a virtual library setting is known from the RPID project. Also, a phone conferencing tool called CoolTalk can be connected to the most recent release of the Netscape Browser called Atlas. In addition, CoolTalk offers a white board, allowing users to collaborate on the same data (text and graphic).Finally, Marc Andreessen has recently announced that Nestcape will be developing a tool called InSoft. With InSoft phone calls will directly be possible from the Netscape navigator.

Synchronous, informal and distributed communication

Spontaneity is a typical characteristic for informal communication. Hence, a virtual library should provide functionalities allowing users to get an overview of who else is on-line in the library. Users should then be able to choose one or several users with whom to communicate. For this, the tools introduced above can be employed.

Asynchronous and non-distributed communication

In conventional libraries, a notice board represents this form of communication. Similar to this, a predefined space in a virtual library can assume the function of a notice board. This space might be an HTML page to which users can add links to the information to be communicated. Another example is the use of annotations to documents. For instance, Hyper-G and its commercial version HyperWave afford users the ability to annotate documents or other annotations. Finally, virtual libraries can use text-based discussion systems, like HyperNews, which are designed for asynchronous and non-distributed communication.

Asynchronous and distributed communication

Basically, asynchronous and distributed communication is found in every virtual library because researchers publish their research results for example in electronic journals which are available in each virtual library that subscribes to them. In addition, there are other possibilities for this form of communication. For instance, Hyper-G provides a service allowing users to see who else is on-line. One can select a single user or all on-line users with whom to start communicating using an integrated message system. Unlike e-mail, the message system displays the message on the screen of the receiver immediately after the sender has sent it. A drawback of this message system is that only one user or all users (but not an arbitrary number of users) can be chosen for communication. Thus, communication within a group is not possible.

New Communication Services

Communication and collaboration will be one of the main research fields in the context of virtual libraries. A big challenge for us is to identify and to implement new communication services for virtual libraries. First results show that communication can be based on digital agents. Basically, a digital agent is a process which carries out a well-defined task. Two new scenarios for communication in virtual libraries then arise. First, digital agents can support the communication between users. Second, users can not only communicate with other users but also with digital agents.

Digital Agents

In conventional libraries, users should be informed about the acquisition of new documents. Hence, libraries often display new documents in extra shelves for a certain period of time before these documents are put in the right place within the library. This can be regarded as an asynchronous and non-distributed communication between librarians and patrons. Virtual libraries can essentially duplicate this way of passing on information about new books.

An extra HTML page for new documents can provide links to them. Similar to extra shelves in conventional libraries, patrons can access this page to see what is new. One drawback of this approach, however, is that patrons have to actively choose to become informed about new documents. Another drawback is that patrons always have to search the entire collection of new books, even though they are only interested in newly acquired books of their particular research domain. In virtual libraries, digital agents can be used to overcome these shortcomings. For example, it should be possible for patrons to define a personal profile.

A patron's profile could comprise the area of interest, an e-mail address etc. On this basis, a digital agent could inform patrons about new books with respect to their profile. Everytime, the library catalogs a new book, the profile service checks who has requested to be informed about it and then sends for example an e-mail to each of such patrons. Further, digital agents can be employed whenever information is to pass on in a stepwise fashion to a number of people. If a message contains more information than is necessary for the receiver, a digital agent can be used as information filter. Thus, only information that is pertinent to the receiver is forwarded.

For instance, cataloging is highly cooperative and communicative, and usually involves more than one person. Since in each step of the cataloging process only parts of the information from the previous steps are needed, a digital agent can be used as information filter when the results of one step are passed on to the subsequent step. In contrast to traditional libraries in which only communication between people is possible, people can also communicate with digital agents in virtual libraries. For instance, the URL-minder is a profile service which keeps track of Web pages. URL-minder allows users to enter URLs they are interested in. Whenever the resource at this URL changes the profile service generates automatically an email and sends it to the user. Similar services are known from the Ariadne project, which is part of the electronic library project MeDoc of the German Association of Computer Science (GI). In this way, users can communicate with digital agents. A core service provided by digital libraries is to helping user find information. Most traditional libraries arrange their collections by subject classification to help browsing.

Classification schemes, such as the Dewey Decimal Classification or the Library of Congress classification, provide both subject information and a hierarchical structure that can be used to organise collections. The most widely used Web information service, Yahoo, is fundamentally a classification of Web resources, augmented by searching. Digital libraries with their hyperlinks lend themselves to strategies that combine searching and browsing. Browsing is the general term for the unstructured exploration of a body of information; it is a popular and effective method for discovering the unexpected.

Descriptive Metadata

Many methods of information discovery do not search the actual objects in the collections, but work from descriptive metadata about the objects. The metadata typically consists of a catalog or indexing record, or an abstract, one record for each object. Usually it is stored separately from the objects that it describes, but sometimes it is embedded in the objects. Descriptive metadata is usually expressed as text, but can be used to describe information that is in formats other than text, such as images, sound recording, maps, computer programmes, and other non-text materials, as well as for textual documents. A single catalog can combine records for every variety of genre, media, and format. This enables users of digital libraries to discover materials in all media by searching textual records about the materials. Descriptive metadata is usually created by professionals. Library catalogs and scientific indexes represent huge investments by skilled people, sustained over decades or even centuries.

This economic fact is crucial to understanding current trends. On one hand, it is vital to build on the investments and the expertise behind them. On the other, there is great incentive to find cheaper and faster ways to create metadata, either by automatic indexing or with computer tools that enhance human expertise.

Catalogs

Library catalogs serve many functions, not only information retrieval. Some catalogs provide comprehensive bibliographic information that can not be derived directly from the objects. This includes information about authors or the provenance of museum artifacts. For managing collections, catalogs contain administrative information, such as where items are stored, either online or on library shelves.

Catalogs are usually much smaller than the collections that they represent; in conventional libraries, materials that are stored on miles of shelving are described by records that can be contained in a group of card drawers at one location or an online database. Indexes to digital libraries can be mirrored for performance and reliability. Information in catalog records is divided into fields and sub-fields with tags that identify them.

Thus, there might be a field for an author, with a sub-field for a surname. MARC cataloguing is used for many types of material including monographs, serials, and archives. Because of the labour required to create a detailed catalog record, materials are catalogued once, often by a national library such as the Library of Congress, and the records distributed to other libraries through utilities such as OCLC.

In digital libraries the role of MARC and the related cataloguing rules is a source of debate. Currently, MARC cataloguing retains its importance for conventional materials; librarians have extended it to some of the newer types of object found in digital libraries, but MARC has not been adopted by organisations other than traditional libraries.

Abstracting and Indexing

The sciences and other technical fields rely on abstracting and indexing services more than catalogs. Each scientific discipline has a service to help users find information in journal articles. The services include Medline for medicine and biology, Chemical Abstracts for chemistry, and Inspec for physics, computing, and related fields. Each service indexes the articles from a large set of journals. The record for an article includes basic bibliographic information (authors, title, date, etc.), supplemented by subject information, organised for information retrieval. The details differ, but the services have many similarities. Since abstracting and indexing services emerged at a time when computers were slower and more expensive than today, the information is structured to support simple textual searches, but the records have proved to be useful in more flexible systems.

Scientific users frequently want information on a specific subject. Because of the subtleties of language, subject searching is unreliable unless there is indexing information that describes the subject of each object. The subject information can be an abstract, keywords, subject terms, or other information. Some services ask authors to provide keywords or an abstract, but this leads to gross inconsistencies. More effective methods have a professional indexer assign subject information to each item. An effective but expensive approach is to use a controlled vocabulary. Where several terms could be used to describe a concept, one is used exclusively. Thus the indexer has a list of approved subject terms and rules for applying them.

The Art and Architecture Thesaurus was developed by the J. Paul Getty Trust as a controlled vocabulary for describing and retrieving information on fine art, architecture, decorative art, and material culture. It has almost 120, 000 terms for objects, textual materials, images, architecture and culture from all periods and all cultures, with an emphasis on Western civilisation. The thesaurus can be used by archives, museums, and libraries to describe items in their collections. It also be used to search for materials. Serious work on the thesaurus began in the early 1980s, when the Internet was still an embryo, but the data was created in a flexible format which has allowed production of many versions, including an open-access version on the Web, a printed book, and various computer formats.

The Getty Trust has explicitly organised the thesaurus so that it can be used by computer programmes, for information retrieval, and natural language processing. The Art and Architecture Thesaurus is arranged into seven categories, each containing a hierarchies of terms. The categories are associated concepts, physical attributes, styles and periods, agents, activities, materials, and objects. A single concept is represented by a cluster of terms, one of which is established as the preferred term, or descriptor. The thesaurus provides not only the terminology for objects, but the vocabulary necessary to describe them, such as style, period, shape, color, construction, or use, and scholarly concepts, such as theories, or criticism.

The costs of developing and maintaining a large, specialised thesaurus are huge. Even in a mature field such as art and architecture terminology is changing continually, and the technical staff has to support new technology. The Getty Trust is extremely rich but, even so, developing the thesaurus was a major project spread over many years.

Dublin Core

Since 1995, an international group, led by Stuart Weibel of OCLC, has been working to devise a set of simple metadata elements that can be applied to a wide variety of digital library materials. This is known as the Dublin Core. The name comes from Dublin, Ohio, the home of OCLC, where the first meeting was held. Several hundred people have participated in the Dublin Core workshops and discussed the design by electronic mail. Their spirit of cooperation is a model of how people with diverse interests can work together. The following fifteen elements form the Dublin Core metadata set. All elements are optional and all can be repeated. The descriptions given below are condensed from the official Dublin Core definitions, with permission from the design team.

— *Creator*: The person or organisation primarily responsible for the intellectual content of the resource. For example, authors in the case of written documents, artists, photographers, or illustrators in the case of visual resources.

— *Subject*: The topic of the resource. Typically, subject will be expressed as keywords or phrases that describe the subject or content of the resource. The use of controlled vocabularies and formal classification schemes is encouraged.

— *Description*: A textual description of the content of the resource, including abstracts in the case of document-like objects or content descriptions in the case of visual resources.

— *Publisher*: The entity responsible for making the resource available in its present form, such as a publishing house, a university department, or a corporate entity.

— *Contributor*: A person or organisation not specified in a creator element who has made significant intellectual contributions to the resource but whose contribution is secondary to any person or organisation specified in a creator element.

— *Date*: A date associated with the creation or availability of the resource.

— *Type*: The category of the resource, such as home page, novel, poem, working paper, preprint, technical report, essay, dictionary.

— *Format*: The data format of the resource, used to identify the software and possibly hardware that might be needed to display or operate the resource.

— *Identifier*: A string or number used to uniquely identify the resource. Examples for networked resources include URLs and URNs.

— *Source*: Information about a second resource from which the present resource is derived.

— *Language*: The language of the intellectual content of the resource.

— *Relation*: An identifier of a second resource and its relationship to the present resource. This element permits links between related resources and resource descriptions to be indicated.

— *Coverage*: The spatial locations and temporal durations characteristic of the resource.

— *Rights*: A rights management statement, an identifier that links to a rights management statement, or an identifier that links to a service providing information about rights management for the resource.

Simplicity is both the strength and the weakness of the Dublin Core. Whereas traditional cataloguing rules are long and complicated, requiring professional training to apply effectively, the Dublin Core can be described simply, but simplicity conflicts with precision. The team has struggled with this tension. Initially the aim was to create a single set of metadata elements, suitable for untrained people who publish electronic materials to describe their work.

Some people continue to hold this minimalist view. They would like to see a simple set of rules that anybody can apply. Other people prefer the benefits that come from more tightly controlled cataloguing rules and would accept the additional labour and cost. They point out that extra structure in the elements results in extra precision in the metadata records. For example, if entries in a subject field are drawn from the Dewey Decimal Classification, it is helpful to record that fact in the metadata. To further enhance the effectiveness of the metadata for information retrieval, several of the elements will have recommended lists of values. Thus, there might be a specified set of types and indexers would be recommended to select from the list.

The current strategy is to have two options, "minimalist" and "structuralist". The minimalist will meet the original criterion of being usable by people who have no formal training. The structured option will be more complex, requiring fuller guidelines and trained staff to apply them.

Cataloguing and indexing are expensive when carried out by skilled professionals. A rule of thumb is that each record costs about fifty dollars to create and distribute. In certain fields, such as medicine and chemistry, the demand for information is great enough to justify the expense of comprehensive indexing, but these disciplines are the exceptions. Even monograph cataloguing is usually restricted to an overall record of the monograph rather than detailed cataloguing of individual topics within a book. Most items in museums, archives, and library special collections are not catalogued or indexed individually. In digital libraries, many items are worth collecting but the costs of cataloguing them individually can not be justified. The numbers of items in the collections can be very large, and the manner in which digital library objects change continually inhibits long-term investments in catalogs. Each item may go through several versions in quick succession.

A single object may be composed of many other objects, each changing independently. New categories of object are being continually devised, while others are discarded. Frequently, the user's perception of an object is the result of executing a computer programme and is different with each interaction. These factors increase the complexity and cost of cataloguing digital library materials. For all these reasons, professional cataloguing and indexing is likely to be less central to digital libraries than it is in traditional libraries. The alternative is to use computer programmes to create index records automatically. Records created by automatic indexing are normally of poor quality, but they are inexpensive.

A powerful search system will go a long way towards compensating for the low quality of individual records. The

Web search programmes prove this point. They build their indexes automatically. The records are not very good, but the success of the search services shows that the indexes are useful. At least, they are better than the alternative, which is to have nothing. Much of the development that led to automatic indexing came out of research in text skimming. A typical problem in this field is how to organise electronic mail. A user has a large volume of electronic mail messages and wants to file them by subject. A computer programme is expected to read through them and assign them to subject areas.

This is a difficult problem for people to carry out consistently and is a very difficult problem for a computer programme, but steady progress has been made. The programmes look for clues within the document. These clues may be structural elements, such as the subject field of an electronic mail message, they may be linguistic clues, or the programme may simply recognise key words. Automatic indexing also depends upon clues to be found in a document.

The author inserted these tags to guide Web browsers in displaying the article. They are equally useful in providing guidance to automatic indexing programmes. One of the potential uses of mark-up languages, such as SGML or XML, is that the structural tags can be used by automatic indexing programmes to build records for information retrieval. Within the text of a document, the string, "Marie Celeste" might be the name of a person, a book, a song, a ship, a publisher, a play, or might not even be a name. With structural mark-up, the string can be identified and labelled for what it is.

Thus, information provided by the mark-up can be used to distinguish specific categories of information, such as author, title, or date. Automatic indexing is fast and cheap. The exact costs are commercial secrets, but they are a tiny fraction of one cent per record. For the cost of a single record created by a professional cataloguer or indexer, computer programmes can generate a hundred thousand or more records. It is economically feasible to index huge numbers of items on the Internet and even to index them again at frequent intervals. Creators of catalogs and indexes can balance costs against perceived benefits.

The most expensive forms of descriptive metadata are the traditional methods used for library catalogs, and by indexing and abstracting services; structuralist Dublin Core will be moderately expensive, keeping most of the benefits while saving some costs; minimalist Dublin Core will be cheaper, but not free; automatic indexing has the poorest quality at a tiny cost. Descriptive metadata needs to be associated with the material that it describes. In the past, descriptive metadata has usually been stored separately, as an external catalog or index. This has many advantages, but requires links between the metadata and the object it references. Some digital libraries are moving in the other direction, storing the metadata and the data together, either by embedding the metadata in the object itself or by having two tightly linked objects.

This approach is convenient in distributed systems and for long-term archiving, since it guarantees that computer programmes have access to both the data and the metadata at the same time. Mechanisms for associating metadata with Web pages have been a subject of considerable debate. For an HTML page, a simple approach is to embed the metadata in the page, using the special HTML tag. These are the meta tags from an HTML description of the Dublin Core Element Set. Note that the choice of tags is a system design decision.

The Dublin Core itself does not specify how the metadata is associated with the material. Since meta tags can not be used with file types other than HTML and rapidly become cumbersome, a number of organisations working through the World Wide Web Consortium have developed a more general structure known as the Resource Description Framework (RDF). The Resource Description Framework (RDF) is a method that has been developed for the exchange of metadata. It has been developed by the World Wide Web Consortium, drawing concepts together from several other efforts, including the PICS format, which was developed to provide rating labels, to identify violence, pornography, and similar characteristics of Web pages.

The Dublin Core team is working closely with the RDF designers. A metadata scheme, such as Dublin Core, can be considered as having three aspects: semantics, syntax, and structure. The semantics describes how to interpret concepts such as date or creator. The syntax specifies how the metadata is expressed.

The structure defines the relationships between the metadata elements, such as the concepts of day, month and year as components of a date. RDF provides a simple but general structural model to express the syntax. It does not stipulate the semantics used by a metadata scheme. XML is used to describe a metadata scheme and for exchange of information between computer systems and among schemes. The structural model consists of resources, property-types, and values. The mark-up in this record makes explicit that the terms description and about are defined in the RDF scheme, while creator and type are terms defined in the Dublin Core (DC).

Information Retrieval

Information retrieval is a field in which computer scientists and information professionals have worked together for many years. It remains an active area of research and is one of the few areas of digital libraries to have a systematic methodology for measuring the performance of various methods. The various methods of information retrieval build on some simple concepts to search large bodies of information. A query is a string of text, describing the information that the user is seeking. Each word of the query is called a search term. A query can be a single search term, a string of terms, a phrase in natural language, or a stylised expression using special symbols.

Some methods of information retrieval compare the query with every word in the entire text, without distinguishing the function of the various words. This is called full text searching. Other methods identify bibliographic or structural fields, such as author or heading, and allow searching on specified field, such as "author = Gibbon". This is called fielded searching. Full text and fielded searching are both powerful tools, and modern methods of information retrieval often use the techniques in combination. Fielded searching requires some method of identifying the fields. Full text searching does not require such support.

By taking advantage of the power of modern computers, full text searching can be effective even on unprocessed text, but heterogeneous texts of varying length, style, and content are difficult to search effectively and the results can be inconsistent. The legal information systems, Westlaw and Lexis, are based on full text searching; they are the exceptions. When descriptive metadata is available, most services prefer either fielded searching or free text searching of abstracts or other metadata. Some words occur so frequently that they are of little value for retrieval. Examples include common pronouns, conjunctions, and auxiliary verbs, such as "he", "and", "be", and so on. Most systems have a list of common words which are ignored both in building inverted files and in queries. This is called a stop list. The selection of stop words is difficult. The choice clearly depends upon the language of the text and may also be related to the subject matter. For this reason, instead of have a predetermined stop list, some systems use statistical methods to identify the most commonly used words and reject them. Even then, no system is perfect.

Computational Linguistics

The words in a document are not simply random strings of characters. They are words in a language, such as English, arranged into phrases, sentences, and paragraphs. Natural language processing is the branch of computer science that uses computers to interpret and manipulate words as part of a language. The spelling checkers that are used with word processors are a well-known application. They use methods of natural language processing to suggest alternative spellings for words that they do not recognise. Computational linguistics deals with grammar and linguistics. One of the achievements of computational linguistics has been to develop computer programmes that can parse almost any sentence with good accuracy. A parser analyses the structure of sentences. It categorises words by part of speech (verb, noun, adjective, etc.), groups them into phrases and clauses, and identifies the structural elements (subject, verb, object, etc.).

For this purpose, linguists have been required to refine their understanding of grammar, recognising far more subtleties than were contained in traditional grammars. Considerable research in information retrieval has been carried out using noun phrases. The content of a sentence can be found by extracting the nouns and noun phrases and searching on them. This work has not been restricted to English, but has been carried out for many languages. Parsing requires an understanding of the morphology of words, that is variants derived from the same stem, such as plurals (library, libraries), and verb forms (look, looks, looked).

For information retrieval, it is often effective to reduce morphological variants to a common stem and to use the stem as a search term. This is called stemming. Stemming is more effective than truncation since it separates words with totally different meanings, such as "computer" from "company", while recognising that "computer" and "computing" are morphological variants from the same stem. In English, where the stem is almost always at the beginning of the word, stemming can be carried out by truncating words and perhaps making adjustments to the final few letters. In other language, such as German, it is also necessary to trim at the beginning of words.

Computational linguists have developed a range of dictionaries and other tools, such as lexicons and thesauruses, that are designed for natural language processing. A lexicon contains information about words, their morphological variants, and their grammatical usage. A thesaurus relates words by meaning. Some of these tools are general purpose; others are tied to specific disciplines. Linguistic can greatly augment information retrieval.

Effectiveness on the User

Information retrieval systems depend for their effectiveness on the user making best use of the tools provided. When the user is a trained medical librarian or a lawyer whose legal education included training in search systems, these objectives are usually met. Untrained users typically do much less well at formulating queries and understanding the results. A feature of the vector-space and probabilistic methods of information retrieval is that they are most effective with long queries. An interesting experiment is to use a very long query, perhaps an abstract from a document. Using this as a query is equivalent to asking the system to find documents that match the abstract.

Many modern search systems are remarkably effective when given such an opportunity, but methods that are based on vector space or linguistic techniques require a worthwhile query to display their full power. Statistics of the queries that are used in practice show that most queries consist of a single word, which is a disappointment to the developers of powerful retrieval systems. One reasons for these short queries is that many users made their first searches on Boolean systems, where the only results found are exact matches, so that a long query usually finds no matches. These early systems had another characteristic that encouraged short queries. When faced with a long or complex query their performance deteriorated terribly. Users learned to keep their queries short. Habits that were developed with these systems have been retained even with more modern systems.

However, the tendency of users to supply short queries is more entrenched than can be explained by these historical factors, or by the tiny input boxes sometimes provided. The pattern is repeated almost everywhere. People appear to be inhibited from using long queries. Another unfortunate characteristic of users, which is widely observed, is that few people read even the most simple instructions. Digital libraries are failing to train their users in effective searching and users do not take advantage of the potential of the systems that they use.

Information retrieval has a long tradition of performance evaluation. Two long-standing criteria are precision and recall. Each refers to the results from carrying out a single search on a given body of information. The result of such a search is a set of hits. Ideally every hit would be relevant to the original query, and every relevant item in the body of information would be found.

In practice, it usually happens that some of the hits are irrelevant and that some relevant items are missed by the search. Precision is the percentage of the hits that are relevant, the extent to which the set of hits retrieved by a query satisfies the requirement that generated the query. Recall is the percentage of the relevant items that are found by the query, the extent to which the query found all the items that satisfy the requirement. Suppose that, in a collection of 10, 000 documents, 50 are on a specific topic. An ideal search would find these 50 documents and reject all others. An actual search identifies 25 documents of which 20 prove to be relevant but 5 were on other topics. In this instance, the precision is 20 out of 25, or 0. 8. The recall is 20 out of 50, or 0. 4. Precision is much easier to measure than recall. To calculate precision, a knowledgeable person looks at each document that is identified and decides whether it is relevant.

10

Challenges of Access Management

Strategic planning concerns the future of the library as a whole while more specific plans may be drawn up for individual services, or to guide a major development such as the selection and implementation of a new library management system. A library might analyse both local and national political factors, the impact of economic factors such as exchange rates and rates of inflation, changes in society's expectations of libraries and the impacts of technological change. Coupled with this, SWOT (Strengths, Weaknesses, Opportunities, Threats) analysis—which focuses on the existing strengths and weaknesses of the organisation, the opportunities it has to develop and the threats to its existence and prosperity - can be used to analyse the internal situation and relate it to likely trends outside.

Having done this, a number of planning assumptions can be stated, making explicit the expectations of the planners about future trends. A useful process is then to write down and discuss a series of scenarios, which are in essence descriptions of or even stories about the future as it might be if particular directions are taken. Some of these scenarios can be fairly outrageous, since the purpose is to stimulate thought about what is desirable - for example, an interesting scenario for a modern academic library to debate might be based around a future without books. Although there are many formal planning systems available, most academic libraries will use processes which are agreed in their university, if only because the library's plans must fit with those of the parent institution.

The process of planning must be clearly understood, and the role of all participants—which should include all library staff, since all have a contribution to make - made explicit. The university will itself develop strategic plans concerning finance, the physical estate, staffing, academic development and many other issues. The library's plans must both contribute to and draw upon these wider considerations. It is also worth noting that the library's plans can be a very effective means of communicating concerns, intentions and problems to the wider community. The library's strategic plan will set out the general direction it is expected to take over the longer term—which because of the rate of change usually means no more than three years.

Managemental Changes

Because, as we have already noted, change is virtually constant in higher education and in librarianship, one of the library manager's most important tasks is to ensure that change is managed and does not just 'happen'. To achieve this it is important to recognise that resistance to change is not born of a wish to be obstructive—or at least, not usually—but because of deeply held beliefs about the values which change may destroy. It is therefore essential that there is a credible vision of the future which change is intended to bring about, and that steps are taken to gain commitment from all stakeholders both to the vision itself and to the path being pursued to achieve it.

Quality of Management

There are many approaches to management and many

schools of thought about management theory and practice. It can be difficult to reconcile all these ideas and schools of thought into a coherent overall approach. To some extent this is a matter of preference, but one approach which has become popular in recent years, not only in libraries, is quality management. Quality assurance is a major issue in higher education in general, and very considerable resources are expended to ensure that the standard of research and teaching in institutions is acceptable. Taking a quality management approach to library services therefore aligns the library closely with institutional concerns.

Quality management focuses first and foremost on two issues: customer satisfaction and continuous improvement. Deriving originally from Japanese and then American business management, quality management became a dominant approach in the UK during the 1990s, and evoked considerable interest among librarians. Under the terminology of total quality management (TQM) it brings together a series of issues in a coherent manner, addressing:

— the need for each organisation to be clear about its purpose; what its mission, aims and objectives really are

— having a consistent focus on customer needs throughout all of the organisation's operations

— senior managers' responsibility for providing leadership, including a vision of the organisation's future

— commitment by all employees to the organisation

— the use of teamwork to bring employees together to work on issues and developments, using the strengths that each member of the team can bring to the task in hand

— involvement of all staff in decision-making and communication—a participative style

— having systematic processes in place so that services are delivered consistently-and users know what to expect

— good resource management with resources understood to encompass not just financial resources but people, buildings, materials and knowledge

— good relationships with suppliers, so that those on whom the organisation depends for its raw materials - in library terms book suppliers, periodicals agents, data services etc. - are committed to the organisation's goals and supported in their efforts to supply the right materials at the right time

— benchmarking, which in essence is a process of comparing yourself against the best in your field, understanding how they operate and seeking to apply that approach in a suitable way to one's own organisation

— monitoring performance, so that the managers know how well the organisation is performing and can take action both to correct problems and to pursue excellence

— training and development of all staff so that they are competent in all the tasks they are asked to perform, knowledgeable about the organisation and all its services or products, and understand the ethos and style of the organisation

— understanding of how the organisation impacts on its environment - in library terms this could be interpreted as the broader role within the local community, or could refer to the contribution that the library makes to society as a whole, perhaps through the preservation of recorded knowledge.

The European Foundation for Quality Management awards a series of quality awards each year to companies which are judged to be offering outstanding quality as defined by its Excellence Model. It is an interesting exercise to examine these criteria and the achievements of award winners. Academic libraries, even when they have not explicitly adopted a quality management approach, have often used particular techniques taken from this school of management practice.

Access Management

The term access management is used to describe the control of access to digital libraries. An obvious reason for controlling access is economic. When publishers expect revenue from their products, they permit access only to users who have paid. Access management would be unnecessary except when revenue is. involved, but that is not the case; there are other reasons to control access to materials in a digital library. Materials donated to a library may have conditions attached, perhaps tied to external events such as the lifetime of certain individuals. A well-managed digital library will keep a record of all changes, so that the collections can be restored if mistakes are made or computer files are corrupted. People from a computing background sometimes assume that every object can be labeled with metadata that lists all the rights, permissions, and other factors relevant to access management. People who come from libraries, and especially those who manage historic collections or archives, know that assembling such information is always time consuming and frequently impossible. Projects, such as the American Memory project at the Library of Congress, convert millions of items from historic collections.

For these older materials, a natural assumption is that copyright has expired and there need be no access restrictions, but this is far from true. For published materials, the expiration of copyright is linked to the death of the creator, a date which is often hard to determine, and libraries frequently do not know whether items have been published. The responsibility for access lies with whoever manages the digital material. The manager may be a library, a publisher, a Webmaster, or the creator of the information. Parts of the responsibility may be delegated. If a library controls the materials and makes them available to users, the library sets the policies and implements them, usually guided by external restraints, such as legal restrictions, licenses from publishers, or agreements with donors. If a publisher mounts materials and licenses access, then the publisher is the manager, but may delegate key activities, such as authorisation of users, to others. When a user accesses a computer system, a two-step process of identification usually takes place.

The first is authentication which establishes the identify of the individual user. The second is to determine what a user is authorised to do. A wide variety of techniques are used to authenticate users; some are simple but easy to circumvent, while others are more secure but complex. A standard method of authentication is to provide each user with a login name and a password. This is widely used but has weaknesses. Passwords are easily stolen.

Most people like to select their own password and often select words that are easy to remember and hence easy to guess, such as personal names, or everyday words. Examples of physical devices that are used for authentication include the magnetically encoded cards used by bank teller machines, and digital smart-cards that execute an authentication programme. Smart-cards are one of the best systems of authentication; they are highly secure and quite convenient to use. A common form of authentication is the network address of a computer. Anybody who has access to a computer with an approved IP address is authenticated.

Data on many personal computers is unprotected except by physical access; anybody who has access to the computer can read the data. Authentication by physical attributes such as voice recognition is used in a few esoteric applications, but has had little impact in digital libraries.

Policies for access management rarely specify users by name. They are usually tied to categories of users or the role of a user. An individual user can have many roles. At different times, the same person may use a digital library for teaching, private reading, or to carry out a part-time business. The digital library may have different policies for the same individual in these various roles.

Most users of digital libraries are people using personal computers, but the user can be a computer with no person associated, such as a programme that is indexing Web pages or a mirroring programme that replicates an entire collection. Some sites explicitly ban access by automatic programmes.

Authentication of Digital Materials

For access management, digital materials must be clearly identified. Identification associates some name or identifier with each item of material. Authentication of digital materials assures both users and managers of collections that materials are unaltered. In most digital libraries, the accuracy of the materials is not verified explicitly. Where the level of trust is high and the cost of mistakes are low, no formal authentication of documents is needed. Deliberate alterations are rare and mistakes are usually obvious. In some fields, however, such as medical records, errors are serious. Digital libraries in these areas should seriously consider using formal methods of authenticating materials. To ensure the accuracy of an object, a digital signature can be associated with it. A digital signature ensures that a file or other set of bits has not changed since the signature was calculated.

Properties of Digital Material

Access management policies frequently treat different material in varying ways, depending upon properties or attributes of the material. These attributes can be encoded as administrative metadata and stored with the object, or they can be derived from some other source. Some attributes can also be computed. Thus the size of an object can be measured when required. Here are some typical examples:

a) *Division into sub-collections*: Collections often divide material into items for public access and items with restricted access. Publishers may separate the full text of articles from indexes, abstracts and promotional materials. Web sites have public areas, and private areas for use within an organisation.

b) *Licensing and other external commitments*: A digital library may have material that is licensed from a publisher or acquired subject to terms and conditions that govern access, such as materials that the Library of Congress receives through copyright deposit.

c) *Physical, temporal, and similar properties*: Digital libraries may have policies that depend upon the time since the date of publication or physical properties, such as the size of the material. Some newspapers provide open access to selected articles when they are published while requiring licenses for the same articles later.

d) *Media types*: A digital library may have access policies that depend upon format or media type, for example treating digitised sound differently from textual material, or computer programmes from images.

Attributes need to be assigned at varying granularity. If all the materials in a collection have the same property, then it is convenient to assign the attribute to the collection as a whole. At the other extreme, there are times when parts of objects may have specific properties. The rights associated with images are often different from those associated with the text in which they are embedded and will have to be distinguished. A donor may donate a collection of letters to a library for public access, but request that access to certain private correspondence be restricted.

Digital libraries need to offer flexibility, so that attributes can be associated with entire collections, sub-collections, individual library objects, or elements of individual objects. Access management policies often specify or restrict the operations and the various actions that a user is authorised to carry out on library materials. Some of the common categories of operation include:

a) *Computing actions*: Some operations are defined in computing terms, such as to write data to a computer, execute a programme, transmit data across a network, display on a computer screen, print, or copy from one computer to another.

b) *Extent of use*: A user may be authorised to extract individual items from a database, but not copy the entire database.

These operations can be controlled by technical means, but many policies that an information manager might state are essentially impossible to enforce technically. They include:

a) *Business or purpose*: Authorisation of a user might refer to the reason for carrying out an operation. Examples include commercial, educational, or government use.

b) *Intellectual operations*: Operations may specify the intellectual use to be made of an item. The most important is the rules that govern the creation of a new work that is derived from the content of another. The criteria may need to consider both the intent and the extent of use.

Systems for access management have to consider both direct operations and subsequent use of material. Direct operations are actions initiated by a repository, or another computer system that acts as a agent for the managers of the collection. Subsequent use covers all those operations that can occur once material leaves the control of the digital library. It includes all the various ways that a copy can be made, from replicating computer files to photocopying paper documents. Intellectually, it can include everything from extracting short sections, the creation of derivative works, to outright plagiarism. When an item, or part of a item, has been transmitted to a personal computer it is technically difficult to prevent a user from copying what is received, storing it, and distributing it to others. This is comparable to photocopying a document. If the information is for sale, the potential for such subsequent use to reduce revenue is clear. Publishers naturally have concerns about readers distributing unauthorised copies of materials.

At an extreme, if a publisher sells one copy of an item that is subsequently widely distributed over the Internet, the publisher might end up selling only that one copy. As a partial response to this fear, digital libraries are often designed to allow readers access to individual records, but do not provide any way to copy complete collections. While this does not prevent a small loss of revenue, it is a barrier against anybody undermining the economic interests of the publisher by wholesale copying. Typical policies in digital libraries are:

a) A publication might have the policy of open access. Anybody may read the material, but only the editorial staff may change it.

b) A publisher with journals online may have the policy that only subscribers have access to all materials. Other people can read the contents pages and abstracts, but have access to the full content only if they pay a fee per use.

c) A government organisation might classify materials, e.g., "top secret", and have strict policies about who has access to the materials, under what conditions, and what they can do with them.

Policies are rarely as simple as in these examples. For example, while D-Lib Magazine has a policy of open access, the authors of the individual articles own the copyright. The access policy is that everybody is encouraged to read the articles and print copies for private use, but some subsequent use, such as creating a derivative work, or selling copies for profit requires permission from the copyright owner.

Simple policies can sometimes be represented as a table in which each row relates a user role, attributes of digital material, and certain operations. Because access management policies can be complex, a formal method is needed to express them, which can be used for exchange of information among computer system. Perhaps the most comprehensive work in this area has been carried out by Mark Stefik of Xerox. The Digital Property Rights Language, which he developed, is a language for expressing the rights, conditions, and fees for using digital works. The purpose of the language is to specify attributes of material and policies for access, including subsequent use.

The manager of a collection can specify terms and conditions for copying, transferring, rendering, printing, and similar operations. The language allows fees to be specified for any operation, and it envisages links to electronic payment mechanisms. The notation used by the language is based on Lisp, a language used for natural language processing. Some people have suggested that, for digital libraries, a more convenient notation would use XML, which would be a straightforward transformation. The real test of this language is how effective it proves to be when used in large-scale applications. Access management is not simply a question of developing appropriate policies. Information managers want the policies to be followed, which requires some form of enforcement. Some policies can be enforced technically. Others are more difficult.

There are straightforward technical methods to enforce a policy of who is permitted to change material in a collection, or search a repository. There are no technical means to enforce a policy against plagiarism, or invasion of privacy, or to guarantee that all use is educational. Each of these is a reasonable policy that is extremely difficult to enforce by technical means. Managing such policies is fundamentally social. There are trade-offs between strictness of enforcement and convenience to users. Technical method of enforcing policies can be annoying. Few people object to typing in a password when they begin a session, but nobody wants to be asked repeatedly for passwords, or other identification. Information managers will sometimes decide to be relaxed about enforcing policies in the interests of satisfying users.

Satisfied customers will help grow the size of the market, even if some revenue is lost from unauthorised users. The publishers who are least aggressive about enforcement keep their customers happy and often generate most total revenue. Data from publishers such as HighWire Press is beginning to suggest the same result with electronic journal publishing. If technical methods are relaxed, social and legal pressures can be effective. The social objective is to educate users about the policies that apply to the collections, and coax or persuade people to follow them.

This requires policies that are simple to understand and easy for users to follow. Users must be informed of the policies and educated as to what constitutes reasonable behavior. One useful tool is to display an access statement when the material is accessed; this is text that states some policy. An example is, "For copyright reasons, this material should not be used for commercial purposes." Other non-technical methods of enforcement are more assertive. If members of an organisation repeatedly violate a licensing agreement or abuse policies that they should respect, a publisher can revoke a license. In extreme cases, a single, well-publicised legal action will persuade many others to behave responsibly.

Policies for Computer Software

Early experience with software for personal computers provides an example of what happens when attempts to enforce policies are unpleasant for the users. Software is usually licensed for a single computer. The license fee covers use on one computer only, but software is easy to copy. Manufacturers lose revenue from unlicensed copying, particularly if there develops widespread distribution of unlicensed copies. In the early days of personal computers, software manufacturers attempted to control unlicensed copying by technical means.

One approach was to supply their products on disks that could not be copied easily. This was called copy-protection. Every time that a programme was launched, the user had to insert the original disk. This had a powerful effect on the market, but not what the manufacturers had hoped. The problem was that it became awkward for legitimate customers to use the software that they had purchased. Hard disk installations were awkward and back-up difficult. Users objected to the inconvenience. Those software suppliers who were most assertive about protection lost sales to competitors who supplied software without copy-protection. Microsoft was one of the companies that realised that technical enforcement is not the only option. The company has become extremely rich by selling products that are not technically protected against copying. Instead, Microsoft has worked hard to stimulate adherence to its policies by non-technical methods. Marketing incentives, such as customer support and low-cost upgrades, encourage customers to pay for licenses. Social pressures are used to educate people and legal methods are used to frighten the worst offenders. Unlicensed copying still costs the software manufacturers money, but, by concentrating on satisfying their responsible customers, the companies are able to thrive.

Policies at a Repository

Most digital libraries implement policies at the repository or collection level. Digital libraries are distributed computer systems, in which information is passed from one computer to another. If access management is only at the repository, access is effectively controlled locally, but once material leaves the repository problems multiply. The issue of subsequent use has already been introduced; once the user"s computer receives information it is hard for the original manager of the digital library to retain effective control, without obstructing the legitimate user. With networks, there is a further problem. Numerous copies of the material are made in networked computers, including caches, mirrors, and other servers, beyond the control of the local repository. To date, most digital libraries have been satisfied to provide access management at the repository, while relying on social and legal pressure to control subsequent use. Usually this is adequate, but some publishers are concerned that the lack of control could damage their revenues. Therefore, there is interest in technical methods that control copying and subsequent, even after the material has left the repository. The methods fall into two categories: trusted systems and secure containers.

Trusted Systems

A repository is an example of a trusted system. The managers of a digital library have confidence that the hardware, software, and administrative procedures provide an adequate level of security to store and provide access to valuable information.

There may be other systems, linked to the repository, that are equally trusted. Within such a network of trusted systems, digital libraries can use methods of enforcement that are simple extensions of those used for single repositories. Attributes and policies can be passed among systems, with confidence that they will be processed effectively. Implementing networks of trusted systems is not easy. The individual systems components must support a high level of security and so must the processes by which information is passed among the various computers.

For these reasons, trusted systems are typically used in restricted situations only or on special purpose computers. If all the computers are operated by the same team or by teams working under strict rules, many of the administrative problems diminish. An example of a large, trusted system is the network of computers that support automatic teller machines in banks. No assumptions can be made about users" personal computers and how they are managed. In fact, it is reasonable not to trust them. For this reason, early applications of trusted systems in digital libraries are likely to be restricted to special purpose hardware, such as smart cards or secure printers, or dedicated servers running rightly controlled software.

Secure Containers

Since networks are not secure and trusted system difficult to implement, several groups are developing secure containers for transmitting information across the Internet. Digital material is delivered to the user in a package that contains data and metadata about access policies. Some or all of the information in the package is encrypted. To access the information requires a digital key, which might be received from an electronic payment system or other method of authentication. An advantage of this approach is that it provides some control over subsequent use. IBM"s Cryptolope system is an example of how secure containers can be used. Cryptolopes are designed to let Internet users buy and sell content securely over the Internet. Information is transmitted in a secure cryptographic envelope, called a Cryptolope container.

Information suppliers seal their information in the Cryptolope container. It can be opened by recipients only after they have satisfied any access management requirements, such as paying for use of the information. The content is never separated from the access management and payment information in the envelope. Thus, the envelope can later be passed on to others, who also must pay for usage if they want to open it; each user must obtain the code to open the envelope. In addition to the encrypted content, Cryptolope containers can include subfiles in clear text to provide users with a description of the product.

The abstract might include the source, summary, author, last update, size, and price, and terms of sale. Once the user has decided to open the contents of a Cryptolope container, a digital key is issued unlocking the material contained within. To view a free item, the user clicks on the abstract and the information appears on the desktop. To view priced content, the user agrees to the terms of the Cryptolope container as stated in the abstract. The content in a Cryptolope container can be dynamic. The system has the potential to wrap JavaScripts, Java programmes, and other live content into secure containers.

In the interest of standardisation, IBM has licensed Xerox"s Digital Property Rights Language for specifying the rules governing the use and pricing of content. Secure containers face a barrier to acceptance. They are of no value to a user unless the user can acquire the necessary cryptographic keys to unlock them and make use of the content. This requires widespread deployment of security service and methods of electronic payment. Until recently, the spread of such services has been rather slow, so that publishers have had little market for information delivered via secure containers.

11

Future of Digital Libraries

Libraries see an expanding base of users and, in many instances, changing service demands. There is ample evidence that when libraries make quality content available through the Web, its use increases and it reaches more people within the institution. In addition, the user base for any individual library has expanded to include users beyond the institution. This has been achieved through more efficient resource-sharing arrangements (often statewide) as well as by targeting new user groups for digitised content and e-services. In many cases, openly accessible digitised collections on the Web are also being used heavily by people from beyond the educational world.

Despite press accounts to the contrary, research libraries report that use of the library's physical facility remains heavy, especially for collaborative learning and research activities and for access to computers and information technologies. As a result, many libraries have moved to provide 24/5 access to the library buildings. At the same time, there is growing evidence in the data collected from ARL member libraries that the service demands of users may be changing. Many libraries see declining use of some traditional services, such as use of some print materials, circulation transactions, and reference transactions.

However, the data confirm that the demands for interlibrary borrowing and for user education are steadily increasing. These trends signal a shift in the behavior of information users that is being closely monitored. Research on the information-seeking behavior of people is growing almost as fast as the Web itself. An overwhelming number of college students reported that the Internet, rather than the library, is the primary site of their information searches.

"Many students are likely to use information found on search engines and various Web sites as research materials....A great challenge for today's colleges is how to teach students search techniques that will get them to the information they want and how to evaluate it....While few universities require college students to take courses on information seeking, many include a session on it during freshman orientation meetings. To better understand how usage patterns are changing, the Digital Library Federation (DLF) and Council on Library and Information Resources (CLIR) commissioned Outsell, Inc., to conduct a large-scale study of over 3,000 undergraduates, graduate students, and faculty members from a wide range of academic institutions. The results revealed that the highest percentage of resources used were print materials, which students ranked higher than library and non-library electronic sources in four out of five factors.

The Internet-based sources scored high only on the factor of convenience, while print materials scored high on the factors that make a difference in the quality of research and learning: generating the information for which the student is looking, the usefulness of the material, its reliability, and the availability of assistance. There are differences across disciplines in terms of how information is used and to what extent new technologies are being embraced; libraries are recognising these differences as they offer new services.

There are also differences in the pace of change in different institutions; institutional cultures that allow, for example, some flexibility in personnel policies and practices as well as in budgetary reallocations, are more accommodating of experimentation and change. In this rapidly changing environment, libraries must continue monitoring trends, assessing their performance by seeking feedback from current users, and anticipating the needs of future users.

To meet and anticipate these needs of the academic and research communities, libraries are collaborating as never before, forming partnerships both within and outside their own institutions, often sharing control in order to effect critical change. While circumstances will vary from library to library, the results of the task force survey demonstrate many ways that libraries are responding to user expectations.

Libraries are expanding the amount and variety of high-quality information resources that are directly available to academic and research users via the Web. They are also expanding the definition of collections to include "born-digital" content that is neither owned nor licensed by the library. The varied efforts toward this goal may be characterised as follows: changing collection development policies to emphasize the acquisition of electronic resources, engaging in digitising and electronic publishing projects, and assuming responsibility for managing and servicing born-digital content that resides outside the domain of the library. Even in the electronic and networked environment, the economic model continues to feature the library as the central agency on campus that buys and/or manages information resources on behalf of the institution. Libraries have shifted the focus of their collection development policies to the acquisition of more electronic content, much of it via consortia.

While aggregate data documenting the quantity of e-resources currently being made available by libraries has proven elusive, there is data on the spending trends. Over the last decade the average percentage of a research library's materials budget that is spent on electronic resources has grown from 4% to 16%. One hundred six ARL university libraries report spending more than $132 million on electronic resources in 2000-01. The vast majority of that was spent on electronic serials and subscription services, expenditures which have increased sharply, from just $11 million in 1994-95 to more than $117 million today. To support this increased spending on electronic content, libraries have reallocated resources from the purchase of print.

The extent of such reallocations will vary depending on institutional user expectations and financial circumstances. Many libraries have adopted a policy of adding the e-version of journals when available and are showcasing titles of e-journals available to users via the Web by making this a staff priority and by applying software management tools for titles included in aggregated electronic databases. The processes for selecting, budgeting, and acquiring electronic materials are continually changing and greatly differ from those for the selection and management of print. The print process is orderly: discrete amounts of money are allocated by discipline, the marketplace is fairly predictable, and materials are selected and ordered using established procedures. By contrast, the processes for selection and management of electronic resources are chaotic.

The migration from print to electronic varies in speed and extent by discipline; electronic products are interdisciplinary and expensive, giving rise to selection by committee; projections for future funding are guesswork; and archiving and content control are problematic. Legal and negotiation skills are now mandatory. To complicate matters, decisions are often made through a consortium.

The process for acquiring electronic resources turns the traditional acquisitions and user service model topsy-turvy. In building electronic collections, libraries must also constantly respond to changing publisher behavior. The most profound influence on a library's collection management and access strategies has been the extraordinary price increases for scholarly journals, combined with publishers' use of licensing to define the terms under which a library may make the content available and to whom. It is reasonable to speculate that these phenomena, driven by some of the larger publishers but now employed widely, make up one of the forces that prompted libraries to blend the previously distinct operations of collection management and access.

Some libraries have fully embraced initiatives stimulated or endorsed by SPARC (the Scholarly Publishing and Academic Resources Coalition) and other affordable publishing venues and are using acquisitions funds as investments in the future of scholarly communication. These libraries focus acquisitions on publications from scholarly societies and less expensive publishers, nonprofit and for-profit, that provide high-quality titles at affordable prices. These less expensive titles tend to be the most highly ranked by faculty but labor intensive to obtain, since each publisher has only a few titles and often lacks sales and technical staff.

These libraries try to consistently view collection expenditures as investments, and to seek out publishers likely to contribute to a sustainable future for scholarly information. Libraries are also supporting open access projects that experiment with alternatives to the current subscription-based funding model or the current journals-based publishing model for scholarly communication. These approaches are seen as those of a good citizen, especially in an institution whose needs for funding include many urgent priorities in addition to library needs. These libraries are investing in initiatives that may help solve the long-term problem of high prices for journals.

Electronic Publishing

Most libraries are also pursuing a proactive strategy to increase user access to quality information resources on the Web by digitising materials and collaborating with others to publish digital collections on the Web. For example, libraries are:

— Creating new electronic collections by digitally reformatting existing collections in the library and institution, including the collections of senior faculty and retired faculty

— Collaborating with other libraries, academic departments, scholarly and historical societies, museums, and others to build virtual collections from originals that are geographically dispersed

— Giving greater emphasis to developing and showcasing special collections of manuscripts and rare books, foreign-language resources, images, music, maps and geospatial data, numeric data sets, and making them accessible to discovery via the Web and in other learning environments

— Supporting faculty's e-publishing efforts by consulting and by offering technological infrastructure to develop the next generation "journal" and to create Web-based research tools and resources for teaching

— Partnering with university presses and other publishers to develop new publishing models

— Partnering with faculty departments and/or societies to mount discipline-based and/or institutional e-print servers

Libraries have expanded the traditional view and definition of collections so that the concept no longer equates with those materials that the library "owns". The boundaries have expanded far beyond the print collections on site or the electronic files mounted locally to include electronic materials licensed or managed by the library and materials available through consortia. Increasingly libraries are taking responsibility for born-digital collections and developing tools for their management and use.

In a growing number of cases, a library's collection also includes resources that reside outside the domain of the library but for which the library takes some responsibility for managing and servicing. An example of the latter is the movement by libraries to support the development of institution-wide knowledge management systems, where an institution's intellectual capital is centralised, preserved, and made accessible.

In a university, this might include collections of digital material created by faculty, research staff, and students, e.g., research collaboratives, graduate student theses, electronic records of the university's administrative offices, courseware content, and streaming audio and video resources generated from courses, conferences, and other campus activities. The content of print collections continues to play a critical role in libraries but that role is changing, as is the way that libraries are managing print collections. Less frequently used print resources are being relocated to storage with paging/retrieval services; more convenient resource sharing makes book collections accessible to wider audiences.

Instead of describing collections as "those things owned", a better definition may be "information resources for which the library invests financial resources—directly or indirectly—to manage, service, or preserve on behalf of library users, regardless of the location of content." "Collections" now include resources owned by the library and those accessed in remote locations; the norm is now an interdependent mix of ownership and access, with the location of the material increasingly irrelevant to users. Libraries are increasingly providing users with services and tools that enhance access to electronic resources and support an integrated approach to discovering and receiving this content—along with library services--in classrooms, on the "desktop", and on PDAs. In many cases, libraries deliver unrestricted content and services to users far beyond those affiliated with the institution. Libraries are pursuing this in many ways, including offering new services, adapting the role of the online catalog, experimenting with the Open Archives Initiative (OAI) metadata harvesting protocol, and writing or adapting software tools.

Role of Online Catalogs

It is clear that the role of the online catalog has changed. That catalog has become one of many databases available to users; libraries are linking to and from the catalog to integrate all of these resources. In recognition of this broader role for the library catalog, some libraries are considering modifying cataloging to favor timely access to a wider variety of formats.

One proposal called for reallocating funds that are devoted to describing books and journals to materials that are proportionately underrepresented in today's catalogs, such as films, music, photographs, and digital objects. Libraries are also reconsidering their current efforts to collect and catalog free Web resources, concluding that these labor-intensive activities can be avoided by perfecting nascent machine harvesting and cataloging techniques.

A small number of libraries and library organisations are participating in experiments funded by The Mellon Foundation to test the application of harvesting and search engine technologies. Using the recently developed OAI metadata harvesting protocol, these libraries are delivering information from the "hidden Web" not normally found by

Internet search engines and from databases with retrieval formats that present special processing or presentation problems.

Several libraries are working with vendors to adapt existing portal software into multifunctional products with features and services desired by users in research communities. Other examples of library involvement in development of software applications are ILL management systems, instructional tutorials, management of content and services for digital libraries, and institutional repositories. Although where information resides matters less to the user, the library as place—the physical entity—remains more important than ever and performs a host of functions vital to learning and research. Much research library space is busier than ever before.

Library facilities are being reconfigured to provide space for collaborative learning and research. There are classrooms and media labs where faculty and librarians may interact in providing student learning experiences, group study spaces, and community spaces where students can meet to discuss ideas. The transformation of library space has also become an opportunity to attract new academic collaborations such as writing studios and academic skills tutoring.

Library space is now seen as learning space on an equal footing with classrooms and laboratories. Libraries are being renovated to expand e-access and foster community by providing electronic classrooms, wireless data networks, offering laptops, and expanding library hours. Libraries are establishing spaces called "information commons" where library reference services are offered jointly with information technology support. At the same time, libraries are responding to decreasing use of in-person reference service by combining service points and shifting resources to online reference service and online tutorials. To make the best use of prime real estate, libraries are adopting new approaches to managing large print collections by using storage centers with delivery services for less frequently used materials and engaging in cooperative approaches to long-term preservation copy retention. The branch or departmental library remains valuable but its role too is changing. While access to information and library services is far less geographically based, branch and departmental libraries still play a role in development of community and serve as sites for collaboration. Yet, in the Internet world there are opportunities to rethink the role of multiple libraries and their configuration within an institution.

One library reported establishing a program to replicate the opportunities for personalised services and contacts that characterise branch library service without the cost of creating additional branches.

Some of the same opportunities for reorganisation may present themselves when libraries work in collaboration with other libraries outside their institutional boundaries. Libraries are active participants in building awareness among researchers, faculty, and students of uses of high-quality content and information technology in teaching and research. Curriculum review and changing expectations for teaching faculty present opportunities for libraries to contribute expertise and resources.

Libraries provide classrooms; training and consulting in finding and evaluating information; and assistance with creating electronic theses and dissertations, displaying and visualising data, publishing journals on the Web, and using geographic information systems (GIS) and remote sensing. Recognising that disciplines are adopting new technology at different rates, librarians are:

— Working with faculty to integrate information literacy skills and digital content into the course curricula

- Expanding the number of people reached by offering basic information literacy and fluency training through online tutorials
- Assisting researchers in acquiring, accessing, displaying, and visualising spatial and numeric data by providing training in use of software and partnering with faculty to provide classroom instruction in its use
- Developing systems and instructional tools for pedagogical use of digital resources, including images
- Managing campus instructional technology initiatives
- Making Organisational Changes within the Library to Innovate and Improve Services

Libraries are embracing change—being willing to change what libraries do and how it is done—and, as a result, are reorganising their operations and re-deploying staff to respond to the new environment. Examples of recent organisational change in ARL libraries include:

- Many libraries report having instituted an integrated approach to collection management, bringing together the activities of building, maintaining, and providing access to library resources in all formats, both in-house and remote, both acquired and locally created.
- Many libraries also report taking interdisciplinary approaches, training library staff to perform across traditional roles and to build bridges between the culture of the library and that of the faculty and information technology. An example is the creation of information commons jointly staffed by the library and information technology, often developing services in collaboration with faculty.
- Others report organisational redesigns to achieve a system-wide view of services to coordinate communications with all library users and to deploy staff more flexibly.

— Libraries are experimenting rigorously with organisational transformation reflecting strategies for team-based decision making, learning organisations, and quality management.

Scholarly Communication Issues

Libraries are assuming leadership within their institutions to advocate for enduring institution-wide knowledge management policies and programs that contribute to a robust system of scholarly communication.

There are specific types of innovation, however, that seem to be related to library or institution size. There is anecdotal evidence that library size has been influential in the development of digital library programs; libraries with more mature digital library programs tend to be libraries with larger collections and more staff members. On the other hand, smaller institutional settings may encourage innovative collaborative activities, either because of the financial necessity to join forces to make something happen or because of the potential in smaller communities for more interaction across campus units. There is also anecdotal evidence that the institutional climate for change and the active support of groups and key individuals within the institution play a central role in the library's orientation and opportunities to innovate; to the extent that the size of the institution impacts this climate, size may be a contributing—if not driving—factor.

Research libraries' ability and desire to collaborate with other research libraries, with non-university libraries, or with other organisations and industries will determine the success of many library programs. Motivations for collaborations vary greatly and include leadership, political support, the lure of available funding, and the desire to transform the library, to move it into the digital age. An increasingly important collaboration is consortial buying of print and electronic content and services.

Consortial buying and licensing for access to electronic resources have become central in every research library's arsenal of strategies for acquiring information more economically than could be accomplished by acting alone. Many libraries find user-initiated consortial borrowing combined with rapid delivery a successful avenue for making their users' access to books as easy as access to electronic resources. There is evidence that fast delivery of books within a consortium has increased book use, especially by undergraduates.

Consortia also offer accompanying services that greatly expedite the discovery and delivery of non-book content for users affiliated with libraries participating in the consortium; some consortia are centrally managing image data banks, electronic theses and dissertations, and other digital materials.

Consortial structures vary and reflect the political framework of the state or region in which they operate and the institutions they represent. In some cases, a state legislature appropriates funds centrally to support consortial activities on behalf of libraries; in others, individual libraries pay to a common fund.

External funding facilitates the process of individual institutions' making the adjustments and compromises that consortia require and tends to support consortial relationships among libraries of varying sizes and characteristics. Consortia funded solely by the participating libraries tend to be formed of libraries of similar size and characteristics. Consortia are on the front line of controversies between libraries and publishers about pricing, the terms of use defined by licenses, and publisher practices that make it difficult for a library to cost-effectively tailor its purchases from the publishers' lists or to reduce the total amount of money spent with that publisher. The tendency of consortia to acquire or license electronic resources from the larger, commercial publishers raises concerns that content from scholarly societies or other smaller publishers will be overlooked. Research library staff are actively working with their partners in consortia to assess the benefits and challenges of consortial licensing and to influence publisher behavior in favor of scholarly communication needs.

A closely related factor to collaboration is the degree to which the organisations involved in a joint effort are willing to share control, at both the intra- and the inter-institutional levels. This sharing of control has implications for many activities such as archiving; consortial buying; expanding online resources; collaborative efforts with faculty, information technology groups, instructional technology centers; and cooperative publishing projects.

Libraries are promoting team operations to advance collaborative projects and to encourage a convergence of different organisational cultures where control is truly shared (for example, between the library culture and faculty culture and computing center culture). Many research libraries are willing to establish new partnerships and share control in order to innovate. Research libraries' ability to recognise their strengths and their willingness to leverage those strengths influences the success of library integration into the research institution.

Libraries have a special kind of space on campus, space that is seen as politically neutral and representative of the intellectual commons--public-good space. This nature of space gives libraries leverage to attract and nurture collaboration with other parts of the institution. Libraries also have human talent they may deploy for the institution. Research library staffs have a wide range of expertise that can support new approaches to meeting user and institutional needs.

Many libraries are leveraging their space and human resources to the advantage of the institution, for example, in creating an information commons, establishing an institutional repository, or providing campus management of copyright clearances. A major factor in innovation is the degree to which research libraries and their institutions are willing and able to embrace change. The willingness of the library leadership (at all levels) to change its vision of what a library is and does, and to transform library operations to reflect that vision, obviously influences innovation. However, the culture of the institution itself also influences how the library engages and supports change.

Many research libraries find themselves in the impossible position of being expected by some disciplines to implement systemic change while continuing to be responsive to the needs of other disciplines that have slower rates of adoption of new technology.19 During this period of transition, this is a major factor influencing how libraries implement change and how that change is received within the institution. The degree to which people in the institution exhibit "interdisciplinarity" or demonstrate effectiveness in working with the various cultures of the institution—library, faculty, and information technology cultures—is another important factor in innovation. Success in collaboration depends on some degree of convergence of these cultures.

Convergence or integration of cultures is being approached in several different ways. Examples include convergence of cultures in shared space; convergence of technical and bibliographic expertise; and convergence of human capital to consolidate efforts, encourage cooperation, and provide institution-wide access to the latest equipment, software, and support as well as a wide and deep collection of high-quality content. Experience reported in the task force survey suggests there is a need to support greater cultural integration. Some libraries pursue this goal by establishing cross-cultural task forces, developing cross-training and mentoring programs for effective performance across and outside traditional roles, adopting position classification schemes that reflect the changes required of staff, providing opportunities for staff to cross boundaries, and by giving people time to work through the process of cultural convergence.

Preserving Digital Content

Converting existing collections and new acquisitions from paper to electronic-only is currently inhibited by the nascent state of strategies for preserving digital content. Internationally, publishers are working with national libraries (or their proxies) for them to assume the role of the publishers' archives for digitised texts; the reliability and terms of use of these archives are still being determined.

When library, publisher, and technology communities reach consensus on how best to manage the preservation of digital resources, the transformation of library collections to largely electronic will accelerate. In this rapidly changing environment, there are many opportunities for entrepreneurial activities, which often require the financial risk of investing resources in new activities even as budget pressures tighten. Entrepreneurship may also create new activities that bypass or challenge the standards, rules, and policies that are part of library operations. Success depends on the library's ability to reach informed judgments, usually with less than complete information, on the strategic importance of an opportunity and whether it warrants the financial and other risks that accompany change.

Research Library Collections

Responding to user expectations for easy searching and convenient access to an expanding array of information sources, libraries are spending increasing amounts of their materials budgets on electronic resources. While up to now many libraries have actually also maintained the print, where dual versions exist, recent budget and space constraints have led many to make a choice of the format they collect. The nascent state of strategies for preserving digital content makes some libraries reluctant to relinquish print editions. However, seeing that these preservation issues are now being addressed, and given the significant advantages of the electronic editions, many libraries have decided to collect electronic-only. Libraries are also offering printing services to meet users' expressed need for print.

As professional print-on-demand technologies become more cost effective, this option may offer, for users who require it, a way to generate high-quality bound printed editions from electronic information resources. At the same time, libraries have not abandoned print. They continue to acquire print in disciplines that are not moving as quickly into the digital world as others and in formats, such as monographs, that are still published primarily in printed form. Thus, integrating print and electronic resources and making print resources almost as easy to access as electronic content are challenges facing libraries in this hybrid environment.

Portal software is being designed to enable users to search library catalogs simultaneously with both open and licensed databases to find content regardless of format, thereby building a bridge between the library's print and digital collections. Timely, self-service resource sharing and other user-initiated services such as book renewals and book- and article-delivery are also making access to print resources much easier. In the future more information will be created, stored, delivered, and preserved digitally, but print—because of its physicality, flexibility, perceived reliability, ease of reading and sharing—will be used for reading and editing for some time to come. Even as print retains importance, the library's physical space has increasing value for other activities, especially collaborative learning and research.

Thus, to free up prime real estate, libraries are moving lesser-used print collections to storage centers (with rapid delivery service) and are exploring cooperative approaches to long-term preservation copy retention. For now, research libraries' print collections continue to play a critical role for users even as that role and how users gain access to the material are changing.

Given the rapidly changing environment, however, libraries are carefully monitoring the information-seeking and reading habits of their users to see how their use of print and digital resources changes or does not change over time. Institutional repositories—digital collections capturing and preserving the intellectual output of a single or multi-university community—provide a compelling response to two strategic issues facing academic institutions. Such repositories:

— Provide a critical component in reforming the system of scholarly communication--a component that expands access to research, reasserts control over scholarship by the academy, increases competition and reduces the monopoly power of journals, and brings economic relief and heightened relevance to the institutions and libraries that support them; and

— Have the potential to serve as tangible indicators of a university's quality and to demonstrate the scientific, societal, and economic relevance of its research activities, thus increasing the institution's visibility, status, and public value.

Institutional repositories represent the logical convergence of faculty-driven self-archiving initiatives, library dissatisfaction with the monopolistic effects of the traditional and still-pervasive journal publishing system, and the availability of digital networks and publishing technologies. This convergence manifests itself in several ways:

— *Attitudinally*: Institutional repositories build on a growing grassroots faculty practice of posting research online, most often on personal web sites, but also on departmental sites or in disciplinary repositories.

— *Economically*: While the variety of institutional contexts and potential implementations make it difficult to project institutional repository development and operational costs with any precision, the evidence so far suggests that the resources required would represent but a fraction of the journal costs that libraries now incur and over which they have little control.

— *Technically*: Digital publishing technologies, ever-expanding global networking, and enabling interoperability protocols and metadata standards are coalescing to provide practical technical solutions that can be implemented now.

The rationale for universities and colleges implementing institutional repositories rests on two interrelated propositions: one that supports a broad, pan-institutional effort and another that offers direct and immediate benefits to each institution that implements a repository.

While institutional repositories centralise, preserve, and make accessible an institution's intellectual capital, at the same time they will form part of a global system of distributed, interoperable repositories that provides the foundation for a new disaggregated model of scholarly publishing.

This model unbundles the principal functions of scholarly communication, thus presenting the potential to realise market efficiencies previously hidden by the vertically integrated publishing model that now characterises academic journal publishing.Altering the structure of the scholarly publishing model will be neither simple nor immediate. The stakes are high for all the well-entrenched participants in the system--faculty, librarians, and publishers--and the inertia of the traditional publishing paradigm is immense.

In the near-term, large journal publishers have both the power and the incentive to maintain the status quo: the prestigious journals they control appear integral to the very structure of academic professional advancement. However, digital publishing and networking technologies, harnessed by an increasingly dissatisfied library market—as well as by authors themselves--are now driving fundamental changes to this publishing model at an accelerating pace. And new communications paradigms, especially when constructed by the scholars themselves, can eliminate seemingly insurmountable publisher advantages in relatively short order. Institutional repositories, by capturing, preserving, and disseminating a university's collective intellectual capital, serve as meaningful indicators of an institution's academic quality. Under the current system of scholarly communication, much of the intellectual output and value of an institution's intellectual property is diffused through thousands of scholarly journals.

While faculty publication in these journals reflects positively on the host university, an institutional repository concentrates the intellectual product created by a university's researchers, making it easier to demonstrate its scientific, social and financial value. Thus, institutional repositories complement existing metrics for gauging institutional productivity and prestige. The current system of scholarly communication limits, rather than expands, the readership and availability of most scholarly research.

Rounds of journal price increases and subsequent subscription cancellations act to reduce the audience further. The role of alternative scholarly publishing models, such as institutional repositories, in breaking the monopolies of publishers and increasing the awareness of university intellectual output grows increasingly clear. Further, institutional repositories can serve this function whether they are implemented on individual campuses or in collaborative consortial projects.

Digital Open Access

The advent of the Internet, the World Wide Web, and digital technologies has revolutionised scholarly communication. Creative applications of these technologies are leading to innovations in the conduct of research as well as in the conveyance of ideas to readers. And the growing availability and application of these technologies has dramatically altered how readers may discover, gain access to, and use information. As positive and liberating as these developments are for many researchers, authors, and readers, they have also accelerated the commodification of information and drives by some content industries to make their channels of information distribution more secure.

As a result, changes are taking place in copyright, license/contract, and related laws that govern the management and use of intellectual property. For the most part, the changes result in more limited access and more restrictive uses for copyrighted material. It is no surprise then that, as the laws change to secure content for publishers, there is a negative impact on those in the educational and research communities where the creation, dissemination, and use of intellectual property is expected and, in fact, forms the very core of learning and research. Historically, the library and academic communities looked to copyright law as the policy framework for balancing competing interests of creators, publishers, and users of copyrighted works.

To achieve its constitutional purpose to promote the progress of science and the useful arts, copyright law provides a copyright owner with a private monopoly to reproduce, distribute, perform, display, and revise a work, while simultaneously providing exceptions for the special circumstances of education and libraries. This balance has been significantly eroded as copyright and other laws have been revised to apply in the digital and networked environment.

Changes in the laws have come from many directions but are largely driven by players who are part of a large and diverse commercial marketplace seeking changes in the legal framework in order to maximise their profits from e-commerce in publishing and entertainment. The rules promoted by these players to govern a sizeable, general marketplace of users do not lend themselves well to the educational and research communities because, with a few notable exceptions, they do not provide for the special qualities and needs of education and scholarship. Even in licensing, where libraries have made some progress in negotiating broad uses for their communities, efforts to legitimise mass-market licenses could eliminate fair use and erode the willingness of providers to negotiate at all.

In the U.S. and Canada as well as other parts of the world, the library community has been actively engaged in policy debates as laws have been revised, consistently advocating the need to retain a balance among the interests of creators, owners, and users. Our involvement has been significant but these efforts have not been able to stop the economic and political forces of the marketplace that now so clearly dominate society.

It is critical that library community advocacy activities be sustained so there is no further erosion of the balance of interests among creators, copyright owners, and users. At the same time, it is essential for the community to step back, assess the current reality, and consider additional strategies for achieving our commitment to "promote equitable access to and effective use of recorded knowledge in support of teaching, research, scholarship, and community service." The current environment clearly favors commercial interests and thus mitigates against effective use of intellectual property for purposes of education and research. After many years of the library community's struggle to retain the balance in copyright law, scientists and scholars have cast a new light on the debate. Researchers have come to depend on new technologies for rapid peer-to-peer communications and sophisticated searching and manipulation of data. They have begun to insist that publishers support articles with large datasets, image files, and simulations. And, as the original authors, they are demanding open, easy access to the literature as soon after publication as possible.

Some publishers have been resistant to open access, fearing loss of revenues and loss of control over their content. To date, librarians have exhibited mixed responses to open-access initiatives. Some librarians, like their scientific and scholarly colleagues, see open access as an opportunity to exploit technology more fully in support of research and teaching; others express concern, particularly with the Public Library of Science, that some libraries will cancel journal subscriptions thereby motivating publishers to raise subscription prices and increasing the overall cost of access. Now is the time for librarians to fully embrace the goal of open access, and join with scholars, scientists, and their institutions in working toward this goal.

Open Archives initiative (OAi)

The goal of the OAi is to contribute in a concrete manner to the transformation of scholarly communication. The proposed vehicle for this transformation is the definition of technical and supporting organisational aspects of an open scholarly publication framework on which both free and commercial layers can be established. The origins of the Open Archives initiative lie in the growing number of electronic preprint (eprint) archives. While several of these began as informal vehicles for the dissemination of preliminary results and non-peer reviewed "gray literature", a number of them have evolved into an essential medium for sharing research results among the colleagues in a field.

These archives demonstrate a shift in the traditional scholarly communication model, which has relied on formally published scholarly journals. There is a growing consensus that the scholarly journal system is facing significant challenges:

— The explosive growth of the Internet has given scholars almost universal access to a communication medium that facilitates immediate sharing of results.
— The rapidity of advances in most scholarly fields has made the slow turn-around of the traditional publishing model an impediment to collegial sharing.
— The full transfer of rights from author to publisher often acts as an impediment to the scholarly author whose main concern is the widest dissemination of results.
— The current implementation of peer-review-an essential feature of scholarly communication-is too rigid and sometimes acts to suppress new ideas, favor articles from prestigious institutions, and cause undue publication delays.
— The imbalance between skyrocketing subscription prices and shrinking or, at best, stable library budgets is creating an economic crisis for research libraries.

The e-print archives exemplify a more equitable and efficient model for disseminating research results. An important challenge is to increase the impact of the e-print archives by layering on top of them services-such as peer review-deemed essential to scholarly communication. This is the focus of the Open Archives initiative.

The aim of the archive initiatives described above is to try to create a more effective scholarly communication mechanism that addresses problems that exist in the established system. The approaches that are taken by individual archives differ in a number of ways. Some initiatives build on a centralised model, others on a distributed departmental, or by extension, institutional model.

Some deal with gray literature only, others incorporate metadata of peer-reviewed papers or try to establish some form of peer-review outside of the established system. Some deal with metadata only, others with both metadata and full content. Yet all share the attribute of offering scholars a vehicle to conveniently and immediately disseminate research results to peers. The reason for launching the Open Archives initiative is the belief that interoperability among archives is key to increasing their impact and establishing them as viable alternatives to the existing scholarly communication model.

The Open Archives initiative has been set up to create a forum to discuss and solve matters of interoperability between author self-archiving solutions (also commonly referred to as e-print systems), as a way to promote their global acceptance. Interoperability is a broad term, touching many diverse aspects of archive initiatives, including their metadata formats, their underlying architecture, their openness to the creation of third-party digital library services, their integration with the established mechanism of scholarly communication, their usability in a cross-disciplinary context, their ability to contribute to a collective metrics system for usage and citation, etc.

Interoperability among archives offers substantial benefits to the scholars that use them. An important attribute of the traditional research library as an information provider is its role as a common entry point for a variety of information resources, not necessarily divided along disciplinary or institutional boundaries. The move from physical to digital sources should not be accompanied by the breakup of this entry point into a collection of fragmented archives. An increasing number of scholars move fluidly in their research across domain boundaries; the technology for delivering digital information should facilitate rather than hinder such fluidity.

Mechanisms for interoperability offer the potential for discovery tools and virtual collections that extend across the contents of multiple archives. Interoperability is also beneficial to the archive and service provider. Rather than having to provide an entire suite of services for its users, individual archives can instead establish a welldefined interface on which external providers can build enhanced services.

A variety of such services can be envisioned, including those that facilitate discovery, linking, and reviewing. An intriguing and essential set of services would be those that provide metrics to assist in the evaluation of the impact of certain scholarship and aid in tenure review and promotion decisions. Although interoperability has been a watchword for a variety of efforts in digital libraries and networked information, the actual meaning of it and the implementation thereof has often proven elusive.

In UK, the Santa Fe Convention presents a technical and organisational framework designed to facilitate the discovery of content stored in distributed e-print archives. It makes easy-toimplement technical recommendations for archives that-when implemented-will allow data from e-print archives to become widely available via its inclusion in a variety of end-user services such as search engines, recommendation services and systems for interlinking documents.

In addition, the convention introduces an organisational framework for making information available about archives that adhere to the technical recommendations of the convention-the data providers-and about trusted parties that build end-user services for data originating from such archives-the service providers. As such it provides a communication mechanism between providers of data and providers of services and creates a community of open archives.

The Santa Fe Convention builds on on a number of definitions and concepts that are essential for its understanding. The Convention considers the following to be crucial components of an e-print archive:

— A submission mechanism;
— A long-term storage system;
— A management policy with regard to submission of documents and their preservation;
— An open machine interface, that enables third parties to collect data from the archive.

The last item is crucial for enabling third parties to create services that support the discovery, presentation and analysis of data in the archive. Most e-print archives will also provide native end-user services. However, facilitating the broad dissemination of archive data through third party services is a crucial feature of an e-print archive. Therefore, the open interface is a key part of the Santa Fe Convention.

The convention uses the notion of a record in an archive. Some archives may store metadata that describes full content without storing the full content itself. In this case, the metadata is a record. Other archives may also store full content. However, the convention assumes that if full content is stored, there will always be associated metadata stored in the archive as well as a mechanism to tie metadata and content together. In this case the combination of metadata and full content is a record.

Open Archives Metadata Set (OAMS)

The Open Archives Metadata Set (OAMS) is a collection of nine metadata elements intended to facilitate coarse granularity resource discovery among the records in distributed and dissimilar archives. The semantics of this set have purposely been kept simple in the interest of easy creation and widest applicability. There is no provision for qualification or extension of the nine elements. The expectation is that individual archives will maintain metadata with more expressive semantics and the Open Archives Dienst Subset provides the mechanism for retrieval of this richer metadata.

Open Archives Dienst Subset

The Open Archives Dienst Subset is a set of protocol requests that are delivered via HTTP. This protocol is a subset of the full Dienst protocol. The protocol requests in the subset provide the following functionality:

— List the full identifiers for records stored in an archive. An optional argument permits the client to specify that the list should only include records added after a specific date. Another optional argument allows the client to specify that the records should be accompanied by the metadata associated with the identifier.

— Return the metadata for a specific record in a requested format.

— Return the list of metadata formats supported by an archive.

— Return the list of metadata formats available for a specific record.

— Return the structure of the partitions by which an archive is organised.

Santa Fe Convention also introduces an organisational framework to facilitate its implementation and to establish a communication mechanism between data providers and service providers. An understanding of this framework can be obtained from an exploration of the core document of the Santa Fe Convention that gives a step by step approach for making an e-print archive or a service comply with the Santa Fe Convention.

Dienst System

The word "Dienst" refers to a number of things:

— A conceptual architecture for distributed digital libraries.

— A protocol for service communication in that architecture.

— A software system that implements that protocol.

Conceptually, Dienst is a system for configuring a set of individual services running on distributed servers to cooperate in providing the services of a digital library. The open architecture of the Dienst system - exposure of the functionality through an defined protocol - makes it possible to combine Dienst services in flexible ways and augment the existing services with other mediator services, which build on the functionality of the existing services.

The Dienst system originated with the Computer Science Technical Reports Project, a DARPA-funded collaboration to establish a digital library of computer science technical reports. Broadly speaking, there are three ways that Dienst is used:

1. Organisations that wish to join an existing digital library built using Dienst.
2. Organisations that wish to create a new distributed digital library with Dienst.
3. Organisations that wish to undertake research in digital libraries using an existing Dienst digital library or by experimenting with the software.

The modular nature of the software encourages researchers who wish explore mechanisms for enhancing existing services or using the interfaces to existing services to built other services. Notice: While the software has been built and tested according to conventional software engineering standards, we stress that it is research software.

Organisations wishing to use it for mission critical applications should consider a thorough review of the architecture, protocol, and software for robustness and security.

The distributed Dienst software is configured to handle textual resources (documents) in a variety of formats. However, the Dienst architecture includes a sophisticated document model that accommodates a wide variety of digital resources. Using the Dienst software for these other resources will require some programming. The Dienst protocol and software is copyrighted but is available for free and can be used and redistributed for non-commercial uses. The Dienst protocol and software is used in a variety of existing digital libraries and projects.

In short, the Open Archives Initiative is providing a framework for the extensive interoperability of archives of scholarly research literature (and potentially other digital materials too). For this initiative to become a widespread reality, the participation of large numbers of individuals and institutions is required. In order to be able to participate, what institutions need is working, interoperable, configurable software that is freely available and easy to set up. It is this need that the EPrints software was developed to fulfill. EPrints is a feature-rich open archive software system that is as simple to install as any normal application. It runs right "out of the box" with a comprehensive default setup that should serve most people's needs. However, it has also been designed to make it extensively and flexibly re-configurable for customised needs; almost any aspect of the archive's operation can be adapted to suit a particular requirement.

Bibliography

Beagrie, N. and Greenstein, D., *A strategic policy framework for creating and preserving digital collections.* JISC/NPO Studies on the Preservation of Electronic Materials. eLib Supporting Study P3. London: South Bank University, Library Information Technology Centre, 1998.

Bearman, D., "Optical media: their implications for archives and museums", *Archives and Museum Informatics Technical Report,* 1 (1). Pittsburgh, Pa.: Archives and Museum Informatics, 1987.

Conway, P., Digitizing preservation. *Library Journal,* 1 February 1994, 42-45.

______________ ., Preservation *in the digital world.* Washington, D.C.: Commission on Preservation and Access, 1996.

______________ ., Selecting mirofilm for digital preservation: a case study from Project Open Book. *Library Resources & Technical Services,* 41 (1), 1996, 67-77.

Cook, T., From information to knowledge: an intellectual paradigm for archives. *Archivaria,* 19, 1984-85, 28-49.

Day, M.W., Metadata for digital preservation: an update. *Ariadne,* no. 22, December 1999.

______________ ., Resource discovery, interoperability and digital preservation: some aspects of current metadata research and development. *VINE,* Issue 117, 2000, pp. 35-48.

Feeney, M. (ed.), *Digital culture: maximising the nation's investment: a synthesis of JISC/NPO studies on the* preservation *of* electronic *materials.* London: National Preservation Office, 1999.

Fishbein, M.H., Appraising information in machine language form. *American Archivist,* 35, 1972, 35-43.

Hills, S., Electronically published material and the archival library. Electronic *Publishing Review,* 5 (1), 1985, 63-72

Lukesh, S.S., E-mail and potential loss to future archives and scholarship or the dog that didn't bark. First Monday, 4 (9, 6 September 1999.

Lynch, C.A., Rethinking the integrity of the scholarly record in the networked information age. *Educom Review,* 29 (2), March/April 1994.

Neavill, G.B., Electronic publishing, libraries and the survival of information. *Library Resources & Technical Services,* 28, 1984, 76-89.

Waters, D.J. and Kenney, A., *The Digital* Preservation *Consortium: mission and goals.* Washington, D.C.: Commission on Preservation and Access, 1994.

Weber, H. and Dörr, M., *Digitisation as a method of* preservation? Amsterdam: European Commission on Preservation and Access; Washington, D.C.: Commission on Preservation and Access, 1997.

Index